THE
TOP TEN
of everything
Chelsea

THE

TOP TEN
of everything

Chelsea

The Best of the Blues
from Azpilicueta to Zola

CLIVE BATTY

First published by Pitch Publishing, 2021

Pitch Publishing
A2 Yeoman Gate
Yeoman Way
Worthing
Sussex
BN13 3QZ
www.pitchpublishing.co.uk
info@pitchpublishing.co.uk

ISBN 978 1 78531 861 0

Typesetting and origination by Pitch Publishing
Printed and bound in India by Replika Press Pvt. Ltd.

CONTENTS

INTRODUCTION

A BIT like the man said in that old Ronseal advert, this is a book which 'does exactly what it says on the tin' – or, rather, the cover. Packed full of trivia, facts and stats, *The Top 10 of Everything Chelsea* revisits every aspect of the club's long and colourful history in dozens of ranked lists which, hopefully, will spark debate and discussion among Blues fans everywhere.

The book features a stellar cast of past and present Chelsea stars, including the best of the British, African, European and South American players who have proudly worn the blue shirt, the great managers who have led the club to domestic and continental silverware, the inspirational skippers from Ron 'Chopper' Harris to John Terry, the most prolific strikers from down the decades and the biggest names in the Chelsea Women's team. It also looks back at the club's most memorable moments, including the Blues' greatest finals, the most celebrated London derby victories, the finest Premier League goals scored by the likes of Didier Drogba, Frank Lampard and Gianfranco Zola, and the most gratefully received own goals gifted by the opposition. Additionally, a host of miscellaneous categories rank the club's best (and worst!) kits, the most popular terrace chants, the most striking Chelsea player tattoos and the bizarre moments on and off the pitch that left supporters scratching their heads.

Blues fans, it must be said, have been rather spoiled in recent years as the club has piled up trophy after trophy.

However, as long-standing supporters like myself will know only too well, Chelsea's history is as much one of pain and disappointment as joy and elation. So, inside these pages, you will also read about the club's most humiliating defeats, the Blues' worst relegation seasons, the players who endured the darkest of nightmare debuts, the scandals that catapulted the club from the back to the front pages and the expensive transfer flops who almost had fans at Stamford Bridge joining in with the away end's taunts of 'What a waste of money!'

At times reading this book, no doubt, you will find yourself nodding along and thinking, 'Yes, I am with the author here; Glenn Hoddle's appearance on *The Masked Singer* was even more of a surprise than Dennis Wise's on *I'm a Celebrity, Get Me Out of Here!* Equally predictably, at other times you may find yourself exploding, 'What idiot wrote this? How on earth can he include Vinnie Jones in a list of "Top 10 Welsh Players"? That clogger couldn't even kick the ball straight … and he was born in Watford!' All I can say in response is that the selections I have made are my own personal choice, based on 50 years supporting Chelsea, since I first went along to the Bridge with my father one Saturday in January 1971 to see John Hollins, Alan Hudson and co. wallop West Brom 4-1.

Inevitably, as I suggest, you will agree with some of my picks and disagree with many others. I very much hope, though, that you will find *The Top 10 of Everything Chelsea* a fun, informative and thought-provoking read throughout.

Clive Batty, June 2021

As well as having no shortage of London adversaries, Chelsea have a number of other arch-rivals dotted around the country – and even one in Europe!

1) Tottenham

Chelsea's intense rivalry with Tottenham goes back at least as far as the 1967 'Cockney Cup Final', which Spurs won 2-1 at Wembley. The Blues, though, have had much the better of things in recent times, leading the north Londoners by 31 wins to seven in the whole of the Premier League era and, incredibly, suffering no defeats at all in any competition between 1990 and 2002. No wonder, then, that Chelsea fans delight in singing 'Can we play you every week?' whenever Tottenham visit the Bridge.

2) Manchester United

There was a time in the late 1990s when belting chants of 'Stand up if you hate Man U!' would reverberate around the Bridge at every Chelsea home game. The Mancs are still hated in SW6, but perhaps not quite as much as they were back then. And, who knows, with their fabled 'Red Empire' now looking rather moth-eaten, it may not be long before some more sensitive Blues fans start to feel just a tiny bit sorry for the once all-conquering Red Devils.

3) Arsenal

For much of the Premier League era, Chelsea's meetings with Arsenal have been the most significant London derby clashes of the season. But there is nothing new in this. In the 1930s, for instance, the encounters between the Blues and the Gunners were the highlights of both clubs' campaigns (Tottenham were languishing in the Second Division at the time), with a then-Football League record crowd of 82,905 attending Chelsea's 1-1 draw with Arsenal at the Bridge in 1935. Whatever Spurs fans and the media may think, Chelsea v Arsenal is the quintessential London football match.

4) Liverpool

The Blues' rivalry with the Reds reached a new level in the Noughties, thanks mainly to four high-profile encounters between the clubs in the latter stages of the Champions League – Liverpool emerging triumphant in 2005 and 2007, with Chelsea taking the honours in 2008 and 2009. Fernando Torres' British record £50m transfer from Anfield to Stamford Bridge in 2011 added an extra element to the mix, while wildly differing fan attitudes to Rafa Benitez – who has coached both teams, of course – have made the clubs' meetings even spicier.

5) Leeds United

Chelsea's rivalry with Leeds goes all the way back to the 1960s, when the swashbuckling Londoners clashed with Don Revie's pragmatic Yorkshiremen in a number of X-rated encounters, the teams' mutual animosity reaching a peak in the epic 1970 FA Cup Final replay at Old Trafford, which the Blues won 2-1. Leeds' decline in the Noughties – partly overseen by former Chelsea chairman Ken Bates, amusingly enough – saw clashes between the two old enemies reduced to a bare minimum, but the Elland Road side's return to the Premier League in 2020 added a new chapter to a classic north-south duel.

6) West Ham

How Chelsea fans loved it when West Ham hate-figure Frank Lampard scored his 200th goal for the club against the despised East Enders in 2013. Still, the Hammers do have their uses, proving to be quite a useful 'feeder club' for the Blues, with the likes of Lamps, Joe Cole and Glen Johnson all making the journey from east to west in the Noughties. Nothing new there, either, as it was West Ham who provided Chelsea with their first superstar striker, George 'Gatling Gun' Hilsdon, way back in 1906!

7) QPR

In 2001, Rangers beat Chelsea 3-1 at Loftus Road in a match described by one QPR fans' website as 'one of QPR's proudest moments in recent years'. What was this momentous occasion? A League Cup Final? An FA Cup semi-final? Or, maybe, a vital Premier League clash that saved the laughably nicknamed 'Superhoops' from the drop? Er, no, it was actually a pre-season friendly. Still, that didn't stop Rangers fans celebrating afterwards as though they'd won the Champions League. Proof, if any were needed, that the QPR-Chelsea rivalry is felt more keenly in Shepherd's Bush than on Fulham Broadway.

8) Barcelona

Blues fans can be justly proud that one of their greatest modern rivalries is with European giants Barcelona – for one thing, it shows just how far the club has come in the past two decades. A staggering 14 Champions League matches between the clubs have created a simmering mutual dislike, as these have been encounters full of managerial point-scoring, dodgy refereeing decisions and last-gasp drama best illustrated by Fernando Torres' breakaway goal in the Nou Camp that took Chelsea to the 2012 Champions League Final.

9) Fulham

Fulham take pride in being London's oldest football club, being founded way back in 43AD at the time of the Roman invasion of Britain. OK, actually the Cottagers started out in 1879, but as they have won precisely nothing since then there's no real reason to take them that seriously. And that, pretty much, sums up Chelsea attitudes to Fulham. Yes, they may be the Blues' nearest neighbours but in terms of being a major rival for silverware they simply don't register, with the result that the meeting of the two west London clubs tends to be one of English football's less passionate 'derbies'.

10) Millwall

Guess who were the visitors the last time there was fighting amongst fans on the pitch at Stamford Bridge? Yes, it was those charming folk from Millwall, in a fourth-round FA Cup replay in 1995. 'No one likes us!' they love to sing, and they're spot on there. Are any Chelsea fans that bothered that the Blues haven't faced the Lions once since that infamous occasion – not even in a pre-season 'friendly'? No, thought not.

TOP 10 MANAGERS

Appointed in January 2021, Thomas Tuchel is the 38th man to have sat in the Chelsea dug out since the club was founded in 1905. Here's the pick of the bunch:

1) Jose Mourinho

Fresh from winning the Champions League with unfancied Porto in 2004, Jose Mourinho described himself as 'a special one' in his first Chelsea press conference. He lived up to the billing, guiding the Blues to two Premier League titles, two League Cups and the FA Cup before a falling-out with Chelsea owner Roman Abramovich led to his departure from the Bridge three years later. After managing Inter Milan and Real Madrid, Mourinho made a sensational return to west London in the summer of 2013, winning the League Cup and Premier League again two years later before a disastrous start to the 2015/16 campaign saw him sacked for a second time. It's probably best to gloss over his subsequent spells with Manchester United and Tottenham.

2) Carlo Ancelotti

After leaving AC Milan, with whom he had won the Champions League as both a player and manager, Carlo Ancelotti enjoyed a tremendous start to his Chelsea career, guiding the Blues to the league and cup Double in exhilarating style in his first season, 2009/10. The following campaign, though, was soured by a three-month-long dip in form – or 'bad moment' as the Italian described it in numerous post-match press conferences – and after failing to add more silverware Ancelotti was sacked on the final day of the season.

3) Antonio Conte

A fiery and tactically astute manager who had previously been in charge of Juventus and the Italian national team, Antonio Conte became Chelsea boss in the summer of 2016. With the help of important signings like N'Golo Kante and Marcos Alonso, he transformed a team that had badly under-performed in the previous campaign, leading the Blues to the Premier League title. However, disagreements between club and manager over subsequent recruitment policy cast a shadow over the following season and although the Italian guided the Blues to an FA Cup triumph in May 2018, he was sacked soon afterwards.

4) Roberto Di Matteo

A former Blues midfielder who had scored vital goals in both the 1997 and 2000 FA Cup finals, Roberto Di Matteo returned to the Bridge in the summer of 2011 as new manager Andre Villas-Boas' assistant. When the rookie Portuguese boss was sacked in March 2012, Di Matteo was made caretaker manager and led the Blues to memorable triumphs in the FA Cup and Champions League. However, it wasn't long before the Italian was shown the door too, following a poor Champions League campaign the following season.

5) Dave Sexton

A thoughtful and studious coach, Sexton guided the Blues to their first-ever FA Cup triumph in 1970 and the European Cup Winners' Cup the following year. However, a talented but occasionally wayward squad tested his sub-par man-management skills to the limit, and he was eventually fired after a disastrous start to the 1974/75 season, which ended with the Blues plummeting into the Second Division.

6) Thomas Tuchel

The former PSG manager replaced club legend Frank Lampard as Blues boss in January 2021 and made an immediate impact, tightening a previously leaky defence, introducing a more tactically astute style of play and improving the form of misfiring strikers Timo Werner and Kai Havertz. Although he suffered the disappointment of seeing his side lose the FA Cup Final to Leicester City, the German was celebrating two weeks later when the Blues defeated Manchester City 1-0 in the Champions League Final in Porto.

7) Ted Drake

The former Arsenal striker famously changed Chelsea's nickname from 'The Pensioners' to 'The Blues' and then led the Londoners to their first-ever league title in 1955 – a totally unexpected success given that much of his reign previously had been spent battling relegation. Over the next few seasons, he introduced a number of promising young players to the team – the so-called 'Drake's Ducklings' included the legendary Jimmy Greaves – before a run of bad results saw him lose his job in 1961.

8) Gianluca Vialli

Appointed player-manager in February 1998 following the surprise dismissal of Ruud Gullit, Gianluca Vialli got off to a great start as Chelsea boss, leading the Blues to triumphs in the League Cup and European Cup Winners' Cup in his first three months in charge. The Italian added the FA Cup in May 2000 but a poor start to the following season amid reports of player discontent resulted in his dismissal just a few months later.

9) Tommy Docherty

The Blues may only have won the League Cup during Tommy Docherty's six-year Chelsea reign, but the Scot's bubbly personality, excellent man-management skills and attack-minded tactical approach ensured that he is remembered with great affection in west London. 'The Doc' also took the Blues to their first Wembley Cup Final in 1967, but a disappointing start to the following campaign combined with an FA ban for misconduct saw him heading for the Bridge exit.

10) Ruud Gullit

The popular choice of the Blues fans to succeed Glenn Hoddle as Chelsea boss, Ruud Gullit took over the reins at Stamford Bridge in May 1996 after an outstanding campaign orchestrating the team on the pitch. His free-flowing side, including exotic continental signings like Gianfranco Zola, Roberto Di Matteo and Frank Leboeuf, claimed the FA Cup in fine style the following year but in February 1998 the Dutchman was sensationally sacked by chairman Ken Bates after failing to agree terms in contract negotiations.

TOP 10 THRASHINGS

The best of the games that the Blues won by seven goals or more:

1) Chelsea 13 Jeunesse Hautcharage 0, European Cup Winners' Cup first round second leg, 29 September 1971

In the biggest win in the club's history, Chelsea annihilated Luxembourg minnows Jeunesse Hautcharage and set a new record score for a European tie with a 21-0 aggregate victory over the two legs. Peter Osgood (5) and Tommy Baldwin (3) both notched hat-tricks, while Ron Harris, Alan Hudson, John Hollins, Peter Houseman and David Webb all chipped in with a goal apiece against a ragtag outfit that included a one-armed midfielder and a bespectacled defender.

2) Chelsea 8 Aston Villa 0, Premier League, 23 December 2012

The Blues set a new Premier League record when seven different players – Fernando Torres, David Luiz, Branislav Ivanovic, Frank Lampard, Ramires (2), Oscar and Eden Hazard – all found the net against Paul Lambert's hapless Aston Villa side. It would have been 9-0, too – and a new domestic football record win for Chelsea – if young substitute Lucas Piazon hadn't missed a late penalty.

3) Chelsea 8 Wigan 0, Premier League, 9 May 2010

The Blues clinched their third Premier League title in some style with an eight-goal rout of ten-man Wigan on the final day of the season. After Nicolas Anelka (2), Frank Lampard and Salomon Kalou had kicked off the party, Didier Drogba helped himself to a 17-minute hat-trick in the second half before Ashley Cole rounded off a memorable victory in the last minute.

4) Chelsea 9 Worksop Town 1, FA Cup first round, 11 January 1908

Prolific striker George 'Gatling Gun' Hilsdon hit six goals

– a feat never since matched by a Chelsea player – as the Londoners racked up their biggest-ever victory in the FA Cup against Midland League side Worksop Town.

5) Chelsea 7 Portsmouth 0, Second Division, 21 May 1963

A young Blues side with an average age of just 21 clinched promotion back to the top flight in dramatic style, crushing Portsmouth on a sunny early summer's evening at the Bridge. New acquisition Derek Kevan opened the scoring after just two minutes, and after that it was plain sailing for the Blues with further strikes from Bobby Tambling (4), Frank Blunstone and Terry Venables delighting fans in the near-55,000 crowd.

6) Chelsea 9 Glossop North End 2, Second Division, 1 September 1906

Nineteen-year-old George Hilsdon enjoyed a tremendous debut after signing from West Ham, rattling in five goals against Glossop North End on the opening day of the 1906/07 season – a campaign that would end with Chelsea winning a first-ever promotion to the top flight.

7) Chelsea 7 Stoke City 0, Premier League, 25 April 2010

Carlo Ancelotti's Double-chasing Blues were heading for a comfortable victory against the Potters thanks to three close-range finishes by Salomon Kalou and a Frank Lampard penalty when they showed their ruthless side, adding three more goals in the final ten minutes. Lampard made it 5-0 with a clever flicked volley, Daniel Sturridge came off the bench to score his first Premier League goal for the Blues and Florent Malouda tapped in number seven with just a minute left to play.

8) Chelsea 7 Ipswich Town 0, FA Cup third round, 9 January 2011

FA Cup holders Chelsea had to wait over half an hour to open their account against Championship strugglers Ipswich, but once Salomon Kalou had fired the Blues ahead the Suffolk side's resistance crumbled. A Daniel Sturridge backheel and an own goal by Carlos Edwards meant the contest was over by half-time, but the Blues continued to pile on the pressure in the second half, adding further goals through Sturridge, Nicolas Anelka and Frank Lampard (2).

9) Walsall 0 Chelsea 7, Second Division, 4 February 1989

The Blues often looked a class above the opposition in their Second Division title-winning campaign in 1988/89, and no more so than in this fixture at relegation-bound Walsall. Scottish international Gordon Durie grabbed the headlines with five goals, while a Graham Roberts penalty and a Kevin Wilson strike completed the scoring.

10) Doncaster Rovers 0 Chelsea 7, League Cup third round, 16 November 1960

The Blues kicked off their first-ever League Cup campaign with a crushing 7-1 win at Millwall and, after disposing of Workington by a 4-2 scoreline in the second round, continued their free-scoring form at fourth-tier Doncaster. Striker Bobby Tambling and wingers Peter Brabrook and Frank Blunstone grabbed two goals apiece, while full-back John Sillett also got his name on the scoresheet.

TOP 10 EXES TO BITE BACK

In Italy, it's known as 'the curse of the ex' – the players who come back to haunt their former clubs after moving on to pastures new. Chelsea have suffered from this phenomenon on numerous occasions, as the following list demonstrates:

1) Bobby Smith

Chelsea boobed big time when they sold burly striker Bobby Smith to London rivals Tottenham in 1955. Not only did Smith go on to help Spurs win the Double in 1961, but he also took delight in dishing it out to his former employers, scoring a total of ten goals against the Blues over the next eight years, including a hat-trick in a 3-1 win at Stamford Bridge in April 1960.

2) Jim McCalliog

The young Scottish midfielder only played a handful of games for Chelsea before being sold to Sheffield Wednesday in 1965 for £37,500 – a then-record fee for a teenager. The following year, McCalliog scored in the Owls' surprise 2-0 win over the Blues in the FA Cup semi-final, adding another a few months later in a 6-1 rout at Hillsborough. He continued to be a thorn in the Blues' side over the next decade, scoring four times against them while with Wolves, and was later part of the Southampton team that knocked the Blues out of the FA Cup in 1977.

3) Kevin De Bruyne

After playing just a few times for the Blues at the start of the 2013/14 season, midfielder Kevin De Bruyne was sold to Wolfsburg for £18m in the 2014 January transfer window. It proved to be a serious error as the Belgian international has emerged as one of the best players in the world since returning to the Premier League with Manchester City, and he has regularly shown what the Blues have been missing, starring in a number of victories over the Londoners and helping himself to four goals in the process.

4) Clive Walker

A Shed End favourite who provided some rare moments of excitement in the grim seasons of the early 1980s, flying winger Clive Walker moved on to Sunderland in 1984. He returned to the Bridge for the second leg of the League Cup semi-final in 1985 and scored twice in his side's 3-2 win (5-2 on aggregate), his second goal prompting serious crowd trouble among disappointed Chelsea fans, which led to Blues chairman Ken Bates announcing plans for electrified fences at the ground.

5) Frank Lampard

With the Blues leading 1-0, Chelsea fans gave former Stamford Bridge hero Frank Lampard a rousing reception when he came on as a late sub for Manchester City at the Etihad in September 2014. What happened next was entirely predictable: Lamps ghosted into the box in his usual manner to volley in a cross and give his new team a share of the spoils. At least Chelsea's all-time record scorer had the good grace not to celebrate his goal, and he was cheered off by both sets of fans at the final whistle.

6) Alan Hudson

Classy midfielder Alan Hudson, a star of the Blues team that won the FA Cup and European Cup Winners' Cup in entertaining style in the early 1970s, received a mixed reception when he returned to the Bridge in April 1974 with Stoke after leaving west London in acrimonious circumstances three months earlier. Huddy, though, had the last laugh after scoring the only goal of the game and remained undefeated against the Blues in seven more matches over the next four years.

7) Tommy Langley

Chelsea Player of the Year in 1979, Tommy Langley joined local rivals QPR the following year. The hard-working striker returned to Stamford Bridge in August 1980 to score the Superhoops' goal in a 1-1 draw and, later in the season, notched the winner in Rangers' 1-0 win at Loftus Road. Happily for Blues fans, Langley then spent much of his career abroad with clubs in Greece, China and the USA.

8) Alan Birchenall

Alan Birchenall set an unlikely record in 1971 when he became the first ex-Chelsea player to score against the Blues for two different clubs in the same calendar year. 'The Birch' struck first for Crystal Palace, who he had joined the previous summer from the Bridge for £100,000, in a 2-2 draw at Selhurst Park in the third round of the FA Cup. Then, after moving to Leicester City in the summer, he was on target again against his old team-mates in a 1-1 draw at Filbert Street in October 1971.

9) Daniel Sturridge

After never quite fulfilling his potential at Chelsea – partly because he was rarely played in his favoured position as a central striker – Daniel Sturridge moved on to Liverpool for £12m in January 2013. In his first match against the Blues three months later, he scored in a 2-2 draw at Anfield – a game best remembered for Sturridge's strike partner Luis Suarez's bite on Chelsea defender Branislav Ivanovic. Then, in September 2018, he scored twice in four days against the Blues in the League Cup and Premier League.

10) Peter Rhoades-Brown

A squad player for four years from 1979–83, lightning-fast winger Peter Rhoades-Brown didn't pull up any trees during his time with Chelsea, scoring just five goals in 109 appearances. However, after moving to Oxford United, he seemed to reserve his best performances for when his old club were the opposition, netting three goals in six games against the Blues.

TOP 10 BLUE TWEETERS

Want to know how Mason Mount felt when he first wore the skipper's armband? Or what Antonio Rudiger thinks of the political situation in Nigeria? Then you need to follow your favourite Chelsea players on social media site Twitter. Mind you, a degree in French, Spanish or German might come in handy when it comes to deciphering the thoughts of some of the club's overseas stars:

1) Olivier Giroud (@_OlivierGiroud_) 2.7m followers
Sample tweet: 'Great night at Sevilla with the 1st place of the group, another clean sheet and 4 goals.'

2) Cesar Azpilicueta (@CesarAzpi) 2.4m followers
Sample tweet: 'Love it lads! Great performance!!'

3) N'Golo Kante (@nglkante) 891,100 followers
Sample tweet: 'I am grateful to my team-mates and to our amazing fans as the adventure continues.'

4) Antonio Rudiger (@ToniReudiger) 731,900 followers
Sample tweet: 'President @mbuhari and the Nigerian Army, stop killing peaceful young protesters. Stop killing the people you are supposed to protect.'

5) Thiago Silva (@tsilva3) 676,500 followers
Sample tweet: 'We are stronger together! That's how we reach the hardest goals.'

6) Mason Mount (@masonmount_10) 624,600 followers
Sample tweet: 'Captaining the club I've been at since

the age of 6, no words can describe the emotion and immense pride!'

7) Christian Pulisic (@cpulisic_10) 589,200 followers

Sample tweet: 'Man it feels great to be back.'

8) Tammy Abraham (@tammyabraham) 512,600 followers

Sample tweet: 'Enjoy Christmas everyone!'

9) Callum Hudson-Odoi (@Calteck10) 462,200 followers

Sample tweet: 'A dream come true, buzzing to get my first goal and assist for the team I've been playing for from the age of 8 years old.'

10) Kurt Zouma (@KurtZouma) 444,900 followers

Sample tweet: 'Another brilliant win and clean sheet! Well done boys!!'

TOP 10 SHIRT SPONSORS

The majority of Chelsea fans would probably prefer that no company's name appears on the club's shirts for advertising purposes. However, the club has embraced shirt sponsorship since the early 1980s, and in the subsequent decades a variety of different companies have had their name emblazoned on the famous blue jersey:

1) Samsung (2005–15)

Chelsea's longest shirt sponsorship deal was struck with South Korean-based multinational Samsung in 2005, the

Blues initially raking in £50m over five years. For the first three years of the partnership 'Samsung Mobile' branding appeared on the club's shirts, but this changed to simply 'Samsung' in 2008. After winning the Champions League in 2012, the club renegotiated the terms of the deal, receiving £18m a year over the following three seasons.

2) Yokohama Rubber Company Ltd (2015–20)

In 2015, Chelsea announced a new shirt sponsorship deal with the Japanese tyre manufacturers. Worth a staggering £40m per season, it was the most lucrative deal in Premier League history behind Manchester United's £53m-a-year contract with Chevrolet. For the next five seasons, the words 'Yokohama Tyres' appeared on Chelsea's shirts alongside the company's distinctive red logo – a small price to pay for all that lovely lolly!

3) Coors (1994–97)

Given the choice, many Chelsea fans would probably feel quite comfortable with a beer company sponsoring the club's famous blue shirts. Mind you, they might have preferred an outfit with a slightly bigger profile in the UK than Colorado beer producers Coors, who signed a three-year £2m deal with the club in 1994 and enjoyed a farewell moment in the sun in 1997 when the Blues won the FA Cup at Wembley.

4) Three (2020–)

The club's current shirt sponsorship deal is with Maidenhead-based telecommunications and internet service provider Three. Thanks to the Covid-19 pandemic and subsequent lockdown, the company was given a head start to its sponsorship, replacing Yokohama from July 2020 with seven matches of the 2019/20 Premier League season still to play. The financial side of the deal has not been made public but it is expected to last three years, by which time Chelsea fans may be used to the sight of their heroes all wearing the number '3' – like an entire team of left-backs!

5) Commodore (1987–93)

After three seasons without a permanent shirt sponsor, Chelsea teamed up with computer manufacturers Commodore in September 1987. The initial three-year deal was for £1.25m, making it the most lucrative in English football at the time. Unfortunately, the Blues were relegated to the Second Division in the first season of the partnership, but it proved to be only a temporary setback and Commodore was happy to renew the deal for £2.1m over five years in 1990.

6) Autoglass (1997–2001)

In April 1997, Chelsea linked up with windscreen replacement company Autoglass in what Blues managing director Colin Hutchinson described as 'a multi-million pound four-year deal'. Strangely, no sooner had the contract been signed than Blues boss Ruud Gullit was in need of the company's services after spotting a crack in the window of his Audi A8 Quattro down at the club's Harlington training ground. If it was an omen, it was a good one, as Autoglass had every reason to be satisfied with the deal, with the Blues winning five trophies over the next four years, while also making their debut in the Champions League and appearing on television with increasing regularity.

7) Emirates (2001–05)

The Gulf airline took over as Chelsea's shirt sponsors in 2001, when Blues chairman Ken Bates agreed a four-year £24m deal – at the time the second-biggest sponsorship deal in English football. When the deal expired, following the Blues' first Premier League success in 2005, the company shifted its allegiance to Arsenal and also acquired naming rights to the Gunners' new stadium when it opened in 2006.

8) Gulf Air (1983/84)

Chelsea wore a sponsor's name on their shirts for the first time when they advertised Gulf Air for the visit of Portsmouth to Stamford Bridge on 27 December 1983. 'Their involvement is good for all of us as it brings more stability to our finances,' said Blues boss John Neal in his programme notes for the game, which finished in a 2-2 draw. However, the partnership proved to be a short one, lasting only to the end of a season, which saw Chelsea crowned Second Division champions. Money was the issue, with Blues chairman Ken Bates stating that Gulf Air's offer of £100,000 a year was inadequate for a top-flight outfit.

9) Amiga (1993/94)

In 1993, Commodore decided to advertise its range of Amiga computers on Chelsea's home shirts, rather than the generic company logo. Confusingly, the name 'Commodore' still appeared on the Blues' second-choice white-with-red-pinstripes second shirt, while the third-choice yellow-with-black-pinstripes top featured the 'Amiga' brand. Perhaps, then, it was all for the best that Commodore International went bust in April 1994, bringing an end to its seven-year association with Chelsea.

10) Bai Lin Tea (1986/87)

The creation of notorious Australian conman Peter Foster, Bai Lin tea was marketed as 'the weight-conscious cuppa' and endorsed by a number of celebrities, including Page 3 girl Samantha Fox, legendary jockey Lester Piggott and Prince Andrew's then-wife Sarah Ferguson. The so-called 'slimming aid' was eventually revealed to be entirely bogus, so it was probably fortunate that the product's name only appeared on the club's shirts for a handful of matches during the 1986/87 season.

TOP 10 EUROPEAN BLUES

Chelsea have had so many great players from Europe over the years that even big names like Ruud Gullit, Gianluca Vialli, Michael Ballack, Arjen Robben and Juan Mata don't make this list.

1) Eden Hazard

One of the finest players of the Premier League era, Eden Hazard joined the Blues from Lille for £32m in 2012, helping his new club win the Europa League in his first season at the Bridge. The Belgian maestro added the League Cup and Premier League title to his list of honours in 2015, his scintillating midfield displays earning him both Footballer of the Year awards, and he enjoyed another outstanding campaign two years later when the Blues again won the league under new boss Antonio Conte. In 2018, Hazard was the matchwinner in the FA Cup Final, scoring the only goal of the game, against Manchester United from the penalty spot, and he was the key man again the following season, signing off his glittering Chelsea career in memorable style by scoring twice in the Europa League Final against Arsenal before joining Real Madrid for a cool £89m.

2) Gianfranco Zola

A wonderfully gifted attacking player, Gianfranco Zola signed from Parma for £4.5m in November 1996. By the end of a glorious campaign, the pint-sized Italian with magic in his boots had helped Chelsea win the FA Cup and scooped the Footballer of the Year award – the first Blues player to earn this coveted accolade. He was a pivotal figure the following season, too, coming off the bench to score a superb winner in the European Cup Winners' Cup Final against Stuttgart in Stockholm. A widely admired figure among fans of all clubs, Zola continued to dazzle into his mid-thirties, collecting a second Chelsea Player of the Year award in 2003 before joining Cagliari in his native Sardinia.

3) Petr Cech

A true Chelsea legend, Petr Cech featured in more games for the Blues (494) than any other overseas player while keeping a club record 228 clean sheets in all competitions. During his 11 years with the west Londoners after signing from French outfit Rennes for a bargain £7m in 2004, the tall and imposing Czech goalkeeper won a vast array of silverware with Chelsea, including, most memorably, the Champions League in 2012 when his penalty-saving heroics were a key factor in the Blues' defeat of hot favourites Bayern Munich on their own patch. After losing his place to Thibaut Courtois he moved on to Arsenal in 2015, with whom he won the FA Cup for a fifth time – a record for a goalkeeper – when the Gunners beat his old club in the 2017 final.

4) N'Golo Kante

Impressed by his immense contribution to Leicester's unlikely Premier League triumph in 2016, the Blues splashed out £32m on energetic defensive midfielder N'Golo Kante that summer. The Frenchman has gone from strength to strength at the Bridge, helping Chelsea win the league in his first season in London, which ended with him being voted Footballer of the Year by both the football writers and his fellow top-flight players. He has since added the FA Cup, the Europa League and the Champions League to his collection of honours.

5) Roberto Di Matteo

A £4.9m recruit from Lazio in the summer of 1996, Italian international Roberto Di Matteo ended his first season with Chelsea in spectacular style, scoring with a thunderous shot from 25 yards in the FA Cup Final against Middlesbrough after just 43 seconds – at the time the fastest-ever goal in the Wembley showpiece. The following season, he was on target again against the same opposition in the League Cup Final and in 2000 he scored the winning goal against Aston Villa in the last FA Cup Final at the old Wembley. Sadly, the elegant midfielder's career was cut short by a triple leg fracture at the start of the 2000/01 campaign but, after making the move into coaching, he returned to the Bridge to lead the Blues to victory in the FA Cup and the Champions League in 2012 before being shown the door after just eight months in charge.

6) Claude Makelele

Then-Chelsea boss Claudio Ranieri dubbed Claude Makelele the team's 'battery' when the Frenchman signed from Real Madrid for £16.8m in 2003. An intelligent, hard-tackling player whose name became synonymous with the defensive midfield role, Makelele was an instrumental figure in the Blues side that won back-to-back Premier League titles under Ranieri's successor, Jose Mourinho. A great favourite with the fans at the Bridge, 'Maka' made his last appearance for the club in the 2008 Champions League Final before joining Paris St-Germain on a free transfer.

7) Marcel Desailly

A former European Cup winner with AC Milan, Marcel Desailly joined the Blues from the Italian giants for £4.6m shortly before helping France triumph in the 1998 World Cup on home soil. Over the next six years 'The Rock', as he was dubbed for his superb defensive qualities, was a mainstay of the Chelsea side that challenged for the Premier League title in 1999 and won the FA Cup the following season. Perhaps, though, his biggest contribution to the team's cause came on the final day of the 2002/03 season when he scored in a 2-1 win against Liverpool, which ensured the Blues' qualification for the Champions League, sparking Roman Abramovich's interest in buying the club.

8) Jimmy Floyd Hasselbaink

Following a then-club record £15m move from Atletico Madrid, Jimmy Floyd Hasselbaink's Chelsea career got off to a great start when he scored 23 goals in the 2000/01 Premier League season to win the Golden Boot. The speedy striker matched that tally the following season, his powerful shooting also helping Chelsea reach the FA Cup Final although, sadly, he was struggling with a hamstring injury on the day and was unable to prevent the Blues losing 2-0 to Arsenal. The goals continued to flow for the Dutch international in his final two years at the Bridge – his total of 87 in all competitions only being bettered by Didier Drogba and Eden Hazard among Chelsea's overseas players – before he joined Middlesbrough on a free transfer in 2004.

9) Cesar Azpilicueta

Chelsea's 'Mr Consistency' has played more than 400 games for the Blues – an achievement matched only by legendary goalkeeper Petr Cech among the club's overseas contingent – since signing from Marseille for £7m in August 2012. In nearly a decade's sterling service, the versatile Spanish international defender has won an impressive seven major trophies with the Blues, including the Premier League title in 2017, when he played every single minute of the campaign, and the Champions League in 2021, when he led his side to victory against Manchester City in the final in Porto.

10) Diego Costa

Fiery, confrontational and extremely aggressive, Diego Costa was once named the most hated footballer in the world, but his value to Chelsea was immeasurable during a three-year stint at the Bridge following a £32m move from Atletico

Madrid in the summer of 2014. In his first season in west London, the Brazilian-born Spanish international was the third-top scorer in the Premier League with 20 goals as the Blues topped the table, while also being voted into the PFA Team of the Year. A strong, muscular striker with a poacher's instincts inside the penalty box, Costa banged in another 20 goals in the 2016/17 campaign, which again ended with the Blues claiming the title. However, a falling-out with boss Antonio Conte that summer led to him rejoining Atletico for £57m in September 2017.

TOP 10 CLASSIC FAN CHANTS

The dozens of different chants Blues fans use to get behind their team include these classics:

1) 'Chel-sea, Chel-sea, Chel-sea, Chel-sea … Chel-sea, Chel-sea, Chel-SEA!'

Not to be confused with the simple bellowed shout of 'Chel-sea' followed by rhythmic clapping, this never-ending melodious chant accompanied by outstretched arms is beloved of travelling Blues fans, especially when they are visiting one of the more intimidating Premier League grounds like Anfield or Villa Park.

2) 'And it's Su-per Chelsea, Su-per Chelsea FC, we're by far the greatest team the world has ever seen'

Even when the Blues were struggling in the Second Division in the early 1980s this was a popular chant, although it reflected reality better as the trophies piled up during the Abramovich era.

3) 'We are the famous, the famous Chelsea' (clap clap clap clap and repeat)

Too right. The Blues are known and loved all around the world now – these days we probably even have fans in remote Amazon villages, in tiny hamlets in the foothills of Mount Everest and in isolated Eskimo communities in the frozen wastes of the Arctic circle. That's famous!

4) 'We love you Chelsea, we do; we love you Chelsea, we do; we love you Chelsea, we do – oh, Chelsea we love you!'

A touching hymn of devotion, which might have been penned by Paul McCartney in his early Beatles days if he hadn't supported Everton.

5) 'Come on you Blues! Come on you Blues!'

Simple and urgent, this chant is frequently used by the vocal Matthew Harding Stand in true '12th man' mode to spur on the team in the closing stages, and it must have helped to create many late equalisers and winners for the Blues over the years.

6) 'Flying high up in the sky, we'll keep the Blue flag flying high; From Stamford Bridge to Wember-lee, we'll keep the Blue flag flying high'

The Blues' own version of the socialist standard 'The Red Flag' is usually rolled out when a Wembley trip is in the offing – which, over the past three decades at least, means pretty often!

7) 'Carefree, wherever you may be, we are the famous CFC, and we don't give a f*** whoever you may be, cos we are the famous CFC!'

Sung to the tune of 'Lord of the Dance', this is a glee-filled Blues classic that often gets an airing when there is a break in play in a match the team are winning easily, the chant spreading rapidly from one part of the ground to the next until even the normally sedate fans in the East stand middle tier are on their feet in full voice.

8) 'One team in London, there's only one team in London, one team in Luuuundon, there's only one team in London'

A great chant for London derbies, just in case the likes of Arsenal, Tottenham or (snigger!) West Ham get any upstart ideas about who the capital's top dogs really are.

9) 'We all follow the Chelsea, over land and sea (and Leicester!); We all follow the Chelsea, on to vic-too-ree!'

Sung to the tune of 'Land of Hope and Glory', many fans have occasionally wondered why this unapologetically optimistic chant mentions Leicester rather than, say, Derby or Norwich. The most plausible explanation is that around the time it was being adopted by fans of various teams in the mid-1960s, Chelsea visited the Foxes, and the away fans added the name of their hosts to the standard lyrics. So, it's been 'and Leicester!' ever since.

10) 'One man went to mow, went to mow a meadow, one man and his dog, Spot, went to mow a meadow ...'

Adapted from the children's counting song by a small group of diehard fans on a Blues pre-season tour to Sweden in 1981, this rather long-winded chant has shown remarkable longevity, remaining in the Chelsea songbook for four decades. Lazier fans generally only join in once the full complement of ten men get mowing (plus the ever-faithful Spot, of course), leading into the eardrum-bursting cries of 'Chel-sea! Chel-sea! Chel-sea!' that finish off this epic number.

TOP 10 WINS V MANCHESTER UNITED

Followers of Arsenal, Liverpool, Manchester City and Tottenham may not agree, but most footy fans would probably say that Chelsea v Manchester United is the biggest, glitziest and most unmissable clash of the season. Still not convinced? Just cast your minds back to these classic encounters:

1) Chelsea 5 Manchester United 0, Premier League, 3 October 1999

Flaky United goalkeeper Massimo Taibi endured a miserable afternoon at the Bridge, being beaten by a powerful Gus Poyet header in the opening minutes and then conceding a further four goals as the 1999 Treble winners fell apart in spectacular style. From a Chelsea perspective, Jody Morris' joyous 'trumpet blowing' celebration after he smashed in the fifth goal was the defining image of a day to remember.

2) Chelsea 3 Manchester United 0, Premier League, 29 April 2006

The Blues clinched back-to-back Premier League titles with an embarrassingly easy win over their nearest rivals in front of an ecstatic crowd at the Bridge. William Gallas got Jose Mourinho's team off to the perfect start with a close-range finish before a solo effort from Joe Cole and a breakaway goal by Ricardo Carvalho signalled the start of a west London party to last long in the memory.

3) Chelsea 1 Manchester United 0, FA Cup Final, 19 May 2007

The first FA Cup Final at the new Wembley was a monumental occasion, with even a leading member of the Royal Family (Prince William) deigning to turn up to present the trophy. In truth, the match itself was a bit of a stinker, but Chelsea fans didn't care about that when Didier Drogba latched on to a return pass from Frank Lampard to poke the ball past United goalkeeper Edwin van der Sar for the winning goal four minutes from the end of extra time.

4) Manchester United 1 Chelsea 2, Premier League, 3 April 2010

The Blues had the Double in their sights when they travelled to Old Trafford for a late-season fixture, but they knew that only victory would suffice against the Premier League leaders. As it turned out, Carlo Ancelotti's men were much the better side and fully deserved their win thanks to a cheeky Joe Cole backheel and a trademark Didier Drogba piledriver before Federico Macheda reduced the arrears for United in the closing minutes.

5) Manchester United 0 Chelsea 3, Premier League, 1 December 2001

Chelsea couldn't match Manchester United for silverware in the late 1990s and early 2000s, but they quite often got the better of the Red Devils in one-off matches – even at Fergie's Old Trafford fortress. This match in late 2001 was a case in point, as goals by Mario Melchiot, Jimmy Floyd Hasselbaink and Eidur Gudjohnsen gave the Blues a comfortable win that was celebrated deliriously by the away fans in a rapidly emptying stadium.

6) Chelsea 6 Manchester United 2, First Division, 6 September 1930

Chelsea's new big-money Scottish signings Alec Cheyne (3) and Hughie Gallacher (2) helped themselves to a combined tally of five goals on their home debuts as the Red Devils were eviscerated at Stamford Bridge. It turned out to be the shape of things to come for United, who were relegated at the end of the season after finishing rock bottom of the First Division.

7) Chelsea 1 Manchester United 0, FA Cup Final, 19 May 2018

On the same day as Prince Harry's wedding to American actress Meghan Markle, it was the Blues who were popping the champagne corks after a narrow win over a United side managed by former Blues boss Jose Mourinho. The crucial moment came in the 21st minute when Eden Hazard was fouled in the box by Phil Jones, the little Belgian dusting himself down to score with ease from the spot.

8) Manchester United 0 Chelsea 4, First Division, 24 August 1968

A couple of months after United won the European Cup at Wembley the Blues sauntered up to Old Trafford and tore George Best, Bobby Charlton et al. apart in front of 55,000 shell-shocked fans; Tommy Baldwin, with a goal in the first minute and another later in the first half, Bobby Tambling and Alan Birchenall grabbing the goals for Chelsea in a famous win.

9) Chelsea 2 Manchester United 1, Premier League, 26 April 2008

On an emotional day at the Bridge, Michael Ballack opened the scoring for the Blues with a powerful header before unveiling a Chelsea shirt dedicated to Frank Lampard's mother, Pat, who had died a few days earlier from pneumonia. Wayne Rooney equalised for United in the second half, but a superbly struck late penalty from Ballack, in possibly his best-ever Chelsea game, wrapped up three points for the Blues.

10) Chelsea 4 Manchester United 0, Premier League, 23 October 2016

Former Blues boss Jose Mourinho endured a miserable return to Stamford Bridge, seeing his United side humiliated by a vibrant Chelsea team. Spanish winger Pedro capitalised on defensive uncertainty to put the Blues ahead after just 30 seconds, a lead that Gary Cahill doubled midway through the first half. Further strikes by Eden Hazard and N'Golo Kante after the break completed an awful afternoon back in west London for Mourinho, who was subjected to gloating chants of 'You're not special any more!' from the Chelsea faithful.

TOP 10 EMERGENCY GOALKEEPERS

We salute the outfield players who donned the keeper's jersey when the first-choice number one was crocked.

1) David Webb

The ultra-versatile Webby pulled on the goalkeeper's gloves for the Blues on a number of occasions, and even played the full 90 minutes between the sticks when Ipswich Town visited the Bridge on 27 December 1971. With injuries ruling out both Peter Bonetti and John Phillips, rookie Steve Sherwood was set to make his debut but failed to arrive at the ground in time after spending Christmas with his family up north. So Webb was handed the green shirt and, after kneeling in front of the Shed in mock prayer, miraculously kept a clean sheet in a 2-0 win for the home side.

2) Bob Mackie

In Chelsea's very first season, Scottish defender Bill Mackie started an FA Cup tie away to south London-based Southern United in October 1905 when both first-choice keeper Willy 'Fatty' Foulke and reserve stopper Michael Byrne were unavailable. Like Webb, he also managed to thwart the opposition forwards, in a 1-0 win. Perhaps he should have stayed in goal for the next round when the Blues were crushed 7-1 by Crystal Palace!

3) Ron Tindall

In an early-season midweek fixture against Tottenham in front of nearly 60,000 at the Bridge, striker Ron Tindall had already scored twice when he replaced injured goalkeeper Reg Matthews on the half-hour mark. A useful cricketer for Surrey who was renowned for his catching ability, Tindall kept Spurs out for 20 minutes until former Blue Bobby Smith pulled one back for the north Londoners. Matthews then returned to the pitch, allowing Tindall to rejoin Jimmy Greaves up front in an eventual 4-2 win for the home team.

4) Reg Williams

A week after losing at Everton in the league, the Blues hosted the Toffees in a fourth-round FA Cup tie in February 1949. Another defeat seemed likely when keeper Peter Pickering went off with a head injury, wing-half Reg Williams taking over his duties. However, Williams proved to be a capable understudy, shutting out the visitors until Pickering returned to the fray, stitched and bandaged. He then went back to his usual position and capped an eventful day by scoring the Blues' second goal in a 2-0 victory.

5) John Terry

In a tempestuous Premier League match at Reading in October 2006, Blues keeper Petr Cech was stretchered off with a fractured skull in the opening minute following a challenge by the Royals' Irish winger Stephen Hunt. Carlo Cudicini came on and performed well until he was knocked unconscious in injury time after a collision with Reading's muscular centre-back Ibrahima Sonko. Skipper John Terry became the Blues' third goalkeeper of the afternoon and was untroubled as the visitors clung on to win 1-0.

6) John Coady

The Irishman, usually a left-sided defender or midfielder, called on his Gaelic football skills when he took over the gloves from Eddie Niedzwiecki after the Welshman's dodgy knee gave way for a final time in a home match against Oxford United in October 1987. Thankfully, Coady was able to keep the United strikers at bay for the final seven minutes as the Blues held on for a 2-1 win.

7) Glen Johnson

The Quadruple-chasing Blues were trailing 1-0 in a fifth-round FA Cup tie at Newcastle in March 2005 and already down to ten men – Wayne Bridge being stretchered off with a broken ankle after all three subs had been used – when goalkeeper Carlo Cudicini was sent off in the last minute of normal time. Right-back Glen Johnson pulled on the keeper's jersey and then dived full length to save Laurent Robert's free kick before the ref blew time on the Blues' cup dreams.

8) David Speedie

Having been knocked out of the League Cup at the quarter-final stage by QPR, Chelsea were hoping for revenge when their neighbours visited the Bridge for a league fixture in March 1986. All was going to plan when winger Pat Nevin gave the Blues the lead but a knee injury to Eddie Niedzwiecki in the second half meant striker David Speedie had to go in goal. The diminutive Scot was always likely to be vulnerable to the high ball, and so it proved – Rangers sub David Kerslake chipping him for the equaliser and a share of the points with just five minutes to play.

9) Vinnie Jones

Hard-nut midfielder Vinnie Jones loved to muck around in goal during the pre-match kickabout, and got the chance to do the job for real when goalkeeper Kevin Hitchcock was sent off at Sheffield Wednesday in December 1991. However, he was unable to stop Wednesday wrapping up the points with a third goal in their 3-0 win and also picked up a yellow card for time-wasting.

10) Tommy Langley

The Blues were leading 1-0 in an Easter relegation battle at West Ham in 1978 when goalkeeper John Phillips was stretchered off after being kicked in the head by Hammers defender Tommy Taylor. Striker Tommy Langley, just on as the only available substitute, gamely volunteered to go in goal but couldn't prevent the Hammers scoring three times in the final 11 minutes. At least he had the last laugh, though, as the East Enders went down at the end of the season while the Blues stayed up.

TOP 10 PEOPLE CALLED 'CHELSEA'

When they sing along to 'Blue is the Colour', these people are literally correct when they say 'Chelsea is our name'!

1) Robert Frederick Chelsea Moore

Better known simply as 'Bobby Moore', England's 1966 World Cup-winning captain's parents apparently chose 'Chelsea' as a middle name for their son to continue a family tradition. Sadly overlooked by the football authorities after his retirement, his magnificent contribution to English football was finally recognised in 2007 when a statue of Moore was erected outside the new Wembley.

2) Chelsea Clinton

The daughter of former US President Bill Clinton and defeated 2016 presidential candidate Hillary Clinton was famously named after the Joni Mitchell song 'Chelsea Morning'. In

2020, she wrote a book about American Olympians but, so far, her interest in sport has not led to her declaring support for her namesake club.

3) Chelsea Manning

Formerly known as Bradley Manning, the one-time US soldier was imprisoned in 2013 for leaking thousands of classified and sensitive military and diplomatic documents to WikiLeaks. In the same year, Manning announced she had adopted a female gender identity and wanted to be known henceforth as 'Chelsea'. Great choice, gal!

4) Chelsea Handler

A popular comedienne in America, Handler is best known for hosting a late-night talk show called *Chelsea Lately*. In 2012, she was named by *Time* magazine as one of the '100 most influential people in the world' alongside the likes of Barack Obama, Harvey Weinstein and Lionel Messi.

Now, there's a trio who'd all love to time travel back to 2012 …

5) Chelsea Kane

No relation of Tottenham's Harry, Kane is an American actress and singer best known for her role as Stella Malone in the Disney channel TV sitcom *Jonas*. One for the kiddies, presumably.

6) Chelsea Peretti

Another American comedienne, Peretti also starred in the police comedy series *Brooklyn Nine-Nine*. No, we haven't seen that one either.

7) Chelsea Wolfe

A singer-songwriter from California, Wolfe's music apparently incorporates elements of gothic rock, doom metal and folk.

Interesting – maybe the Stamford Bridge DJ should give one of her songs a spin some time? On second thoughts, maybe not …

8) Chelsea Quinn Yarbro

A veteran American writer of historical horror novels, Quinn Yarbro has been awarded the 'Knightly Order of the Brasov Citadel for the Transylvanian Society of Dracula'. Don't snigger at the back – in the world of historical horror writing, that's like winning the Champions League!

9) Chelsea Cooley

Crowned Miss USA in the annual beauty pageant in Baltimore in 2005, 21-year-old Chelsea then moved to a Trump Tower apartment in New York, which she shared with Miss Universe and Miss Teen USA. Wonder if 'the Donald' ever dropped in to visit the three lovely ladies?

10) Chelsea Green

A professional wrestler and model, the Canadian has also competed in 'Queens of Combat' bouts under the names 'Jaida' and 'Laurel Van Ness'. Just stick to 'Chelsea' would be our advice!

TOP 10 SECOND DIVISION GAMES

Since being voted into the Second Division of the Football League in 1905, Chelsea have spent a total of 19 seasons in the second tier – most recently a single title-winning campaign in 1988/89 – but happily have never dropped any lower.

No fewer than seven of those seasons ended with the Blues celebrating promotion to the top flight, so it's no surprise that many of the games in this list come from those joyfully remembered campaigns.

1) Chelsea 5 Leeds United 0, 28 April 1984

After a five-year absence, Chelsea returned to the top flight in some style with this emphatic victory over Leeds United. Mickey Thomas got the party started with an early goal before star striker Kerry Dixon hit a brilliant hat-trick to put the Blues out of sight. Sub Paul Canoville joyfully fired home the fifth in the closing minutes and was promptly mobbed by hundreds of ecstatic pitch invaders. Understandably, the visiting Leeds fans found the afternoon altogether less enjoyable and took out their frustrations on the Bridge's electronic scoreboard at the final whistle.

2) Sunderland 0 Chelsea 1, 18 May 1963

After leading the Second Division earlier in the season, Chelsea's form had slumped after the 'Big Freeze' left the Blues unable to play a single league game for six post-Christmas weeks. Travelling up to Roker Park, Tommy Docherty's team knew they had to win to keep their promotion hopes alive, and they picked up the points thanks to a flukey goal by veteran midfielder Tommy Harmer and some outstanding saves by goalkeeper Peter Bonetti. Three days later the Blues returned to the top flight in glorious style, smashing Portsmouth 7-0 at the Bridge to pip Sunderland to second place on goal average.

3) Chelsea 4 Hull City 0, 14 May 1977

After having clinched promotion with a hard-earned draw at champions Wolves the previous week, Eddie McCreadie's young Chelsea side celebrated their achievement with a four-goal hammering of Hull in front of nearly 44,000 pumped-up fans at the Bridge. Against pretty feeble opposition, striker Steve Finnieston helped himself to a hat-trick while diminutive midfielder Ian Britton also got on the scoresheet, all of the goals prompting gleeful pitch invasions that almost led to the match being abandoned in the second half.

4) Bolton 0 Chelsea 1, 7 May 1983

After a disastrous nine-game run without a win, the Blues had dropped into the bottom three and were facing relegation to the Third Division for the first time in their history. John Neal's misfiring side desperately needed to win at fellow strugglers Bolton in their penultimate match to avoid the drop and possible financial meltdown, and thanks to winger Clive Walker's excellent second-half goal they took all three points. The following week, a 0-0 draw with Middlesbrough back at the Bridge was enough to ensure that the nightmare scenario of third-tier football was averted.

5) Chelsea 4 Wolverhampton Wanderers 0, 13 April 1907

In only their second season as a Football League club, Chelsea achieved promotion to the First Division with this crushing defeat of Wolverhampton Wanderers. Striker Jimmy Windridge and winger John Kirwan were the heroes of the hour, grabbing two goals apiece to all but guarantee the west Londoners' ascent to the elite division. When news came through that promotion rivals Leicester and West Brom had both lost, even the most pernickety of statisticians were satisfied that the Pensioners would accompany champions Nottingham Forest into the top flight. After winning their last two matches, Chelsea finished nine points clear of third-placed Leicester.

6) Chelsea 4 Newcastle United 0, 12 November 1983

Against a Newcastle side featuring former England captain Kevin Keegan and future internationals Peter Beardsley and Chris Waddle, John Neal's Blues side put on a five-star show that confirmed their promotion credentials. Midfielder Nigel Spackman, winger Peter Rhoades-Brown and striker David Speedie (2) grabbed the goals, but the outstanding performer was Scottish wing wizard Pat Nevin, whose first-half 80-yard dribble past five bemused Newcastle defenders had the home crowd roaring their approval.

7) Chelsea 1 Bradford Park Avenue 0, 27 April 1912

In their final match of the season, Chelsea needed to better the result Burnley achieved at Wolves to ensure a return to the top flight after a two-year absence. The west Londoners took care of their own business at Stamford Bridge, beating Bradford Park Avenue 1-0 thanks to inside-forward Charlie Freeman's second-half goal. The 40,000 crowd then had an agonising wait until the result from Molineux was announced. Finally, it came through: Burnley had lost 2-0 and Chelsea were back in the big time.

8) Chelsea 1 Leeds United 0, 22 April 1989

A week after defeat at Leicester ended a then-club record 27-match unbeaten league run, Chelsea clinched promotion and the Second Division title with a narrow home win over old rivals Leeds United. Midfielder John Bumstead, whose only other Chelsea goal that season came in a 2-0 victory at Elland Road earlier in the campaign, scored the winner in the second half to ensure that the Blues could crack open the bubbly with four games still to play.

9) Chelsea 2 Nottingham Forest 1, 16 April 1977

After away defeats over Easter to Fulham and Charlton, the Blues badly needed a win against promotion rivals Nottingham Forest to keep alive their dream of a return to the top flight. Victory seemed unlikely at half-time when Forest deservedly led through Martin O'Neill's well-taken goal, but Chelsea upped the pressure after Ian Britton equalised, and took the points when striker Steve Finnieston smashed home from close range in the dying minutes.

10) Chelsea 5 Hull City 1, 11 September 1905

Chelsea's first-ever Football League game at Stamford Bridge couldn't have gone any better as striker Jimmy Windridge (3) and inside-forward David Copeland (2) put Hull to the sword.

Played on a Monday afternoon the match attracted a curious crowd of just 6,000, but by the following April an incredible 67,000 fans were pouring through the Bridge turnstiles for the visit of Manchester United, suggesting that the new club was very much a viable concern.

TOP 10 CHELSEA HARD MEN

They are the players the opposition fear. The choppers and the stoppers, the destroyers and the enforcers. Whatever you call them, these Chelsea players were rock hard, and you'd certainly want them on your side if things got ugly ...

1) Ron Harris

Chelsea's all-time top appearance maker is so hard that even now, some 50 years after his heyday, the simple mention of his nickname, 'Chopper', is enough to get strikers of his era shaking in their boots. Yes, he was a tough defender, but Ronnie was also a brilliant leader on the pitch for the Blues, skippering Dave Sexton's team to victory in the FA Cup in 1970 and triumph in the European Cup Winners' Cup the following year.

2) Branislav Ivanovic

The burly Serb was a bit of a throwback to an earlier age, when defenders would let opponents know they were in for an unpleasant afternoon with a painful 'reducer' soon after the first blow of the referee's whistle. In addition to being an intimidating presence whether at right-back or in the centre of the defence, Ivanovic was also a huge threat at set pieces and scored a number of vital goals for the Blues – most notably, the winner in the 2013 Europa League Final against Benfica.

3) Micky Droy

Gargantuan centre-half Micky Droy was the Blues' main defensive enforcer in the late 1970s and early 1980s. It was a role the 6ft 4in, 15-stone former Slough Town player was ideally suited for, even though off the pitch he was the archetypal 'gentle giant'. After 14 years' loyal service at the Bridge, which included many a bone-crunching challenge, Droy moved on to Crystal Palace in 1985.

4) Vinnie Jones

Many Chelsea fans were aghast when then-Blues boss Ian Porterfield bought former Wimbledon 'Crazy Gang' stalwart Vinnie Jones from Leeds in 1991. The one-time hod carrier had a reputation as a talentless destroyer, but during a short spell at the Bridge he showed himself to be more than just a brutal hatchetman. There were, though, moments when the old red mist descended, notably when he was booked after just four seconds in an FA Cup tie against Sheffield United for a typically no-holds-barred tackle.

5) John Terry

Chelsea's most successful-ever captain, John Terry always gave the impression of enjoying the physical aspects of the game. Whether it was flying into 50-50 challenges, blocking piledriver shots with his chest, legs or head, or playing while nursing an injury, his devotion to the cause was never questioned. However, JT's commitment to the Blues came at some cost, notably when he was knocked out during the 2007 League Cup Final against Arsenal after diving head first into a six-yard box full of raised boots.

6) Eddie McCreadie

According to the late, great Peter Osgood, the star Chelsea player of the early 1970s, the Blues team of that era was very much divided into two: in midfield and attack, Ossie and co. attempted to weave their magic and artistry; meanwhile, at the back, the Londoners had 'four assassins' who took great delight in kicking lumps out of the opposition. One of the chief 'lump kickers' was Scotland international 'Eddie Mac', whose physical approach to the game probably reached a zenith when he nearly decapitated Leeds' Billy Bremner with a throat-high kung-fu kick in the 1970 FA Cup Final replay at Old Trafford.

7) Graham Roberts

A former FA Cup winner with Tottenham Hotspur, Graham Roberts joined the Blues from Glasgow Rangers in 1988 shortly after the Londoners had suffered a shock relegation to the Second Division. Manager Bobby Campbell soon installed the robust 'Robbo' as captain and it proved to be an inspired decision as the hard-as-nails defender stiffened up the Blues back line and led the club back into the top flight while also chipping in with a club record 13 penalties in a season.

8) Dennis Wise

Then-Manchester United manager Sir Alex Ferguson once famously remarked that 'Dennis Wise could start a fight in an empty room', and while Chelsea fans might have disagreed with Fergie, there was no doubt that the Blues skipper of the 1990s was a very combative figure. The little midfielder's battling qualities made him an iconic figure with the Bridge faithful, but a tendency to overstep the mark on occasions led to a club record nine red cards during an 11-year Blues career that saw him lift an impressive six trophies.

9) Joey Jones

A tough-tackling left-back who joined the Blues from Wrexham in 1982, Joey Jones was a key figure in the Chelsea side that won the Second Division title two years later. Voted Player of the Year in his first season at the club, the Welsh international built up a strong rapport with the fans on the terraces, thanks to his trademark pre-match clenched-fist salute and enthusiastic chopping down of opposition wingers.

10) Stan Willemse

Every successful team needs a player who can get a foot in, win a few 50-50s, and put the opposition under physical pressure. Left-back Stan Willemse fulfilled that role perfectly in the Blues side that won the league title for the first time in the club's history in 1955. Signed from Brighton in 1949 for £6,000, Willemse's crunching tackles soon made him a firm favourite with the Stamford Bridge crowd, and it was a sad day for many fans when he moved on to Leyton Orient a year after he collected his title winner's medal.

TOP 10 CHELSEA FC WOMEN

Formed in 1992 as Chelsea Ladies and rebranded as Chelsea FC Women in 2018, the club is now established as one of the powerhouses of the women's game. After years of steady progress, the girls won the league and cup Double in 2015 – a feat the Blues repeated in 2018 – and in 2020 claimed the Women's Super League (WSL) again on a points-per-game basis after the season was disrupted by the Covid-19 pandemic. A further WSL title followed in 2021, the same year the Blues reached the Champions League Final for the first time in their history.

Key players during the club's recent years of success include:

1) Fran Kirby

Now happily recovered from a debilitating bout of pericarditis, Fran Kirby is back to showing the form that led ex-England manager Mark Sampson to dub her 'the mini Messi' and in December 2020 she became the Blues' all-time leading scorer with a brace against Benfica in the Champions League. An all-action striker who loves to dribble past defenders, Kirby was named the PFA Player of the Year and the Football Writers' Women's Footballer of the Year in 2018 following a great season with the Blues, which ended in her scoring with a delightful curling shot in the 3-1 defeat of Arsenal in the Women's FA Cup Final at Wembley.

2) Ji So-Yun

Instantly recognisable with her pudding-bowl haircut, Ji is a five-time winner of the Korean Footballer of the Year award and was also named PFA Player of the Year at the end of her first season with Chelsea in 2015, which culminated in her scoring the winning goal in the FA Cup Final against Notts County. She has gone on to play for the Blues more than 150 times, invariably catching the eye with her sublime skills on the ball and trademark defence-splitting passes.

3) Beth England

Beth signed for the Blues from Doncaster Rovers Belles in 2016 before spending the 2017/18 campaign on loan at Liverpool. An excellent all-round striker who packs a powerful shot, she has gone from strength to strength since returning to London, winning both the PFA and FA Player of the Year awards in 2019/20, when she finished second in the WSL scoring charts behind Arsenal's Vivianne Miedema with 14 goals.

4) Millie Bright

A hard-tackling and dependable central defender who is also a threat in the air at attacking set pieces, Millie has been a mainstay of the Blues team since signing from Doncaster Rovers Belles in 2014. Her consistent performances in the WSL saw her nominated for the PFA Women's Player of the Year award in 2018 and have made her a regular fixture in the England Women's side.

5) Eniola Aluko

The sister of Reading striker Sone Aluko, former England international Eniola was once described as 'the Wayne Rooney of women's football'. A pacy striker, she enjoyed two spells with the Blues, scoring nearly 50 league goals while helping the club win five major honours. After spending the final season of her career with Juventus in 2018/19, she returned to England to become Sporting Director of Aston Villa Women.

6) Claire Rafferty

A reliable left-back who could also play as a winger and was renowned for her crossing ability, Claire Rafferty made over 100 league appearances for the Blues between 2007 and 2018 and was part of the Chelsea team that beat Notts County 1-0 in 2014 to win the FA Cup for the first time in the club's history. Capped 18 times for England, Rafferty also played for Great Britain at the 2012 Olympics in London.

7) Magdalena Eriksson

Chelsea's current captain joined the club from Swedish outfit Linkopings in 2017, and she has gone on to enjoy great success with the Blues, winning the league and cup Double in 2018 and another WSL title two years later. A composed left-sided central defender, Eriksson has won over 60 caps for Sweden and was part of her country's squad that won silver at the 2016 Olympic Games in Rio.

8) Sam Kerr

Previously with Perth Glory and the Chicago Red Stars, Australia captain Sam Kerr joined the Blues halfway through the 2019/20 season, scoring her first goal with a thumping header in a superb 4-1 win at Arsenal. The following campaign, she was top scorer in the WSL with 21 goals. A talented attacker who never gives the opposition a minute's rest, Kerr first played for the Matildas as a 15-year-old and starred for her country at the 2019 World Cup in France, scoring an impressive five goals.

9) Erin Cuthbert

The 23-year-old has become an important player for the Blues since joining the club from Glasgow City in December 2016. A lively and hard-working midfielder who likes to get into the opposition box, Erin was named Chelsea Player of the Year in 2019 and took her good form into that summer's World Cup, scoring for Scotland in an exciting 3-3 draw with Argentina.

10) Pernille Harder

Shortly after joining Chelsea from German outfit Wolfsburg for a world-record £250,000 in September 2020, Pernille Harder was named runner-up to England's Lucy Bronze in the Best FIFA Women's Player award. An attacking player who possesses flair in abundance, the multi-capped Danish international grabbed her first goal for the Blues with a brilliant backheel in a 9-0 demolition of Bristol City.

TOP 10 SPORTING ALL-ROUNDERS

The Chelsea players who were not only nifty on the football pitch but excelled at other sports:

1) Max Woosnam

Sometimes described as Britain's greatest-ever sportsman, Max Woosnam was an amateur who played three times for Chelsea in 1914 before helping Manchester City finish second in the league in the first post-World War I campaign. An accomplished tennis player, he won the Wimbledon doubles title in 1921, a year after capturing gold and silver medals at the Antwerp Olympics. His other sporting feats included making a century at Lord's in a schoolboy match, scoring a 147 maximum in snooker and beating Charlie Chaplin at table tennis while using a butter knife instead of a bat!

2) Benjamin Howard Baker

Another hugely talented sporting all-rounder, Benjamin Howard Baker is best known to Blues fans as the only goalkeeper to score for the club. However, he was also an international water polo player, a title-winning tennis player and a superb athlete, who held British records in the high jump and triple jump and represented his country in these events at the 1912 and 1920 Olympics.

3) Petr Cech

Shortly after rejoining the Blues as technical and performance advisor in the summer of 2019, the legendary former Chelsea goalkeeper made his debut as goaltender for Guildford Phoenix in the National Ice Hockey League Division 2. Having previously played the sport as a child in his native Czech Republic, Cech was no novice and his shot-stopping abilities helped his side win a shoot-out victory against Swindon Wildcats.

4) Ron Tindall

Jimmy Greaves' regular strike partner in the late 1950s, Tindall had an unusual clause in his contract allowing him to miss the first month of the football season while he played cricket for Surrey. An all-rounder, he scored a total of 5,446 runs for the county and took 150 wickets before retiring from the sport in 1966.

5) Clive Allen

Briefly on the Blues' books during the 1991/92 season, the former England striker returned to the Bridge in 1997 as the placekicker for the London Monarchs in the World League of American Football. A prolific goalscorer for his clubs, Allen fared reasonably well too with the oval ball, notching a total of 25 points in his one season with the Monarchs.

6) Eric Parsons

An ever-present on the right wing in Chelsea's 1955 championship-winning season, 'The Rabbit' took up bowls in his hometown of Worthing when he retired from the game and won a number of significant titles in singles, pairs and triples.

7) Ralph Oelofse

Born in Johannesburg, Ralph Oelofse became the first-ever African to play for the Blues when he made his debut against West Brom in 1952. He only made eight appearances in total for the club but enjoyed more success in rugby union, earning international caps with the Springboks. He was also a decent boxer who once fought the South African middleweight champion.

8) Boudewijn Zenden

Part of the Chelsea team that reached the FA Cup Final in 2002, Dutch midfielder Zenden earned his black belt in judo when he was just 14 and was a three-times champion of his home province, Limburg.

9) Roy Wegerle

A skilful if inconsistent attacker, Wegerle played a handful of games for the Blues in the mid-1980s before moving on to Luton Town and then achieving cult status at QPR. After his career ended he became a pro golfer, qualifying for the 2001 European Tour. The following year, he competed in the Alfred Dunhill Championship in his native South Africa but, sadly, finished last.

10) John Coady

A bit-part player with the Blues in the late-1980s, Coady played Gaelic football at senior level for Synge Street GAA in Dublin as a teenager before deciding to concentrate on his budding football career with Shamrock Rovers.

TOP 10 UNLIKELY TV APPEARANCES

We're used to seeing current or former Blues on programmes like *Football Focus* or *A Question of Sport*, but these TV appearances were altogether more unexpected.

1) Glenn Hoddle, *The Masked Singer*

Presumably, back in the mid-1990s when he was player-manager of Chelsea, Glenn Hoddle never imagined for a moment that one day he would be prancing around a TV studio belting out 'Rock Around the Clock' while wearing a giant 'Grandfather Clock' outfit. Yet, bizarrely enough, that's precisely what happened in February 2021 when the former England boss appeared on the second series of ITV's popular entertainment show *The Masked Singer*. Hoddle didn't fare badly, either, being voted off after professional warblers Mel B and Sophie Ellis-Bextor in a contest that was eventually won by 'Sausage', aka singer Joss Stone.

2) Teddy Maybank, *Blind Date*

A bit-part striker for the Blues in the mid-1970s, Maybank appeared on an early edition of the ITV dating show in 1986. Introduced by presenter Cilla Black as 'our Edward from Brighton', he was selected by a woman called Claire as her 'date' but later had to admit to her that he had a fiancée back home. Claire was understanding but Cilla, by all accounts, was furious.

3) Dennis Wise, *I'm a Celebrity, Get Me Out of Here!*

Former Chelsea captain Dennis Wise appeared in the 2017 series of the Down Under-based jungle challenge show, alongside the likes of boxer Amir Khan, footballer's wife Rebekah Vardy and the eventual winner, *Made in Chelsea* star Georgia Toffolo. Wisey performed with his customary determination and single-mindedness, winning meals for his camp-mates in a scary underwater Bushtucker Trial despite being bitten by a large crab, before being the sixth contestant to be voted off.

4) Peter Osgood, *Never Mind the Quality, Feel the Width*

In December 1970, Blues fans were somewhat startled to see Shed hero Peter Osgood turn up in the then-popular sitcom about two argumentative tailors, one Catholic and the other Jewish. Ossie featured in an episode centred around a football match between a synagogue and a Catholic church, playing himself as a 'ringer' for one of the teams.

5) Kerry Dixon, *Celebrity Eggheads*

The Blues hotshot of the 1980s took on the brainy regulars in the BBC2 quiz show in December 2011, featuring in a team of ex-footballers alongside fellow former internationals Tony Currie, Alan Kennedy, Alan Rough and Frank Worthington.

Alas, Kerry and co. were so thoroughly trounced that one TV reviewer described the episode as 'car crash television'. Perhaps the five players should have challenged the self-satisfied know-it-alls to a game of footy afterwards and given them a good kicking …

6) Graeme Le Saux, *Dancing on Ice*

As a speedy left-sided defender or midfielder with the Blues in the 1990s, Soxy was pretty light on his feet, but he was certainly no Christopher Dean when he took part in the fourth series of *Dancing on Ice* in January 2009. Partnered by dancer Kristina Leko, he was the first celebrity to be eliminated in a contest that was eventually won by actor and singer Ray Quinn.

7) Peter Bonetti, *The Weakest Link*

Legendary Blues goalkeeper Peter Bonetti risked being the victim of presenter Anne Robinson's waspish wit when he went on the BBC quiz show in 2001. Appearing alongside a panel of former footballers, including Martin Peters, Geoff Hurst and eventual winner Martin Chivers, 'The Cat' was by no means 'the weakest link', surviving to the last five before being unlucky to be voted off.

8) Dave Beasant, *You Bet!*

Shortly after joining Chelsea from Wimbledon in January 1989, goalkeeper Dave Beasant appeared with DJ Janice Long and former Liberal Party leader David Steel on the Bruce Forsyth-hosted game show, which saw a panel of celebrities bet on whether members of the public could perform various challenges and stunts.

9) Pat Nevin, *Pointless Celebrities*

The former Chelsea winger was partnered by ex-Wimbledon midfielder Lawrie Sanchez when he appeared on a special sports stars edition of the tea-time quiz show in May 2019. The pair didn't embarrass themselves at all, reaching the final where they lost out to snooker players Stephen Hendry and John Parrott.

10) Gavin Peacock, *Songs of Praise*

Former Blues midfielder Gavin Peacock was famously part of then-Chelsea manager Glenn Hoddle's 'God squad' in the mid-1990s, so maybe it wasn't completely surprising to see him present a Costa del Sol-based episode of the BBC's Christian singalong show back in 2008.

TOP 10 NIGHTMARE DEBUTS

These players all dreamed about pulling on the Chelsea shirt for the first time but, sadly, it all went wrong on their big day ...

1) Stanley Macintosh

Then-Chelsea manager David Calderhead must have been tempted to use the old Oliver Hardy line – 'That's another fine mess you've got us into, Stanley!' – after giving a debut to Brighton-born goalkeeper Stanley Macintosh at Derby in December 1930. The 25-year-old had a grim afternoon at the Baseball Ground, conceding half a dozen goals in a 6-2 defeat and, although he continued to play for the reserves for a few more years, was never seen in the first team again.

2) Paul McMillan

Signed a few weeks earlier from Scottish junior side Lennox Castle, 17-year-old Paul McMillan was surprisingly thrown into first-team action against Southampton at the Bridge in September 1967. The young attacking midfielder made little impact as the Blues crashed to a shocking 6-2 defeat, with

Saints striker Ron Davies grabbing four of his team's goals, and he promptly disappeared from view before moving on to Clydebank the following year.

3) Les Fridge

Some might say that 17-year-old goalkeeper Les Fridge 'froze' on his Chelsea debut, conceding some soft goals in a dismal 5-1 home defeat to Watford in May 1986 – but this book firmly refuses to stoop to that basic level of 'humour'. The young Scot stayed another year in west London, but didn't feature in the first team again before joining St Mirren and spending the rest of his career north of the border.

4) John Dempsey and Alan Hudson

After dropping a quartet of established players for indulging in a boozy Friday afternoon lunch in Barbarella's, the restaurant just outside Stamford Bridge, Blues boss Dave Sexton gave debuts to new defensive signing John Dempsey and teenage midfield prodigy Alan Hudson for the following day's trip to Southampton in February 1969. With reserves Stewart Houston and Joe Fascione also getting rare outings, this was an unfamiliar-looking Blues team and the Saints took full advantage, winning 5-0. Happily, both Dempsey and Hudson would quickly move on from their disappointing starts and go on to enjoy some great days with the club.

5) Billy Sinclair and Jim Smart

After eight Chelsea players, including skipper Terry Venables, John Hollins and George Graham, had broken a curfew at a Blackpool hotel and gone out to sample the late-night attractions of 'the Golden Mile', Blues boss Tommy Docherty reacted furiously, sending them all home in disgrace. A number of reserve players, including young Scots Billy Sinclair and Jim Smart, were hastily summoned from London and the pair made their debuts at Burnley in the penultimate match of the 1964/65 season. Predictably, the much-weakened Blues team went down to a heavy defeat, losing 6-2 to the Clarets, for whom striker Andy Lochhead scored five goals. Neither Sinclair nor Smart ever played for Chelsea again.

6) Fernando Torres

Stamford Bridge was agog with excitement when striker Fernando Torres made his debut in February 2011. Not only had the Spanish hitman joined the Blues for a then-British record fee of £50m, he would also be playing for Chelsea for the first time against his old club Liverpool. It was all set up for Torres to be the hero, but his performance was a huge disappointment. Failing to gel with his strike partners Didier Drogba and Nicolas Anelka, he almost looked as though he didn't know which side he should be playing for and few were surprised when he was subbed midway through the second half of a limp 1-0 defeat. Sadly, it was a sign of things to come for the 26-year-old, who had to wait until his 14th game for the Blues before scoring his first goal.

7) Sylvan Anderton and Pat Holton

After a dispiriting 5-0 defeat at Blackpool in March 1959, Chelsea manager Ted Drake rang the changes for the following day's match at Leeds, bringing in former Reading midfielder Sylvan Anderton and Scottish left-back Pat Holton for their club debuts. However, neither enjoyed a day to remember as the Blues were trounced 4-0 and, indeed, Holton would never wear the blue shirt again before moving on to Southend United.

8) Errol McNally

Deputising for Peter Bonetti at Goodison Park in March 1962, 18-year-old Errol McNally endured a torrid debut against Everton, conceding four goals in a 4-0 defeat. The young Northern Irishman featured another eight times in the Blues' goal over the next two years, but never once finished on the winning side. Viewed by some fans as something of a 'Jonah', there were sighs of relief around Stamford Bridge when he moved on to Glenavon in 1964.

9) Erland Johnsen

Back in the late 1980s it was a rarity for the Blues to sign a non-British player, let alone one from a top European club. However, that's what happened in December 1989 when Chelsea bought Norwegian international defender Erland Johnsen from German giants Bayern Munich. Much was expected of the 22-year-old, but his first outing for the Londoners was nothing short of disastrous – a 4-2 defeat at QPR during which he was given such a runaround by Rangers striker Les Ferdinand that he was replaced in the second half. However, once he had adjusted to English football, Johnsen proved to be a useful acquisition and he would go on to play for the Blues until 1997.

10) Teddy Maybank

A few days after seeing him score the winner against Fulham in a friendly in April 1975, Chelsea boss Eddie McCreadie decided to give 18-year-old striker Teddy Maybank his debut in a vital relegation battle against Tottenham at White Hart Lane. The high-stakes gamble didn't pay off as the Blues slumped to a dismal 2-0 defeat while Maybank's inexperience at senior level was exploited by the cunning Spurs defenders. 'I had been on the pitch for about ten minutes and one of the Tottenham players said something to me that I can't repeat, and then ran off,' he later recalled in an interview with the official Chelsea website. 'It took me aback and I was wandering around in a daze for ten minutes! He completely did me, but that used to happen in those days.'

TOP 10 EUROPEAN GOALS

Some of the Blues' best goals in European competition have come against the cream of the continent, including the likes of Barcelona, Juventus and AC Milan:

1) Dennis Wise, AC Milan 1 Chelsea 1, Champions League group stage, 26 October 1999

Having just fallen behind to an Oliver Bierhoff header, the Blues immediately hit back at the San Siro with a goal of exceptional quality. Just inside the Milan half, Roberto Di Matteo miscontrolled a pass from Tore Andre Flo, but the ball broke kindly for the Italian, who hit a superb lofted drive over three defenders straight to the onrushing Dennis Wise. Controlling the ball on his right foot, the Chelsea skipper surged into the penalty area before hitting a low left-foot shot through the legs of Milan keeper Christian Abbiati and into the far corner of the net. The goal earned the Blues a vital point in their first-ever Champions League campaign and is still recalled in song by fans over 20 years later.

2) Oscar, Chelsea 2 Juventus 2, Champions League group stage, 19 September 2012

Two minutes after scoring on his Champions League debut with a deflected shot, new signing Oscar doubled the Blues' lead against Italian giants Juventus with a sensational strike. Receiving a pass from Ashley Cole with his back to goal on the edge of the box, the Brazilian midfielder knocked the ball away from a couple of defenders before swivelling sharply and rocketing an unstoppable shot into the top corner. Arguably the best-ever goal seen at the Bridge in a European fixture.

3) Michael Essien, Chelsea 1 Barcelona 1, Champions League semi-final second leg, 6 May 2009

After a battling 0-0 draw in Barcelona, the Blues' hopes of reaching a second consecutive Champions League Final were given a boost when midfielder Michael Essien struck in spectacular fashion after just nine minutes of the return leg at the Bridge. Following some neat passing between Florent Malouda, Frank Lampard and Ashley Cole, the ball deflected off a Barça defender and spun towards the Ghanaian some 25 yards out. Connecting beautifully, Essien sent a powerful dipping volley crashing against the crossbar, the ball bouncing down over the line and back into the roof of the net. Sadly, his wonder goal was not enough to take the Blues through to the final as a late strike by Andres Iniesta gave Barça the advantage on the away goals rule.

4) John Spencer, Austria Vienna 1 Chelsea 1, European Cup Winners' Cup second round second leg, 3 November 1994

Hampered by injuries and UEFA's 'four foreigners maximum' rule, Chelsea were under pressure from Austria Vienna when the ball ran loose to Blues striker John Spencer deep inside his own half. Incredibly, all the Austrian defenders had pushed up for a corner allowing the diminutive Scotsman a free – if rather long – run on goal. Chased by a pack of opposition players, Spencer raced forwards, his little legs pumping hard, before rounding the Vienna goalkeeper and coolly planting the ball into the net. A superb solo goal, but also a vital one that allowed the Blues to progress to the quarter-finals of the Cup Winners' Cup on the away goals rule.

5) Alex, Chelsea 4 Liverpool 4, Champions League quarter-final second leg, 14 April 2009

After winning 3-1 at Anfield in the first leg, the Blues put their fans through the ringer before going through to the Champions League semi-finals for a third consecutive season. The highlight of a pulsating match at the Bridge was this sensational free kick by Blues defender Alex. The Brazilian took a fast bowler's run-up before blasting a thunderbolt of a shot with the outside of his right foot that sped past the Liverpool wall and crashed into the roof of the net, leaving Reds goalkeeper Pepe Reina little more than a helpless spectator.

6) Olivier Giroud, Atletico Madrid 0 Chelsea 1, Champions League last 16 first leg, 23 February 2021

Despite dominating possession, the Blues were finding Atletico Madrid a hard nut to crack in this last 16 Champions League match which, because of the Covid-19 pandemic, had been moved from the Spanish capital to Bucharest. The goal, when it finally came in the 68th minute, was worth the wait, Olivier Giroud flinging himself in the air to send a spectacular left-footed overhead kick into the bottom corner past Atletico keeper Jan Oblak. Initially, a lineman's flag cut short Chelsea celebrations but the VAR officials eventually ruled that Giroud's wonderful piece of improvisation should stand. Now, who says that VAR is ruining football?

7) Ramires, Barcelona 2 Chelsea 2, Champions League semi-final second leg, 24 April 2012

Trailing 2-1 on aggregate to a Lionel Messi-inspired Barcelona and down to ten men after John Terry was sent off, Chelsea's chances of reaching the 2012 Champions League Final looked desperately slim. However, in a rare attack just before half-time, the Blues' hopes were revived when Frank Lampard played an astute through ball to the speedy Ramires. Spotting that Barça keeper Victor Valdes had advanced off his line, the Brazilian midfielder casually dinked the ball over him with a perfectly executed lob into the far-bottom corner and then celebrated his priceless goal with a dance borrowed from American rapper 50 Cent.

8) Mark Hughes, Chelsea 3 Vicenza 1, European Cup Winners' Cup semi-final second leg, 16 April 1998

The Blues were trailing Italian side Vicenza on the away goals rule with 15 minutes to play in an exciting Cup Winners' Cup semi-final at the Bridge when goalkeeper Ed de Goey launched a huge kick downfield. Grappling with a defender, Mark Hughes headed the ball on and then was first to reach it when it dropped, sending a ferocious left-foot shot from just inside the penalty area into the far corner of the net to spark ecstatic celebrations around the ground.

9) Frank Lampard, Barcelona 2 Chelsea 2, Champions League group stage, 31 October 2006

In yet another dramatic encounter with Barcelona, the Blues were trailing to an early Deco goal when Frank Lampard collected the ball just before it bobbled out for a goal kick to the home side. A cross to the lurking Didier Drogba appeared to be Lamps' best bet, but instead he turned quickly and from an almost impossible angle audaciously chipped the ball over Barça goalkeeper Victor Valdes and into the net off the far post for a remarkable goal.

10) Peter Osgood, Chelsea 2 AC Milan 1, Fairs Cup third round second leg, 16 February 1966

Four days short of his 19th birthday, Blues striker Peter Osgood scored a stunning goal against AC Milan in front of a huge crowd of nearly 60,000 at the Bridge. Controlling a high ball with his right foot just outside the penalty area, Ossie cut inside his man before unleashing a powerful left-footer that left Milan goalkeeper Luigi Balzarini rooted to the spot as it flew into the top corner. The wonder goal helped the Blues draw the tie 3-3, and they eventually progressed on the toss of a coin after a play-off in the San Siro finished 1-1.

TOP 10 JOSE MOURINHO QUOTES

Since he first rocked up at Stamford Bridge in 2004, Jose Mourinho has proved to be the most quotable manager in the business. Here are some of the most famous quips and comments from the mouth of 'The Special One'.

1) 'Please don't call me arrogant, but I'm European champion and I think I'm a special one.'
At his first Chelsea press conference, 2004

2) 'There are some guys who, when they are at home, have the big telescope to look into the homes of other people and see what is happening. Wenger must be one of them – and it is a sickness. He speaks, speaks, speaks about Chelsea.'
Launching a spectacular attack on Arsenal manager Arsene Wenger, 2005

3) 'I was very surprised to see Mr Ranieri so popular, but without a trophy in four years.'
Putting the boot in on his underachieving predecessor, 2004

4) 'Everybody is waiting for Chelsea not to win every game and one day when we lose there will be a holiday in this country.'
After Chelsea won the first nine games of the 2005/06 Premier League season

5) 'I am the happy one.'
On his return to Chelsea, 2013

6) 'In the supermarket, you have eggs class one, class two, class three. Some are more expensive than others and give you better omelettes. So

when the class one eggs are in Waitrose, and you cannot go there, you have a problem.'
After a limited transfer budget saw him sign a batch of mediocre players, 2007

7) 'My philosophy in football is that there is only one winner. The second is the first of the last.'
Revealing his ultra-competitive nature, 2004

8) 'He is a specialist in failure. I'm not. The reality is he's a specialist because, eight years without a trophy, that's failure. I did that in Chelsea I'd leave and not come back to London.'
Firing another bullet at Arsene Wenger, 2014

9) 'It was a goal that came from the moon – from the Anfield stands.'
After Liverpool's controversial winner in the Champions League semi-final, 2005

10) 'You have your pundits. Jamie Redknapp is a brilliant football brain, they can explain you everything.'
When asked by Sky Sports to explain how Chelsea won 2-0 at Anfield to dent Liverpool's title hopes, 2014

TOP 10 DRAWS

The American view of drawn sporting fixtures is that they are like 'kissing your sister'. Blues fans who witnessed these nail-biting matches would beg to disagree.

1) Barcelona 2 Chelsea 2, Champions League semi-final second leg, 24 April 2012

The Blues' 1-0 lead from the first leg at the Bridge looked as thin as a supermodel's waist when they fell two goals behind on the night and were reduced to ten men after skipper John Terry was sent off. However, right on half-time, Brazilian midfielder Ramires restored some hope with a clever chip from Frank Lampard's pinpoint pass to put the Blues ahead on the away goals rule. Roared on by the vast Nou Camp crowd, Barça launched a siege on the Chelsea goal in the second half, but missed a great chance to go ahead when Lionel Messi smashed a penalty against the bar. Then, in the last minute, Fernando Torres collected Ashley Cole's desperate hoof up the pitch and sprinted unchallenged from the halfway line before calmly rounding Barça keeper Victor Valdes and slotting home to confirm the Blues' place in the Champions League Final.

2) Chelsea 2 Leeds United 2, FA Cup Final, 11 April 1970

On a poor-quality Wembley pitch that resembled a dirty beach, Leeds were the better team and Chelsea were simply grateful to have a second chance to win the cup in the replay at Old Trafford. Don Revie's men took the lead midway through the first half when Jack Charlton's header from a corner just bobbled over the line, but the Blues fought back to equalise through winger Peter Houseman shortly before half-time. An 83rd-minute goal from Mick Jones appeared to have given victory to the Yorkshiremen, but a flying header by Ian Hutchinson three minutes later took an engrossing final to extra time. The additional 30 minutes produced no more goals so, after a well-deserved lap of honour by both teams, it was on to Manchester.

3) Chelsea 2 Tottenham 2, Premier League, 2 May 2016

Tottenham needed to win this midweek fixture to keep their title hopes alive and started brightly, taking a two-goal lead through Harry Kane and Son Heung-Min. Chelsea, though, fought back after the break, Gary Cahill scoring with a shot from a corner. As the Blues piled on the pressure Spurs became increasingly rattled, collecting a Premier League record nine yellow cards, but their physical approach couldn't prevent sub Eden Hazard waltzing past a couple of defenders before curling a superb shot into the far corner seven minutes from time. The final whistle was greeted jubilantly by the home fans, confirming as it did that the title would be heading not to north London but to Leicester City, managed by former Blues boss Claudio Ranieri.

4) Leicester City 0 Chelsea 0, League Cup Final second leg, 5 April 1965

Thanks to a late wonder goal by Eddie McCreadie, Tommy Docherty's Blues were 3-2 up from the first leg of the League Cup Final at the Bridge and turned up at Filbert Street determined to protect that lead at all costs. A fine defensive display allied to some excellent goalkeeping by Peter Bonetti saw Chelsea do just that, grinding out a gritty 0-0 draw. The home fans, though, were unimpressed by the Blues' negative tactics and gave vent to their feelings by booing loudly when skipper Terry Venables was presented with the cup by Football League president Joe Richards.

5) Tottenham 2 Chelsea 2, League Cup semi-final second leg, 5 January 1972

Leading 3-2 after the first leg at the Bridge, Dave Sexton's Blues knew they would need to be at their best to get a result at White Hart Lane to take them to the League Cup Final. Trailing to Martin Chivers' goal at half-time, a fine effort from Chris Garland restored Chelsea's aggregate lead, only for the referee to award Spurs a controversial penalty when Alan Hudson unintentionally handled in the box. Martin Peters calmly converted and extra time seemed inevitable until, in the very last minute, 'Huddy' fired in a low free kick from near the corner flag that somehow bounced through a forest of legs and into the net to book the Blues a place at Wembley.

6) Chelsea 4 Liverpool 4, Champions League quarter-final second leg, 14 April 2009

A thrilling match at the Bridge saw the Blues concede their 3-1 lead from the first leg by half-time, Liverpool deservedly going two goals up on the night. Chelsea, though, were a different proposition after the break – a clever finish by Didier Drogba, a stunning free kick by Brazilian defender Alex and a close-range shot from Frank Lampard seemingly killing off the Reds' challenge. However, two quickfire goals in the closing stages by Lucas and Dirk Kuyt gave the Merseysiders a sniff of a chance, before Lamps tied the scores at 4-4 – easily enough to take the Blues through to the semis.

7) Wolverhampton Wanderers 1 Chelsea 1, Second Division, 7 May 1977

Officially, Chelsea fans were banned from attending away matches after crowd trouble at a number of games during the 1976/77 season but thousands headed up to the Midlands for this vital promotion clash – the Blues needing a point to ensure their return to the top flight after a two-year absence. Tommy Langley's well-taken goal from Ray Wilkins' defence-splitting pass gave the visitors a half-time lead, but Wolves hit back with a late equaliser from John Richards. The draw, though, suited both teams, confirming Wolves as Second Division champions and Chelsea as runners-up.

8) Sheffield Wednesday 4 Chelsea 4, League Cup quarter-final replay, 30 January 1985

Overpowered by a physical Wednesday team, the Blues could have no complaints about going into the break 3-0 down.

However, sub Paul Canoville immediately pulled a goal back, sparking a remarkable recovery that saw the Blues level the scores thanks to further strikes from Kerry Dixon and Mickey Thomas. Five minutes from time, Canoville banged in what appeared to be the winner, but a last-gasp penalty for the home side meant the Blues had to settle for a draw and a second replay at the Bridge, which they won 2-1.

9) Chelsea 5 West Ham United 5, First Division, 17 December 1966

The Blues and the Hammers served up a pre-Christmas cracker in front of nearly 48,000 fans at the Bridge, sharing ten goals. The visitors dominated the early proceedings, scoring twice in the first half before Tommy Baldwin halved the deficit just before the break. A crazy spell of five goals in just 17 minutes at the start of the second half saw Chelsea lead 3-2 thanks to strikes from Tony Hateley and Charlie Cooke, only for the Hammers to hit back with three quick goals themselves. With ten minutes to go, Bobby Tambling gave Chelsea hope from the penalty spot, and then the same player shinned one in right at the death to round off an incredible afternoon's entertainment.

10) West Bromwich Albion 3 Chelsea 3, Premier League, 26 September 2020

One of a handful of occasions that the Blues have fought back from three goals down to draw 3-3, a series of catastrophic defensive errors gave West Brom a commanding lead at the break. However, a rejigged Chelsea side performed much better in the second half and got back into the match when Mason Mount fired in from outside the box. Substitute Callum Hudson-Odoi reduced the arrears further with a well-placed shot following a neat passing move before Tammy Abraham tapped in to level the scores in injury time.

TOP 10 LOAN SIGNINGS

Many might see them as footballing mercenaries with no real attachment to the Blues, but some of these short-term fixes served the club extremely well.

1) George Weah

With record signing Chris Sutton enduring a nightmare season in front of goal, Chelsea boss Gianluca Vialli bolstered his attacking options by signing former World Player of the Year George Weah on loan from AC Milan in January 2000. The Liberian legend made an immediate impact in west London, coming off the bench on his debut to head home the only goal of the game in a derby against Spurs at Stamford Bridge. Although some way past his spellbinding best, Weah's undimmed goalscoring prowess proved invaluable to the Blues over the next few months and the 33-year-old fully deserved the FA Cup winner's medal he picked up after the Londoners beat Aston Villa in the last final at the old Wembley.

2) Mateo Kovacic

The Croatian midfielder joined Chelsea on a season-long loan from Real Madrid in August 2018, but initially struggled to make a real impact at Stamford Bridge. Although industrious and energetic, his passing lacked penetration and his shooting was invariably terrible – more likely to worry fans in the upper tier than the opposition goalkeeper. However, as the campaign wore on, Kovacic's performances improved and, following an outstanding display in the Europa League Final against Arsenal, most Chelsea fans were happy enough when the club paid the Spanish giants £40m to make the move permanent. His good form continued throughout the 2019/20 season, at the end of which he was voted the club's Player of the Year.

3) Tony Godden

With first-choice goalkeeper Eddie Niedzwiecki crocked and his deputy Steve Francis performing like a rabbit trapped in the headlights while conceding ten goals in two matches, Blues boss John Hollins acted swiftly to bring in experienced West Brom custodian Tony Godden on loan until the end of the 1985/86 campaign. The boyhood Chelsea fan performed so well in his run in the side, particularly in impressive away wins at Manchester United and West Ham, that the Blues signed him full-time on a free transfer and he played 30 more games in the following campaign before moving on to Birmingham City.

4) Laurent Charvet

Signed on loan from French side Cannes midway through the 1997/98 season, attack-minded right-back Charvet impressed on his Blues debut, setting up Mark Hughes for a vital goal in the League Cup semi-final first leg against Arsenal – a tie the west Londoners eventually won on aggregate. He scored twice in his 13 appearances for the club – a stunning 25-yarder in a 3-1 defeat at Leeds demonstrating his technical qualities – and was an unused sub for the European Cup Winners' Cup victory against Stuttgart in Stockholm. Keen to stay in England when his loan ended, he signed for Newcastle in the summer of 1998 and later also played for Manchester City.

5) Craig Forrest

Signed on a short-term loan from Ipswich Town as goalkeeping back-up while Ruud Gullit's Blues played out their remaining league games before the 1997 FA Cup Final, Forrest made his debut for the club as a sub for the injured Frode Grodas at Newcastle in April that year. Chelsea were trailing 3-0 after just 35 minutes when the Canadian international came on, but he managed to keep the rampant Geordies at bay in an eventual 3-1 defeat before playing the full 90 minutes in wins against Leicester and Wimbledon, conceding just one goal. An impressed Gullit wanted Forrest to play in the Wembley final against Middlesbrough but, sadly for the 29-year-old, the two clubs could not agree a deal to extend his loan.

6) Maniche

A member of Porto's 2004 Champions League-winning side, Maniche teamed up with his old boss Jose Mourinho in January 2006, joining the Blues on loan from Dynamo Moscow. The shaggy-haired midfielder made a number of substitute appearances before starting his first Premier League match against West Ham in April, only to be sent off after just 17 minutes. More happily, Maniche was on the pitch (as a sub for Didier Drogba) later that month when the Blues secured the title for a second consecutive season with a 3-0 home drubbing of Manchester United. Dynamo then tried to interest Chelsea in a £5m permanent deal but the Blues declined to pay up for a player who had failed to dazzle during his extended audition.

7) Gonzalo Higuain

Arriving at the Bridge in January 2019, Argentinian striker Gonzalo Higuain was reunited with Chelsea manager Maurizio Sarri, who had previously been his boss during a free-scoring spell at Napoli. The goals, though, did not flow as expected for the 31-year-old in London – just five in 18 slightly lethargic appearances. It was not a tally likely to interest the Blues in meeting Inter's £31m valuation of their asset, and it was no surprise when Higuain returned to Italy in May.

8) Ricardo Quaresma

The talented Portuguese winger arrived on loan at Chelsea from Inter Milan in February 2009, during the last days of

Luiz Felipe Scolari's ill-fated reign at the Bridge. He made his debut as a sub in a drab 0-0 draw with Hull City, catching the eye with a couple of his signature crosses with the outside of his right boot. However, he barely figured under caretaker boss Guus Hiddink – his sole memorable moment coming when he crossed for Alex to head home in a 2-0 victory at Coventry in the sixth round of the FA Cup – and in June 2009 he returned to Inter.

9) Alexandre Pato

At 26, the former AC Milan striker should have been at his peak when he pitched up at the Bridge on loan from Brazilian side Corinthians in April 2016. However, injuries had taken their toll and he was a shadow of the young player who had ripped through Serie A defences a few years earlier. Pato, though, did manage to get on the scoresheet for the Blues on his debut, converting a penalty he had won himself in a 4-0 win at Villa Park. After that, he played just once more – in a 1-0 defeat at Swansea – before returning to Brazil.

10) Radamel Falcao

While with Atletico Madrid, Colombian hitman Radamel Falcao had destroyed Chelsea in the 2012 Super Cup, scoring a superb hat-trick in a 4-1 win for the Spanish outfit. However, when he arrived at the Bridge on a season-long loan from Monaco in the summer of 2015, a severe ACL injury had blunted his edge while a disappointing loan at Manchester United the previous season had affected his self-belief. It was no surprise, then, that Falcao failed to make much of an impact at the Bridge, scoring just one goal – a diving header in a home defeat against Crystal Palace – before disconsolately heading back to the south of France.

TOP 10 PREMIER LEAGUE-ERA KITS

The classic kits that made the Blues look especially stylish:

1) Home, 2006–08

After cutting ties with Umbro, Chelsea signed an eight-year kit deal worth £100m with Adidas in January 2005. The first home strip produced by the company the following year was a stonker, featuring the three classic Adidas stripes down the sleeve, a white rimmed crew neck and FlowMapping technology designed to allow heat and sweat to escape. 'The technology and style of the shirt is typical of the modern game and will help our performance,' was Frank Lampard's verdict at the launch. He was proved right, as the Blues won both domestic cups in the 2006/07 campaign and reached the Champions League Final in the same kit in 2008.

2) Away, 2003/04

In the mid-1970s, Chelsea wore a stunning white away kit with two block stripes of red and green running down the front – the colours inspired by those sported by the great Hungary side of the 1950s. Taking their cue from that classic Blues kit, Umbro revisited it in 2003 although this time the large horizontal stripes contrasting with the white background were black and blue. Fittingly, perhaps, the stylish design was on show for the first match of the Roman Abramovich era, a 2-0 win away to Slovakian side MSK Zilina in a Champions League qualifier.

3) Home, 1999–2001

After producing a pig's ear of a home kit two years earlier, Umbro returned to form in 1999 with a sleek design featuring a 60s-style round-neck collar and discreet white piping on an attractive royal blue shirt. The kit was an instant hit with fans, who voted it the best in the club's history in a poll in the official Chelsea magazine in early 2000. It proved to be a successful strip, too, as the Blues lifted the FA Cup later that year after beating Aston Villa in the last final played at the old Wembley.

4) Away, 2008/09

Yellow has been a popular choice for the Blues' change strip since the early 1960s, and arguably the best kit of this type was produced by Adidas for the 2008/09 campaign. A clean and unfussy design, the deep yellow of the shirt contrasted delightfully with the blue round-neck collar and three stripes down the sleeves. Memorably, the Blues won the FA Cup in this kit, beating Everton 2-1 in the final at Wembley.

5) Home, 2005/06

Chelsea's centenary season naturally required a top-class kit reflecting the club's history, traditions and heritage, and Umbro came up with the goods with an eye-catching design. Gold piping on the royal blue shirts and shorts hinted at the club's status as reigning Premier League champions while fans were delighted to see the much-missed 'lion rampant' return on the new club badge. Even better, that gold trim acquired an extra shine when the Blues reclaimed their title with a 3-0 tonking of Manchester United at the Bridge.

6) Away, 2013/14

A somewhat bizarre publicity campaign saw Chelsea midfielder Juan Mata launch this Adidas away kit with his hands and feet covered in blue paint. The gimmicky approach, though, was unnecessary as the plain white shirt with blue trim, offset by a thin horizontal red and blue band, made a spectacular first impression. 'Arguably the nicest kit we've seen so far this summer,' was the verdict of *The Mirror*.

7) Home, 2014/15

Influenced, perhaps, by a famous Chelsea strip of the mid-1980s, Adidas came up with a home kit in two tones of blue, the horizontal stripes of the darker tone gradually getting larger lower down the shirt. The imaginative design went down well with fans and brought the players good luck, the Blues going unbeaten at home in the league as they won the Premier League title for a fourth time.

8) Home, 2017/18

After ending a long-standing partnership with Adidas six years early, Chelsea announced a new mega kit supply deal with Nike worth a reported £900m over 15 years in October 2016. The American giants' first creation the following season was a strikingly unfussy home kit, influenced by the classic Blues kit of the early-1970s. The minimalist design was a hit with fans and meant the Blues looked the part at Wembley when they lifted the FA Cup after beating Manchester United in the 2018 final.

9) Away, 2002–04

According to the Umbro team who designed it, this striking away kit's colours were 'midnight blue and carbon'. However, to most fans it looked remarkably similar to the black strip Manchester United had worn in the mid-90s. Either way, the radical change from the Blues' more traditional yellow or white kits gave the players a slightly more menacing air on their travels.

10) Away, 2012/13

Launched by Chelsea stars Frank Lampard, Gary Cahill, Fernando Torres and Daniel Sturridge, this Adidas white away kit featured an eye-catching light blue sash and a darker blue V-neck collar. The chic design proved popular with fans and lucky for the team, who wore it a number of times during their ultimately successful Europa League campaign.

TOP 10 NON-CHELSEA MATCHES AT STAMFORD BRIDGE

As well as being the home of Chelsea, Stamford Bridge has hosted numerous important football matches not involving the Blues, including these memorable encounters:

1) London XI 2 Barcelona XI 2, Inter-Cities Fairs Cup Final first leg, 5 March 1958

The forerunner of the UEFA Cup and Europa League, the Inter-Cities Fairs Cup was originally conceived as a competition for sides representing cities rather than clubs. This first series kicked off in 1955 but the final between a London XI featuring Chelsea players Jimmy Greaves and Peter Sillett was not held until three years later. The first leg attracted a crowd of 45,466 to the Bridge, with the young Greavsie inevitably on target in a 2-2 draw. The Londoners made seven changes to their team for the second leg in Barcelona two months later, but their rejigged side slumped to a 6-0 defeat.

2) Aston Villa 1 Huddersfield Town 0, FA Cup Final, 24 April 1920

The first post-World War I FA Cup Final and the first of three to be played at Stamford Bridge might easily have featured Chelsea, who had earlier lost 3-1 in the semi-final to Aston Villa at Bramall Lane. And it was Villa who took home the silverware for a then-record sixth time after Billy Kirton's goal in the tenth minute of extra time finally saw off the challenge of plucky Huddersfield.

3) England 4 Switzerland 1, Victory International, 11 May 1946

After hosting England internationals against Scotland (1913), Wales (1929) and Austria (1932), Stamford Bridge was chosen as the venue for a prestigious 'Victory International' against

79

Switzerland less than a year after the end of World War II. A massive crowd of 75,000 watched England fall behind before romping to a 4-1 victory, with Chelsea centre-forward Tommy Lawton nabbing one of the goals.

4) Huddersfield Town 1 Preston North End 0, 29 April 1922

In the last FA Cup Final before the opening of the original Wembley Stadium, Huddersfield lifted the trophy for the first and only time in front of a crowd of 53,000 at the Bridge. The key moment arrived midway through the second half when the Terriers were awarded a penalty following a foul that looked to have been committed outside the box, and Billy Smith converted past Preston's bespectacled goalkeeper James Mitchell.

5) Wolfsburg 1 Lyon 0, Women's Champions League Final, 23 May 2013

The absence of an English side contributed to a slightly disappointing crowd of just under 20,000 turning up at the Bridge for the 2013 Women's Champions League Final between holders Lyon and German outfit Wolfsburg. However, those who made the effort were rewarded with a tight and absorbing spectacle, won by the underdogs from Lower Saxony thanks to a second-half penalty by Martina Muller.

6) Brazil 1 Russia 1, friendly international, 25 March 2013

In the first senior international match to be played at the Bridge for 67 years, five-times World Cup winners Brazil took on Russia just over a year before hosting the 2014 finals. The South Americans, managed by ex-Blues boss Luiz Felipe Scolari and featuring three Chelsea players in their line-up in David Luiz, Oscar and Ramires, fell behind after a pinball-style scramble in their box but salvaged a deserved draw thanks to a last-minute equaliser by Fluminense striker Fred.

7) Manchester United 8 Swindon Town 4, Charity Shield, 25 September 1911

The most entertaining of ten Charity Shield matches played at the Bridge saw reigning league champions Manchester United beat Southern League title winners Swindon in fine style, with future Chelsea striker Harold Halse grabbing no fewer than six of United's eight goals. Proceeds from the match were later donated to survivors of RMS *Titanic*, which sank in the Atlantic in April 1912.

8) Arsenal 3 Orient 0, FA Cup semi-final, 8 April 1978

In the last of ten FA Cup semi-finals played at the Bridge, Arsenal easily overcame a second-tier Orient side who had earlier beaten Chelsea at the same venue in a fifth-round replay. One of the Gunners' goals was scored by a 20-year-old Graham Rix, who would go on to become the Blues' assistant manager under Glenn Hoddle and Ruud Gullit.

9) England 2 World XI 2, Soccer Aid 2019, 16 June 2019

The annual charity fundraiser for UNICEF featured female players for the first time, with ex-Blue Katie Chapman lining up alongside former Chelsea stars Joe Cole, Glen Johnson and John Terry in the England team. The pros, though, were let down by their celebrity team-mates in the penalty shoot-out that followed an exciting 2-2 draw, handing victory to a World XI skippered by sprint legend Usain Bolt.

10) Tottenham Hotspur 1 Wolverhampton Wanderers 0, FA Cup Final, 23 April 1921

The 'news' that Spurs have won the FA Cup at Stamford Bridge will have Chelsea fans reading this reaching for the sick bucket – but, fear not, this unpalatable event happened over a century ago and so can safely be filed away under 'ancient history'. Anyway, in case you're interested, the only goal of a dull affair was scored by Tottenham's outside-left Jimmy Dimmock early in the second half.

TOP 10 GOLDEN OLDIES

The Chelsea players who were still turning out for the club aged 37 – or even older!

1) Didier Drogba
After returning to west London for a single season during which he helped the Blues win the Premier League and the League Cup, Didier Drogba enjoyed an emotional farewell against Sunderland at the Bridge on the final day of the 2014/15 campaign. Substituted after 28 minutes, the 37-year-old was chaired off by his team-mates in recognition of his immense contribution to the Chelsea cause since first arriving at the club from Marseille in the summer of 2004.

2) Dickie Spence
One of a handful of players to represent Chelsea both before and after World War II, Yorkshireman Dickie Spence turned out for the last time for the Blues against Bolton in September 1947 when nearly two months past his 39th birthday – making him the club's oldest-ever outfield player. After quitting the game, the tricky right-winger played a big role in developing the club's youth system, helping to bring through a host of young players over the next two decades.

3) Mark Schwarzer
Signed as back-up to Petr Cech in the summer of 2013, the Australian goalkeeper made a total of 12 appearances for the Blues, becoming the club's oldest player by some distance

when he turned out in a 2-1 win at Cardiff on the last day of the 2013/14 campaign aged 41 years 218 days. The following season he moved on to Leicester City, and was still on the club's books when they won the Premier League title in 2016.

4) John Harris

Chelsea captain in the immediate post-war period, John Harris was the oldest member of the Blues' 1955 title-winning team, making most of his 31 appearances at right-back rather than in his usual centre-half role following an injury to Peter Sillett. The following season, he played the last of his 364 games for the club in a 2-1 defeat against Sheffield United in April 1956 aged 38 years and nine months before becoming player-manager of Chester City.

5) John Hollins

After returning to the Bridge as player-coach in the summer of 1983, John Hollins made the last of his 592 appearances for the club away to Grimsby on the final day of the 1983/84 season when just two months shy of his 38th birthday. It proved to be a good day for the veteran midfielder-turned-defender to sign off, as the Blues won 1-0 thanks to a Kerry Dixon header to clinch the Second Division title on goal difference ahead of Sheffield Wednesday.

6) Glenn Hoddle

Appointed Chelsea player-manager in 1993, Glenn Hoddle immediately installed himself as sweeper in the Blues' back line, earning rave reviews for his still-superb ball control and visionary passing. Later in the season he reverted to his usual midfield role, featuring mainly as a sub as he led the Blues to the FA Cup Final. The following campaign he made a number of cameo appearances, culminating in a start against Arsenal on the final day of the season, before calling time on his playing career aged 37 years and six months.

7) Sam Irving

A year after being part of the Cardiff City side that famously beat Arsenal in the 1927 FA Cup Final at Wembley, Irish half-back Sam Irving moved from south Wales to west London. Already 34, his experience proved invaluable as the Blues finally won promotion to the top flight in 1930 after six years in the second tier. He played his last game for the Blues – a 2-0 win against Liverpool in October 1931 – when two months past his 38th birthday, before ending his career with Bristol Rovers.

8) Willy Caballero

Signed on a free transfer from Manchester City in the summer of 2017, Argentinian goalkeeper Willy Caballero became the oldest player to represent Chelsea in the FA Cup Final when he turned out in the 2-1 loss to Arsenal in 2020 aged 38 years 308 days. The following season, he was just two days short of his 39th birthday when he played in the Premier League against West Brom at the Hawthorns.

9) Peter Bonetti

Nearly two decades after making his Chelsea debut as an 18-year-old, Peter Bonetti was still flinging himself around the Blues' goal, making the last of his 729 appearances for the club against Arsenal in May 1979 when he was aged 37 years and seven months. After a sojourn in Scotland, where he occasionally played for Dundee United, 'The Cat' returned to the Bridge in 1985 as goalkeeper coach, even pulling on the gloves once again for a reserve match when he was 44.

10) Graham Rix

Appointed Chelsea youth coach by new Blues boss Glenn Hoddle in 1993, Graham Rix must have imagined his playing days were over. However, the following year an injury crisis saw him make his debut as a sub in a European Cup Winners'

Cup tie against Viktoria Zizkov when just a month short of his 37th birthday. The stylish midfielder was well past that landmark when he came on against his old club Arsenal in the final match of the 1994/95 season, after which he decided to hang up his boots for good.

TOP 10 HUMILIATING DEFEATS

Like all clubs, Chelsea have had a fair few 'bad days at the office' over the years. Be warned: the following makes for grim reading. Fans of a delicate disposition who have wiped these miserable encounters from their personal memory banks may wish to skip to page 89.

1) Wolverhampton Wanderers 8 Chelsea 1, First Division, 26 September 1953

Fast becoming a power in the land, Wolves swept aside a Chelsea side that was reduced to nine men by the end due to injuries, inflicting the Blues' heaviest-ever defeat. Two goals down at half-time, the Londoners completely capitulated after the break, former England winger Johnny Hancocks helping himself to a hat-trick as the champions-to-be rammed in six more goals to render Roy Bentley's 76th-minute strike the scantest of consolations for the visitors.

2) Manchester City 6 Chelsea 0, Premier League, 10 February 2019

Chelsea suffered their worst-ever defeat in the Premier League at the hands of a rampant Manchester City side, for whom star striker Sergio Aguero scored three times to equal Alan Shearer's long-standing record of 11 Premier League hat-tricks. Manager Maurizio Sarri's much-vaunted 'Sarri-ball' was more like 'sorry-ball' as the Blues barely laid a glove on the home side and defended abjectly from start to finish.

Four down after just 25 minutes, the visitors had reason to be thankful they only conceded two more in arguably the poorest Chelsea performance of the Abramovich era.

3) Rotherham United 6 Chelsea 0, Second Division, 31 October 1981

The early 1980s were a desperate period for the Blues, with this crushing defeat at a packed Millmoor one of the lowest moments. Maverick Yugoslav goalkeeper Petar Borota had a personal nightmare in what turned out to be his last-ever game for the Londoners, gifting the Millers their opener and then needlessly conceding a penalty as the home side romped into a three-goal lead after just 13 minutes. Rotherham added three more after the break, veteran striker Rodney Fern completing his hat-trick, while the Blues' misery was compounded when midfielder John Bumstead missed twice from the spot with a retaken penalty.

4) Chelsea 0 Notts County 6, First Division, 9 February 1924

With the Blues engaged in a desperate (and ultimately vain) struggle against relegation, the cover of the *Chelsea FC Chronicle* for the visit of mid-table Notts County featured a cartoon under the hopeful headline 'Something to change the luck'. The footballing fates, though, were not smiling on the home side, who conceded in the first 60 seconds and were three down after just nine minutes. The match was over as a contest but County didn't let up, adding three more goals in the second half as the Blues went down to a painful defeat that remains their worst-ever home reverse.

5) QPR 6 Chelsea 0, First Division, 31 March 1986

Stuffed 4-0 at the Bridge by fellow title-chasers West Ham two days earlier, the Blues made it a truly 'Black Easter' for their fans by suffering another heavy London derby defeat, this time on the plastic pitch at Loftus Road. QPR's slick passing on the fast-paced surface proved too much for a rickety Chelsea defence, while Rangers strikers Gary Bannister and John Byrne were in deadly form, grabbing the first five of their team's goals between them. A dreadful day for the Blues got even worse when striker David Speedie was sent off for violent conduct before Rangers sub Leroy Rosenoir gleefully slammed in the Hoops' sixth and final goal.

6) Leeds United 7 Chelsea 0, First Division, 7 October 1967

A day after Tommy Docherty's resignation as Chelsea boss, the Blues' players were, understandably, not in the best frame of mind to face a powerful Leeds side eager to avenge their FA Cup semi-final defeat against the Londoners a few months earlier. Three early goals for the Yorkshiremen set the tone, prompting the home fans to chant 'Ey-aye-addio, we're only warming up'. Sadly for the visitors, they were right, as Peter Lorimer smashed in a trademark piledriver before half-time to make it 4-0. After the break, a long-distance shot from Eddie Gray, a Marvin Hinton own goal and a spectacular overhead kick by Leeds skipper Billy Bremner completed the rout.

7) Nottingham Forest 7 Chelsea 0, First Division, 20 April 1991

An end-of-season game against a Forest side with half an eye on the following month's FA Cup Final against Tottenham did not look especially daunting on paper, but if the Blues were guilty of complacency they certainly paid the price. Buoyed by an early Roy Keane goal, Forest sensed blood and went for the jugular, tearing the Blues' defence apart with wave after wave of swift attacks. Three down at half-time, the visitors were unable to stem the tide and conceded four more goals after the break, two of them scored by legendary Forest skipper Stuart 'Psycho' Pearce.

8) Wolverhampton Wanderers 7 Chelsea 1, First Division, 15 March 1975

The glory days of the early-1970s were just a distant memory when Chelsea's somewhat threadbare mix of old-stagers and inexperienced youngsters arrived at Molineux in desperate need of points in what would prove to be an unsuccessful relegation battle. Wolves, though, were in unsympathetic mood and took control of the game with two goals midway through the first half. A Bill Garner header briefly gave the Blues hope, but they were soon overwhelmed by a home side inspired by new £100,000 midfielder Willie Carr, who was one of six different Wolves players to get on the scoresheet on a truly dire afternoon for Chelsea.

9) Crystal Palace 7 Chelsea 1, FA Cup third preliminary round, 18 November 1905

Thanks to the FA's insistence that Chelsea would not be exempted from the preliminary rounds of the FA Cup, the Blues were forced to send a reserve team to south London while the first team played Burnley in a Second Division match at Stamford Bridge. Palace were in the second tier of the Southern League at the time, so a heavy defeat for the 'stiffs' was far from inevitable, but the Eagles took full advantage of the bizarre double-booking to win 7-1 – still a record win for a non-league side against Football League opposition. At least there was better news from west London, where the 'real' Chelsea won 1-0.

10) Nottingham Forest 6 Chelsea 0, First Division, 28 March 1979

A young Blues side heading inexorably for the drop did well to keep the reigning champs and soon-to-be European

Cup winners at bay until shortly before half-time in this rearranged midweek fixture, when Forest's Martin O'Neill opened the scoring. The Northern Irish midfielder added two more after the break as the floodgates opened with his teammates Tony Woodcock (2) and Garry Birtles also breaching a shaky Chelsea defence lacking in top-flight experience and genuine quality.

TOP 10 SURPRISE CHELSEA APPEARANCES

Fans were rubbing their eyes in disbelief when they spotted these unlikely figures in the famous blue shirt:

1) Jimmy Tarbuck
The comedian and keen Liverpool fan came on as a substitute for Alan Birchenall against QPR in Ken Shellito's testimonial at Stamford Bridge on 6 May 1968. Presumably, manager Dave Sexton wasn't too impressed by the tubby comic's cameo as he didn't rush to sign him up for the following season!

2) George Best
Given that he spent much of his free time in the drinking dens of the King's Road, it was hardly surprising that wayward Northern Ireland star George Best was sometimes linked with a move to Chelsea. However, the only time he wore the club's colours was while turning out for a Past XI against the then-current Blues team in Peter Osgood's testimonial at the Bridge in November 1975. Despite being without a club at the time, Bestie showed his peerless dribbling skills were still intact, scoring twice in his side's 4-3 defeat.

3) Ian Botham
England's greatest-ever cricket all-rounder was also a decent footballer, making a number of appearances in the Football

League for Scunthorpe United in the early-1980s. The only time Chelsea fan Botham played at Stamford Bridge, however, was in Ron Harris' testimonial in May 1980 when he helped a Past Chelsea XI beat the then-current first team 1-0, thanks to a goal by a 40-year-old Jimmy Greaves.

4) Dave Cash and Graham Dene

Fans in the Shed were more than a little bewildered when the two Capital Radio DJs came on for the Blues at half-time in Ian Hutchinson's testimonial against QPR at the Bridge in November 1978. The pair didn't exactly cover themselves in glory as the home side let slip a two-goal lead and ended up drawing 2-2.

5) Alan Ball

The ginger-haired 1966 World Cup-winning midfielder turned out as a guest for the 1970 Chelsea team against the 1977 vintage in a fundraising match at Stamford Bridge for Peter Houseman's children, after the former Blues winger was tragically killed in a car accident with his wife and two friends while travelling home after playing for Oxford United.

6) Ossie Ardiles and Graeme Souness

Two of the finest midfielders of their generation took to the field in Chelsea colours for a one-off occasion, representing a Past Blues XI in Eddie Niedzwiecki's testimonial against Bobby Campbell's Second Division title winners at Stamford Bridge in May 1989. It proved to be an exciting match, with the then-current team winning 5-4.

7) Terry Byrne

Former Chelsea masseur and massive Blues fan Terry Byrne was rewarded with a brief run-out for the Londoners in a tour match against Brunei in May 1997, coming on for French defender Frank Leboeuf in the closing stages of an emphatic 6-0 victory.

8) Leon Lenik

The manager of the Chelsea club restaurant traded his dinner jacket for a football jersey in November 1983, coming on for skipper Colin Pates in Micky Droy's testimonial against Arsenal at Stamford Bridge. Fittingly, Droy scored one of the Blues' goals in a 2-1 win over the Gunners.

9) Hugh Hastings

Two days after the Blues won the Second Division title in May 1984, the then-Chelsea programme editor was a surprise substitute for Kerry Dixon in the second half of a testimonial for Brentford's Eddie Lyons at Griffin Park. Hastings didn't disgrace himself but was unable to match the standard set by Dixon, who helped himself to five goals in the Blues' 6-3 victory.

10) Antonio Pintus

The Blues' Italian fitness trainer came on for Danish winger Bjarne Goldbaek five minutes from the end of the Londoners' tour match against Instant District of Hong Kong in May 1999. Chelsea won the game 2-1, with goals from Gianfranco Zola and Mikael Forssell.

TOP 10 PENALTY SHOOT-OUTS

The Blues have endured their fair share of misery in shoot-outs, but in recent years especially have enjoyed some great wins too in the battle of nerves between penalty-taker and goalie.

1) Bayern Munich 3 Chelsea 4, Champions League Final, 19 May 2012

A night of high drama in Munich took yet another stomach-churning twist when spot kicks were required to decide the destiny of the Champions League trophy after a pulsating 1-1 draw. The Germans edged ahead in the contest after Bayern keeper Manuel Neuer saved from Juan Mata, but David Luiz and Frank Lampard drilled home to keep the Blues in the fight. When Petr Cech saved from Croatian striker Ivica Olic it gave Ashley Cole the chance to level the scores, which he did in convincing fashion. Finally, the odds moved in Chelsea's favour when Cech tipped Bastian Schweinsteiger's shot on to a post, giving Didier Drogba the opportunity to become the matchwinner and a Blues hero for all time. Showing remarkable composure, he carefully placed the ball on the spot, took a short run-up and then expertly slotted his penalty into the corner of the net to spark wild celebrations in the Allianz Arena and among Blues fans around the world.

2) Chelsea 4 Tottenham 2, League Cup semi-final second leg, 24 January 2019

Inspired by a lively Eden Hazard, the Blues won 2-1 on the night to wipe out Spurs' one-goal lead from the first leg and then had the advantage of taking penalties in front of the Matthew Harding Stand. A wild shot by Eric Dier, who blasted his penalty high over the bar, had the home fans cheering and when Kepa Arrizabalaga saved from Lucas Moura it fell to David Luiz to seal the Blues' victory with a confident finish right in the corner.

3) Chelsea 4 Eintracht Frankfurt 3, Europa League semi-final second leg, 9 May 2019

After two 1-1 draws a tightly contested semi-final went to spot kicks, the Germans taking an early advantage when Cesar Azpilicueta's penalty was brilliantly saved by Eintracht goalkeeper Kevin Trapp. However, the tide turned the Blues' way when Kepa Arrizabalaga blocked Martin Hinteregger's low drive with his legs and then dived to his right to palm away Goncalo Paciencia's shot. The Blues had kept regular penalty-taker Eden Hazard back till last, and it proved to be a wise move as he expertly drilled home the winner to take the Blues through to the final against Arsenal in Baku.

4) Newcastle United 2 Chelsea 4, FA Cup third-round replay, 17 January 1996

After an exciting 2-2 draw at St James' Park, the Blues were gifted early presents in the shoot-out when Peter Beardsley smashed his penalty against the bar and then Steve Watson saw his shot saved by Kevin Hitchcock. Untroubled by the home fans' catcalls, the visitors rattled home their spot kicks with ruthless efficiency, Eddie Newton wrapping up a superb victory with a low strike into the corner of the net.

5) Chelsea 4 Manchester United 1, Community Shield, 9 August 2009

Pegged back to 2-2 by an injury-time goal from Wayne Rooney, the Blues gained some semblance of revenge for their Champions League defeat on penalties by United in the Champions League Final in Moscow a year earlier by convincingly beating Alex Ferguson's men in this Wembley shoot-out. Petr Cech gave the Londoners a great start by saving Ryan Giggs' penalty with his legs and when he pounced on Patrice Evra's tame effort, it was just left to Salomon Kalou to clinch victory from 12 yards, which he did with some ease.

6) Chelsea 5 Norwich City 3, FA Cup third-round replay, 17 January 2018

Reduced to nine men in extra time after both Pedro and Alvaro Morata were sent off, the Blues were relieved to take this tie to penalties following a 1-1 draw. The key moment came early, when Chelsea's penalty-saving specialist Willy Caballero leapt to his right to turn away Nelson Oliveira's shot – a truly magnificent save. The ball kept hitting the back of the net after that, leaving Eden Hazard to clinch a hard-fought victory when he stroked home the Blues' fifth penalty.

7) Ipswich Town 1 Chelsea 4, League Cup quarter-final, 7 January 1998

After rallying from two goals down to draw 2-2, Ipswich must have fancied their chances in the shoot-out, but the Tractor Boys reckoned without the Blues' Dutch goalkeeper Ed de Goey, who saved from both James Scowcroft and Mauricio Taricco. Chelsea made no such blunders, Frank Leboeuf, Gianfranco Zola, Roberto Di Matteo and Mark Hughes all scoring to book the Blues a mouthwatering two-legged semi-final with arch-rivals Arsenal.

8) Chelsea 4 Leicester City 3, League Cup second round second leg, 25 October 1983

Two goals up after an impressive display in the first leg at Filbert Street, the promotion-hunting Blues made things difficult for themselves by losing 2-0 on the night to the Foxes at the Bridge. In Chelsea's first-ever penalty shoot-out, goalkeeper Eddie Niedzwiecki was the hero, saving two Leicester spot kicks while only Scottish striker David Speedie failed to convert from 12 yards for the Blues.

9) Chelsea 4 Fulham 3, League Cup third round, 21 September 2011

Following a 0-0 draw on the night, the Blues got off to a bad start in the shoot-out when Frank Lampard's spot kick was superbly saved by Fulham keeper Mark Schwarzer. However, Chelsea's substitute goalkeeper Ross Turnbull then saved from Mousa Dembele to level things up and when Florent Malouda put the home side 4-3 ahead, the pressure was on the Cottagers' Costa Rican striker Bryan Ruiz. He smashed his penalty against the bar and down on to the line – but, crucially, not over it – and the Blues were through.

10) Chelsea 4 Blackburn Rovers 1, League Cup third round, 15 October 1997

After a 1-1 draw on the night the Blues were indebted to goalkeeper Kevin Hitchcock, who saved from both Chris Sutton – a foretaste of his miserable season in front of goal in a Chelsea shirt two years later – and Lars Bohinen, to allow young midfielder Mark Nicholls to round off the evening with the winning penalty for the home side after defenders Frank Leboeuf, Frank Sinclair and Steve Clarke had all scored from the spot.

TOP 10 MANAGERS' QUOTES

Jose Mourinho had an extended say earlier. Now let's hear from some other Chelsea bosses:

1) 'Chelsea are the greatest club I've known. The people here have taken it on the chin for 50 years and always come up smiling. That takes some doing.'

Ted Drake, manager of the Blues' first title winners in 1955

2) 'My favourite moment has to be winning the FA Cup. I was a new manager, and Chelsea were a new club, in terms of winning trophies. I didn't expect it but all of a sudden it clicked, and it was an amazing time.'

Ruud Gullit, who led the Blues to FA Cup glory in 1997

3) 'At Chelsea, you have to have the intention to win and if I didn't say that then I shouldn't be here.'

Frank Lampard, on becoming Chelsea boss in 2019

4) 'I want the prima donnas to play and sing for the team, not for me. If they want to sing for themselves they'll no longer be a part of the orchestra and they'll become solo artists. They will be singing on their own.'
Claudio Ranieri, shortly after becoming Chelsea manager in 2000

5) 'I had a better quality player at Swindon and I had better facilities at Swindon. For example, I had to do a deal for Andy Townsend on a pay phone, putting 50p in the slot. And that was a £2.1 million deal!'
Glenn Hoddle, manager between 1993 and 1996, remembering his early days at the club

6) 'I was perfectly happy with Arsenal, and would have left them for only one club – Chelsea.'
Dave Sexton, after his appointment as Chelsea boss in 1967

7) 'If I am a Chelsea fan, I want to be excited when I go to the stadium, when I switch on the TV. I want to feel a certain level of energy, to feel a special bond with the players.'
Thomas Tuchel, after becoming Chelsea manager in 2021

8) 'I walk in here every day and you look out there and you get a tingling down your back. It's a tremendous set-up. Tremendous supporters.'
John Neal, 1981

9) 'I like to have this chance at Chelsea because this is a great team in Europe, with the possibility of winning the Champions League.'
Carlo Ancelotti, after becoming Chelsea manager in 2009

10) 'I'll be like a sponge, absorbing things from everybody, learning, then making decisions. And I will make decisions because it's me whose botty is on the line.'
Gianluca Vialli, after being named player-manager in 1998

TOP 10 SCOTTISH PLAYERS

From the Blues' foundation in 1905, there has invariably been a strong Scottish streak running through the club. Here's the pick of the talent hailing from north of the border:

1) Charlie Cooke

Sporting a Zapata moustache straight out of a spaghetti western, Charlie Cooke had a flamboyant image that matched his style of play. A master dribbler, his feints, dummies, shimmics and drag-backs bamboozled opponents while his pinpoint crosses set up numerous chances for the likes of Peter Osgood, Ian Hutchinson and Tommy Baldwin. Tommy Docherty, who signed Cooke from Dundee in 1966, called him 'my best signing, a marvellous player', but it was Dave Sexton who benefited most from his wing wizardry as the Scottish international helped the Blues win the FA Cup in 1970 and the European Cup Winners' Cup a year later. He was voted Chelsea Player of the Year in 1968 and, following a brief stint away from the Bridge with Crystal Palace, for a second time in 1975.

2) Hughie Gallacher

One of the Scottish 'Wembley Wizards' who famously thrashed England 5-1 in 1928, Hughie Gallacher joined the Blues from Newcastle two years later amid much excitement for a then-club record £10,000. Despite being just 5ft 5in tall, he was famed for his heading ability as well as his shooting prowess, qualities that brought him 81 goals in four and a bit seasons at the Bridge. However, a number of drink-related incidents didn't impress the Chelsea top brass and in 1934 he was sold to Derby County.

3) Eddie McCreadie

Tough-tackling left-back Eddie McCreadie joined the Blues from minnows East Stirling for just £5,000 in 1962. Three years later, he was a surprise pick at centre-forward for the first leg of the League Cup Final against Leicester but justified manager Tommy Docherty's decision by scoring a dramatic late winner. Back in defence, he helped the Blues win the FA Cup in 1970, and by the time he retired four years later McCreadie had played over 400 times for the club, as well as winning 23 caps for Scotland. Appointed Chelsea manager in 1975, he led the Blues to promotion two years later before abruptly quitting over a contract dispute.

4) Steve Clarke

Signed from St Mirren in January 1987 to bolster a leaky Chelsea back line, Steve Clarke went on to serve the club for over a decade. His excellent positional play, tidy defending and well-timed overlapping runs down the right wing earned him the club's Player of the Year award in 1994 as well as six Scotland caps, but he had to wait until the Blues' FA Cup triumph in 1997 before getting his hands on major silverware. He later worked as the club's assistant manager under Jose Mourinho and Avram Grant, and in May 2019 was appointed manager of Scotland.

5) Pat Nevin

A twinkle-toed dribbler who could befuddle any defence with his intricate footwork, Pat Nevin was signed from Clyde for £95,000 in 1983. He had an immediate impact, helping the Blues gain promotion to the top flight and winning the Chelsea

Player of the Year award in his first season at the Bridge. He went on to win the first of his 28 caps for Scotland in 1986, collected another Player of the Year award the following year but was sold to Everton for a then-club record £925,000 after the Blues were relegated to the second tier in 1988.

6) John Harris

Having first played for Chelsea as a guest during World War II, John Harris became a full-time Blue in 1945 and was immediately appointed club captain by boss Billy Birrell. In the same year, he became the first Chelsea skipper ever to collect silverware at Wembley when he was presented with the Football League (South) Cup by the Prime Minister, Winston Churchill, after a 2-0 win against Millwall in April 1945. A commanding presence at the heart of the Londoners' defence, he was still a regular in the side in his late 30s, playing the majority of the games when the Blues won the league title in 1955. He left the Bridge the following season to become player-manager at Chester.

7) David Speedie

A bargain £80,000 signing from Darlington in 1982, David Speedie was a fiery striker with a prodigious leap that enabled him to outjump much taller defenders. During the 1983/84 season he formed a terrific partnership with Kerry Dixon, the duo being instrumental in the Blues' Second Division title-winning campaign. The goals continued to flow for 'Speedo' in the top flight, earning him a much-deserved Scotland call-up as well as the club's Player of the Year award in 1985, before he moved on to Coventry City for a then-club record £750,000 in July 1987.

8) Andy Wilson

Signed from Middlesbrough in 1923 for a then-club record fee of £6,500, Andy Wilson was a skilful playmaker whose abilities on the ball seemed unaffected by an almost totally disabled left arm – the result of an injury suffered during World War I. The Scot's eight seasons with the Blues were mostly spent in the Second Division but, after a series of near misses, he helped the club back into the top flight in 1930, contributing ten goals to the successful promotion campaign. The following year, he moved on to QPR.

9) John McNichol

A talented inside-forward who was equally adept at creating or scoring goals, John McNichol joined the Blues from Brighton in 1952 and three years later was a key member of the Chelsea side that won the title for the first time. His total of 14 league goals that season was only bettered by skipper Roy Bentley and it was surprising that his excellent all-round play did not earn him a single Scotland cap. After losing his place to a young Jimmy Greaves, he signed for Crystal Palace in 1958.

10) John Boyle

Called up to the first team aged 19, Motherwell-born John Boyle got his Chelsea career off to a great start when he fired in a 20-yard winner against Aston Villa in the League Cup semi-final in January 1965. A few weeks later, 'Boylers' picked up a winner's medal in the same competition after the Blues beat Leicester City in a two-legged final. A hard-running midfield workhouse, he could also do a good job at full-back as he demonstrated in the 1971 European Cup Winners' Cup Final against Real Madrid, when he marked legendary winger Francisco Gento out of the game. Three years later, he moved on to Brighton after making 266 appearances for the Blues.

TOP 10 GOAL-FILLED THRILLERS

Chelsea fans certainly got their money's worth on these occasions; a Blues win and a total of nine goals or more:

1) Chelsea 5 Manchester City 4, Full Members Cup Final, 23 March 1986

The brainchild of Chelsea chairman Ken Bates, the Full Members Cup was a half-cocked competition that attracted meagre crowds and mocking headlines. However, this inaugural final provided an entertaining spectacle for over 67,000 fans at Wembley the day after both teams had been in league action. After falling behind early on, the Blues hit back to take a commanding 5-1 lead, thanks to a superb hat-trick by David Speedie and two goals from his strike partner Colin Lee. Three defensive lapses in the last five minutes, including a comical headed own goal by Doug Rougvie, left Blues fans waiting nervously for the final whistle but the cup was soon in the hands of Chelsea skipper Colin Pates.

2) Chelsea 6 Newcastle United 5, First Division, 10 September 1958

A see-saw midweek encounter saw the Blues trail 2-1 in the first half before two quickfire goals from Jimmy Greaves gave the home side a narrow lead at the break. However, Newcastle rallied to score three times in the first 15 minutes of the second half. The points seemed to be heading to the North East until the final ten minutes when a goal from midfielder Tony Nicholas and two by striker Ron Tindall gave Chelsea an unlikely, and pretty extraordinary, victory.

3) Chelsea 5 Manchester United 4, League Cup fourth round, 31 October 2012

Three days after losing 3-2 to United in a Premier League game at Stamford Bridge, the Blues appeared to be heading out of the League Cup to the Red Devils by the identical score. However, a foul on Brazilian midfielder Ramires allowed sub Eden Hazard to convert a last-minute penalty and take the tie to extra time. Daniel Sturridge then gave the Blues the lead in the 97th minute and when Hazard set up Ramires for number five the contest was over, making Ryan Giggs' late penalty for United a mere footnote.

4) Chelsea 7 Portsmouth 4, First Division, 25 December 1957

Chelsea boss Ted Drake recalled 17-year-old Jimmy Greaves to the first team after a six-week absence, and the decision paid off handsomely as the tyro striker helped himself to a quickfire first-half hat-trick before adding a fourth after the break. Both teams were in generous mood for this Christmas Day fixture, gifting each other an own goal apiece in a match that kept the 27,000 fans at Stamford Bridge entertained from start to finish.

5) Orient 3 Chelsea 7, Second Division, 10 November 1979

Recently appointed Chelsea manager Geoff Hurst enjoyed watching a comprehensive victory at Brisbane Road, 21-year-old Lee Frost helping himself to a hat-trick while strike partner Clive Walker bagged two. Orient were never really in the contest: 3-0 down at half-time, they were facing an utter trouncing midway through the second half when losing 6-1 before rallying with two late goals to give the scoreline a semblance of respectability.

6) Preston North End 4 Chelsea 5, First Division, 19 December 1959

When these teams met earlier in the campaign at the Bridge, it ended all square after an exciting 4-4 draw, Jimmy Greaves grabbing a hat-trick for the Blues. At Deepdale, though, Greavsie went one better – or rather, two better – scoring all of Chelsea's goals in a remarkable 5-4 victory, despite being man-marked by future England international Gordon Milne. Unlucky Preston striker Tommy Thompson notched a hat-trick of his own but, presumably, didn't even get a signed match ball as a consolation.

7) Derby County 4 Chelsea 6, First Division, 15 December 1990

A topsy-turvy match at the Baseball Ground saw the Blues lead 3-1 at half-time only to concede three quick goals midway through the second half to trail 4-3 with just 15 minutes to play. However, after winning their five previous games, Chelsea were full of confidence, and soon equalised through Dennis Wise's header. Then Gordon Durie collected goalkeeper Dave Beasant's throw to run half the length of the pitch before scoring with a well-drilled shot. It was left to Graeme Le Saux to put the seal on a tremendous away win with a close-range finish in the last minute.

8) Everton 3 Chelsea 6, Premier League, 30 August 2014

The Blues got off to a sensational start at Goodison Park, scoring twice in the opening three minutes through Diego Costa and Branislav Ivanovic. A Kevin Mirallas header reduced the arrears for the Toffees just before half-time, and it remained 2-1 until midway through the second half. A crazy spell of five goals in just 12 minutes – including one for ex-Chelsea striker Samuel Eto'o on his Everton debut – ended with Ramires poking home to make it 5-3 to the Blues, before Costa finished off the Toffees' stubborn resistance, firing in after being set up by John Obi Mikel's clever backheel pass.

9) Birmingham City 4 Chelsea 5, First Division, 31 December 1977

Newly promoted Chelsea had struggled for goals throughout the campaign – averaging less than a goal a game – when they suddenly found their shooting boots on a New Year's Eve trip to St Andrew's. Fighting back from a goal down, the Blues responded brilliantly to lead 5-2, thanks to a Tommy Langley hat-trick and one apiece from veteran striker Bill Garner and speedy winger Clive Walker. Brum rallied with a couple of late goals but it wasn't enough to prevent the Blues taking two very welcome points back to London.

10) Chelsea 6 Manchester City 3, First Division, 19 November 1960

Three days after scoring seven in a League Cup tie at Doncaster, the Blues almost matched that impressive tally but had to be satisfied with just six in a mid-table clash with Manchester City at the Bridge. Inevitably, Jimmy Greaves was on the scoresheet for the home side, grabbing a first-half hat-trick, while his strike partner Ron Tindall scored two, with 19-year-old Bobby Tambling also on target.

TOP 10 PLAYER CHANTS

The best of the chants Blues fans have devised for their favourite stars:

1) 'Su-per, su-per Frank, su-per, su-per Frank, su-per, su-per Frank, su-per Frankie Lampard '

A chant that had previously been used for the recently departed Romanian wing-back Dan Petrescu was aimlessly hanging around the Bridge when Frank Lampard signed for the Blues from West Ham in the summer of 2001. It didn't take long for the chant to be revamped and, as he kept banging in the goals, for 'young Frank Lampard' to swiftly evolve into a player on an altogether higher plane – 'Super Frankie Lampard'.

2) 'Osgood, Osgood, Osgood, Osgood, born is the king of Stamford Bridge'

It's rather appropriate that the Shed's song in tribute to legendary striker Peter Osgood should be based on a Christmas carol ('The First Noel') as it was only nine days before Christmas 1964 that the 'rising young star' made his debut for the Blues, scoring both goals in a 2-0 win against Workington Town in a League Cup quarter-final replay at the Bridge.

3) 'He's won more than you, he's won more than you, John Terry, he's won more than you'

When Chelsea skipper John Terry was picked on by opposition fans – a regular occurrence, especially in the latter years of his Stamford Bridge career – the home crowd had a simple retort. And, given that he won a total of 15 major trophies with the Blues, this chant was literally correct in many cases.

4) 'Gianfranco Zola, la la la la la, Gianfranco Zola, la la la la la'

When he first arrived at the Bridge from Parma, the brilliant little Sardinian was serenaded with a version of The Kinks' 'Lola'. However, pretty soon the Chelsea choir decided that Zola was more of an 'easy listening' kind of guy and adapted the 'I love you, baby' chorus of the old Frankie Valli hit 'Can't Take My Eyes Off You' to salute their star player.

5) 'Oh Dennis Wise, scored a f***ing great goal, in the San Siro, with ten minutes to go'

A rare case of a player chant referring to a particular incident, in this case Dennis Wise's famous goal away to AC Milan in a Champions League group game in October 1999. Latching on to a brilliant pass from Roberto Di Matteo, Wisey controlled the ball superbly before tucking it under Milan keeper Christian Abbiati to give the Blues a valuable point in a 1-1 draw. A moment worth celebrating in song for years to come!

6) 'One Kerry Dixon, there's only one Kerry Dixon, one Kerrrrie Dixon, there's only one Kerry Dixon'

Not the most original of chants, perhaps, but throughout most of the 1980s and into the early 1990s it did the job in unfussy style – just like the blond striker himself, who proudly sits third in the list of Chelsea's all-time top scorers.

7) 'Oi, oi, oi, Hudson-Odoi, oi, oi, oi, Hudson-Odoi'

This ode to Blues winger Callum Hudson-Odoi begins with well-crafted lyrics ('Local boy from Wandsworth, been Chelsea since birth' etc.) sung to the tune of Bob Marley's 'Buffalo Soldier' before seguing into a chorus that has more than a hint of the frenetic *Banana Splits* theme tune, 'The Tra La La song' or, even, the manic cover by punk band The Dickies, which reached number seven in the charts in 1979. The question is: was the reggae great influenced by the madcap *Splits* quartet of Fleegle, Bingo, Drooper and Snorky when he commemorated the black soldiers who fought in the Indian wars? One to ponder, certainly ...

8) 'Eden, Eden, Eden, Eden, Eden, Eden, Hazard, Eden'

Chelsea fans struggled for a while to come up with a chant for Belgian trickster Eden Hazard, but in the end settled on this frenetic number, which nicely matched the little man's all-action style of play.

9) 'Oh Tammy, Tammy, Tammy, Tammy, Tammy, Tammy Abraham'

This chant in praise of the young Chelsea striker has been around a while, and is actually based on the Chicory Tip song 'Son of my Father', which topped the UK charts in February 1972 – incidentally, exactly the same time as 'Blue is the Colour' reached the Top 10.

10) 'We'll just call you Dave, we'll just call you Dave, Azpilicueta, we'll just call you Dave'

A tongue-in-cheek tribute to Spanish defensive stalwart Cesar Azpilicueta, set to the tune of the old Beach Boys number 'Sloop John B'. At this point, some readers may be wondering, 'Yes, I get that "Azpilicueta" is a bit of a mouthful, but why "Dave" rather than, say, Paul, Pete or Pedro?' Well, it all goes back to the popular sitcom *Only Fools and Horses* and the dim-witted Trigger's insistence on calling Rodney Trotter 'Dave'. All a bit too meta? Maybe, but remember we are Chelsea, we are quite a droll bunch down here in SW6.

TOP 10 PREMIER LEAGUE HAT-TRICKS

The Blues have scored 26 hat-tricks since the Premier League began in 1992, including these crackers:

1) Jimmy Floyd Hasselbaink, Chelsea 4 Tottenham 0, 13 March 2002

Jimmy Floyd Hasselbaink scored a joint club-record three Premier League hat-tricks for Chelsea, but there is no doubt which one was the best. Three days after thrashing Spurs 4-0 in an FA Cup quarter-final tie at White Hart Lane, the Blues gave the north Londoners another mauling at the Bridge, with the Dutch striker very much to the fore. His first goal after 21 minutes was a lovely curling right-footer from just outside the penalty area. Then, in the second half, he powered in a header from Jesper Gronkjaer's right-wing cross before rounding off his evening with another curler from the edge of the box, this time with his left foot, to complete a perfect hat-trick.

2) Christian Pulisic, Burnley 2 Chelsea 4, 26 October 2019

New signing Christian Pulisic hadn't scored for Chelsea since moving from Borussia Dortmund for a cool £58m, but he made up for a slightly slow start to his Blues career on this trip to Turf Moor. His first two goals were rather similar efforts: capitalising on poor Burnley passes in midfield, the American surged forward before shooting low past Clarets goalkeeper Nick Pope, on the second occasion aided by a slight deflection. For his third goal, Pulisic was indebted to Mason Mount, who whipped in a fine cross that the unmarked winger was able to head home with some ease.

3) Gianfranco Zola, Chelsea 4 Derby County 0, 29 November 1997

Incredibly, the brilliant Gianfranco Zola had never scored a hat-trick in a competitive match before this trio against an outclassed Derby side at the Bridge. The little Sardinian opened the scoring with a fierce low shot from the edge of the box after just 11 minutes and then added two more goals in the second half: the first was a rather scrappy effort, but the second was superb – a composed side-foot finish after he had played a delightful one-two with fellow Italian Roberto Di Matteo.

4) Gianluca Vialli, Barnsley 0 Chelsea 6, 24 August 1997

Italian striker Gianluca Vialli scored Chelsea's first-ever Premier League hat-trick at an opponent's ground with a four-goal burst at newly promoted Barnsley. His first goal was the pick of the bunch, a magnificent shot on the turn from the edge of the penalty area after being put through by Dan Petrescu. Three typical poacher's goals – two shots and a header, all from close range – in the second half completed a great day for the shaven-headed hitman.

5) Tammy Abraham, Wolves 2 Chelsea 5, 14 September 2019

Chelsea centre-back Fikayo Tomori may have scored the best goal of the day with a stunner from 25 yards, but it was Tammy Abraham who took the headlines with a well-taken hat-trick. Opening his account with a shot on the turn from eight yards, the Blues striker then doubled his tally with a powerful stooping header. However, he saved the best for last: a burst of acceleration past a Wolves defender followed by a low drive into the far corner. We won't mention the unlucky own goal he also scored!

6) Tore Andre Flo, Tottenham 1 Chelsea 6, 6 December 1997

On a glorious afternoon for Chelsea at White Hart Lane, lanky Norwegian striker Tore Andre Flo set the ball rolling in the first half with a well-directed near-post header. After the break, he took advantage of a clever pass by strike partner Gianfranco Zola to score emphatically with a powerful right-foot shot, before rounding off a memorable derby rout with a cheeky chip over Spurs goalkeeper Ian Walker.

7) Andre Schurrle, Fulham 1 Chelsea 3, 1 March 2014

German winger Andre Schurrle pounced three times in just 16 second-half minutes to give the Blues the points against neighbours Fulham. His first goal demonstrated his pace and power, as he ran in behind the Cottagers' defence to finish with aplomb. Then an astute pass by Eden Hazard set him up for a low left-footer, before he completed his hat-trick with another decisive shot from Fernando Torres' through ball.

8) Alvaro Morata, Stoke City 0 Chelsea 4, 23 September 2017

The Spanish striker's day got off to a great start when he scored after just two minutes, outpacing the Stoke defence and then finishing with cool certainty. He had to wait until 13 minutes from the end to get his second, but it was a beauty: a powerful run past a couple of toiling defenders followed by a deft shot into the far corner from an acute angle. Then, just five minutes later, he claimed the match ball with a tap-in from just a couple of yards out.

9) Diego Costa, Chelsea 4 Swansea City 2, 13 September 2014

Fiery Spanish striker Diego Costa endeared himself to the Chelsea faithful with a hat-trick in just his fourth match for the Blues following a summer move from Atletico Madrid. His first, just before the break, was a powerful downward header from a corner at the Shed End. Eleven minutes into the second half, Costa nabbed his second with a high shot into the roof of the net from a cross by Cesc Fabregas. Finally, he made it three with another close-range finish, diverting a Ramires shot into the net while the Swans appealed in vain for offside.

10) Gavin Peacock, Chelsea 5 Middlesbrough 0, 4 February 1996

Chelsea fans had to wait almost four years before seeing one of their players hit a Premier League hat-trick, attacking midfielder Gavin Peacock coming up with the goods in a five-star demolition of Middlesbrough at Stamford Bridge. His first goal was a bobbling shot from the edge of the box, his second a tap-in after Ruud Gullit unselfishly squared the ball following a surging run before he rounded off a wonderful team performance with a close-range finish from John Spencer's superb defence-splitting pass.

TOP 10 ONE-GOAL WONDERS

The long-serving players who found the net just once for the Blues:

1) Benjamin Howard Baker

An all-round sportsman who held British records in the high jump and triple jump as well as playing cricket, water polo and tennis to a high level, Howard Baker joined Chelsea from Everton in October 1921. The following month, the Blues goalkeeper took and scored a late penalty at Stamford Bridge against Bradford City – the only goal of the game. He was less fortunate against Arsenal later that season, missing from the spot and having to dash back to his penalty area, but he remains the only goalkeeper ever to have scored for the Blues.

2) George Barber

A regular in the Chelsea side throughout the 1930s, George Barber was a tall full-back who signed on a free transfer from Luton Town. Although he gave the club sterling service, he only managed to get on the scoresheet once for the Blues in 294 games. His sole goal came in an FA Cup tie at Brighton in 1933, which the home side were leading 2-0, when he made a rare foray forward and grabbed a late consolation.

3) Erland Johnsen

Norwegian defender Erland Johnsen played in almost 200 games for the Blues between 1989 and 1997, and has fond memories of his single goal for the club in a 2-0 home win against Southampton in April 1994. 'A corner was taken from the left,' he later recalled. 'It was flicked on by the near post, and I jumped above the defender on the far post to head the ball down in the bottom corner. I was very surprised to see the ball go in, but the feeling was great!'

4) Graham Wilkins

The older brother of Chelsea skipper Ray, full-back Graham Wilkins didn't have a bad scoring record with the Blues, scoring five times in 149 games, but unfortunately four of those were at the wrong end! The goal he would prefer to remember came in a 2-1 win against Middlesbrough at Stamford Bridge in April 1979. 'I'd pushed up from right-back to the edge of the box, by the angle, caught the ball on my chest and volleyed it into the top left-hand corner at the Shed End,' he later recalled. 'I was absolutely flabbergasted!'

5) John Sillett

The brother of 1955 title winner Peter Sillett, full-back John made his Blues debut in 1957 but had to wait three years before getting on the scoresheet with a long-range shot in a 7-0 demolition of Doncaster Rovers in the League Cup. 'It felt wonderful to score and not to be congratulating my brother – who used to take our penalties and free kicks – for a change,' he later told the official Chelsea magazine.

6) Alec Ormiston

The Scottish centre-half turned out 102 times for the Blues before World War I, missing just one game when the Londoners won promotion back to the First Division in 1912. It was during that season that Ormiston scored his only goal for the club in a 2-1 home win against Leicester Fosse, the original name of Leicester City.

7) Albert Ferrer

Strangely, Spanish defender Albert Ferrer's only goal for Chelsea came in the same match that French midfielder Didier Deschamps also got on the scoresheet for the only time – a 2-0 Champions League win against Hertha Berlin at the Bridge in November 1999. Ferrer's goal was set up by Dennis Wise, who found him running unmarked in the inside-right position with a clever chipped pass that Ferrer converted with surprising confidence.

8) Frank Mitchell

An Australian-born wing-half who also played cricket for Warwickshire, Mitchell signed for the Blues from Birmingham City in January 1949. Two months later, he scored in a 1-1 draw away to Aston Villa but he failed to find the net again before moving on to Watford three years later.

9) Stan Wicks

In January 1954, Blues boss Ted Drake raided his former club Reading to bring centre-half Stan Wicks to the Bridge for £10,500. After a spell in the reserves, he eventually replaced future England manager Ron Greenwood at the heart of the Chelsea defence midway through the club's title-winning campaign in 1954/55. Wicks' sole goal for the Blues was an important one, coming in a 4-2 win against Tottenham at White Hart Lane in April 1955.

10) Yuri Zhirkov

Signed from CSKA Moscow for £18m in July 2009, midfielder Yuri Zhirkov helped the Blues win the Double in his first season at the Bridge. However, he had to wait until the following campaign to notch his only goal for the club during his two years in west London, a stunning left-footer from outside the box in a 2-0 victory away to Spartak Moscow in the group stages of the Champions League.

TOP 10 BLUE FIRSTS

Chelsea have always been an innovative, forward-looking club, an attitude reflected by the number of significant 'firsts' that the Blues have achieved:

1) First British club to win all four UEFA trophies

When the Blues beat Benfica in the final of the Europa League in Amsterdam in 2013, they became the first club from these shores to have won all four of the historic UEFA competitions, adding to their successes in the Champions League (2012), European Cup Winners' Cup (1971 and 1998) and the UEFA Super Cup (1998). Since then, Chelsea have won the Europa League again, in 2019, to become the first British club to win the trophy twice under its latest name.

2) First London club to win the Champions League

As league title winners in 1955, Chelsea were invited to take part in the inaugural edition of the European Cup but were persuaded by a sceptical FA not to participate in the exciting new venture. It was an opportunity lost but, after several agonising near misses, the Blues eventually won the competition – by then known as the Champions League – in 2012 when they beat Bayern Munich on penalties in the final at the Allianz Arena to become the first London club to win UEFA's foremost club competition.

3) First club to win the FA Cup at the new Wembley

In 2007, Chelsea had the honour of playing in the first FA Cup Final at the new £798 million Wembley Stadium. Appropriately, the Blues beat Manchester United 1-0 – the same score by which they had beaten Aston Villa seven years earlier in the last final played at the original Wembley.

4) First Premier League club to score 100 goals in a season

Under attack-minded manager Carlo Ancelotti, the Blues won the Premier League title in 2009/10 in thrilling style. In their last match of the season, they needed to beat Wigan Athletic at Stamford Bridge to be sure of pipping Manchester United to top spot, but also knew that they would become the first team to hit three figures in a single Premier League campaign if they scored five or more goals. An emphatic 8-0 win ensured the west Londoners achieved both their aims.

5) First British club to host a European final

On 5 March 1958, Stamford Bridge became the first British ground to host a European final when it staged the first leg of the inaugural Inter-Cities Fairs Cup Final between a team representing London and another from Barcelona. Two Chelsea players, Jimmy Greaves and Peter Sillett, were in the London team that drew 2-2 at the Bridge before losing the second leg 6-0 at the Nou Camp.

6) First Premier League club to field an entirely foreign XI

Chelsea were at the forefront of the 'overseas invasion' of English football, signing the likes of Dutchman Ken Monkou and Norwegian Erland Johnsen even before the start of the Premier League in 1992. However, on Boxing Day 1999 the Blues really annoyed the 'Little Englanders' in the press by fielding the Premier League's first all-foreign XI for a 2-1 win at Southampton. The Chelsea line-up consisted of two Frenchmen (Didier Deschamps and Frank Leboeuf), two Italians (Roberto Di Matteo and Gabriele Ambrosetti), a Romanian (Dan Petrescu), a Nigerian (Celestine Babayaro), a Dutchman (Ed de Goey), a Norwegian (Tore Andre Flo), a Uruguayan (Gustavo Poyet), a Brazilian (Emerson Thome) and a Spaniard (Albert Ferrer).

7) First club to host the Charity Shield

In April 1908 the first-ever Charity Shield match was played at Stamford Bridge, league champions Manchester United taking on Southern League title winners QPR. After a rain-soaked 1-1 draw, the teams agreed to a replay that wasn't held until August, United winning 4-0. The two matches raised £1,275 (around £155,000 in today's money) for charitable causes.

8) First English club to wear shirt numbers

Along with Arsenal, Chelsea were the first English club to wear shirt numbers, adopting an idea of Gunners boss Herbert Chapman for a Second Division game against Swansea Town on 25 August 1928. The spectator-friendly innovation didn't upset the Blues in the slightest, who tonked the Welshmen 4-0. However, the football authorities remained unconvinced by the experiment and didn't make shirt numbers obligatory for another 11 years.

9) First Football League club to fly to an away fixture

On 19 April 1957, Chelsea became the first Football League team to fly by aeroplane to an away fixture. Joining the jet-set seemed to suit the Blues, who won 2-1 at Newcastle. The Londoners were back in action the following day and showed no sign of jet lag as they thrashed Everton 5-1 at the Bridge.

10) First top-flight club to play on a Sunday

The Blues took part in the first-ever First Division match to be played on a Sunday, losing 1-0 away to Stoke City on 27 January 1974. Previously, Football League teams were prohibited from playing on Sundays and were only given special dispensation in 1974 because a national fuel crisis caused by a long-running miners' strike meant that they were not allowed to play matches under floodlights.

TOP 10 AFRICAN PLAYERS

The list of Chelsea players to hail from Africa is an impressive one and, of course, it is headed by a genuine club legend:

1) Didier Drogba

A phenomenally powerful striker who could batter a defence into submission more or less on his own, Didier Drogba joined the Blues from Marseille for £24m in 2004. Over the next eight years he was a central figure in Chelsea's success, winning the Golden Boot in the 2009/10 Double season, scoring in four victorious FA Cup finals, three League Cup finals and, most famously, the winner from the spot in the shoot-out against Bayern Munich in the 2012 Champions League Final after his trademark power header had saved the Blues from defeat two minutes from the end of normal time. After leaving the Bridge that summer the Ivorian icon returned to west London two years later for a single season, adding a fourth Premier League title to his impressive collection of honours.

2) Michael Essien

The Ghana international became the most expensive African player ever when he joined Chelsea from Lyon for £24.4m in August 2005. It proved to be money well spent as the powerful and energetic midfielder cemented a place in the Blues team that went on to win the Premier League for a second season running. The following campaign he was voted Chelsea Player of the Year, the first African ever to achieve this award, and in 2008 he helped the Blues reach a first Champions League Final. Sadly, two serious knee injuries blighted his later Chelsea career, and in 2012 he moved on to Real Madrid.

3) Salomon Kalou

A hard-working, direct and pacy striker who usually preferred to operate from a wide position, Salomon Kalou joined the

Blues for around £9m from Feyenoord in the summer of 2006. The Ivorian struggled to hold down a regular starting berth, but was always part of the matchday squad and made some vital contributions off the bench. His final match for the club was the 2012 Champions League Final victory against Bayern Munich, after which he joined French side Lille.

4) John Obi Mikel

The Blues signed the Nigerian teenager from Norwegian club Lyn in controversial circumstances in 2006, Manchester United claiming that Chelsea had 'kidnapped' Obi Mikel after he had already committed himself to the Old Trafford club. United's loss proved to be Chelsea's gain as the strongly built defensive midfielder overcame some initial disciplinary problems to serve the Blues for a decade, helping the west Londoners win a host of silverware, including two Premier League titles and the Champions League in 2012.

5) Edouard Mendy

With first-choice goalkeeper Kepa Arrizabalaga suffering a dismal run of form at the start of the 2020/21 season, then-Blues boss Frank Lampard moved quickly in the transfer window to bring Rennes goalkeeper Edouard Mendy to the Bridge for £22m. The Senegal international immediately shored up a previously leaky Blues defence, conceding just one goal in his first seven appearances, while using his long reach to make some spectacular saves and bringing a much-needed sense of calm authority to his vital position. He ended his first season in west London by helping the Blues win the Champions League, keeping yet another clean sheet in the 1-0 win over Manchester City in the final in Porto.

6) Celestine Babayaro

Chelsea signed the Nigerian left-back from Anderlecht in the summer of 1997 when he was only 18, the £2.25m fee setting a new club record for a teenager. An injury-hit first season meant he missed out on the Blues' triumphs in the League Cup and European Cup Winners' Cup, but he picked up a winner's medal in the FA Cup in 2000. Famed for his eye-catching acrobatic goal celebrations, Babayaro played over 200 games for the club before joining Newcastle in January 2005.

7) Mark Stein

The slightly built South Africa-born striker joined Chelsea from Stoke for £1.5m in October 1993 and later that season scored in a then-record seven consecutive Premier League matches. However, goals became harder to come by for Stein after that purple patch and the arrival of Mark Hughes in 1995 limited his first-team opportunities. In 1998, after three different loans away from the Bridge, he moved on to Bournemouth.

8) Geremi

A £6.9m signing from Real Madrid in the summer of 2003, the Cameroon international was a hard-tackling midfielder who could also fill in at right-back. His Chelsea career got off to a bad start when he was sent off on his home debut against Leicester, but his versatility made him a handy squad member in the Blues' Premier League title-winning seasons during Jose Mourinho's first spell in charge. However, his last action for the club before joining Newcastle is not one fans will remember with fondness – a missed penalty in the 2007 Champions League semi-final shoot-out defeat by Liverpool.

9) Samuel Eto'o

African Footballer of the Year a joint-record four times, Samuel Eto'o joined the Blues from Russian side Anzhi Makhachkala on a one-year contract in August 2013. Aged

32, the Cameroon striker was some way past his best but did enjoy one memorable afternoon at the Bridge when he scored a hat-trick in a 3-1 defeat of Manchester United. After leaving the Blues he stayed in the Premier League, signing for Everton.

10) Hakim Ziyech

After impressing for Ajax in the sides' two Champions League meetings in 2019, the Blues splashed out £33.3m on Moroccan winger Hakim Ziyech the following year. His Chelsea career got off on the right foot, with goals against FK Krasnodar and Burnley in his first two starts, while he also showed his ability as a creator with some dangerous left-footed crosses. He then came out of a bad dip in form to get back to his best in the spring of 2021, scoring a number of vital goals, including the winner in the FA Cup semi-final against Manchester City.

TOP 10 FA CUP SHOCKS

The Blues have a great record in the FA Cup, winning the trophy an impressive eight times. However, the west Londoners have also occasionally been the victims of a giant-killing by a lower-league team, ending their supporters' dreams of cup glory in the most painful manner possible.

1) Chelsea 2 Bradford City 4, FA Cup fourth round, 24 January 2015

Sitting pretty at the top of the Premier League, the Blues must have anticipated a routine cup win against lower-league opposition when Gary Cahill and Ramires both scored in the first half. However, the Bantams refused to buckle and pulled a goal back before the break, John Stead firing a powerful drive past Petr Cech. With 15 minutes to go, former

Chelsea reserve Felipe Morais equalised from close range and then, incredibly, the League One side took the lead through Andrew Halliday's well-placed side footer. Desperate for an equaliser, the Blues piled on the pressure, but Didier Drogba was wide with a header and Kurt Zouma blazed over from close range before Bradford wrapped up one of the greatest shocks in FA Cup history with a last-minute goal by Mark Yeates.

2) Chelsea 1 Crewe Alexandra 2, FA Cup third round, 7 January 1961

After losing 6-0 at Manchester United and 6-1 at Wolves over Christmas, Chelsea continued their wretched form by going out of the FA Cup to Fourth Division Crewe. Two goals by the visitors in the first 25 minutes put the Blues on the back foot, and although ex-Alex winger Frank Blunstone soon pulled one back it wasn't enough to prevent the Londoners slumping out of the competition at the first hurdle.

3) Darlington 4 Chelsea 1, FA Cup fourth-round replay, 29 January 1958

In the original match at Stamford Bridge, Chelsea were 3-0 down at half-time to fourth-tier Darlo before fighting back to earn a draw. The replay on a muddy pitch saw the Blues dominate for long periods, but they were held to a 1-1 draw in the 90 minutes. Then, in a remarkable six-minute spell at the start of extra time, Darlington scored three times without response to pull off the biggest cup shock in their history.

4) Barnsley 1 Chelsea 0, FA Cup sixth round, 8 March 2008

On a hard, bobbly pitch, Chelsea's team of international superstars failed to perform to their normal high standards and fell behind to the struggling Championship side midway through the second half when Kayode Odejayi outjumped

Blues keeper Carlo Cudicini and headed in – one of just five goals the Nigerian striker scored for the Tykes in 82 appearances. Despite increasing Chelsea pressure the Yorkshiremen stayed firm, making it through to the semi-finals of the cup for the first time since 1912.

5) Orient 3 Chelsea 2, FA Cup fifth round, 26 February 1972

Dave Sexton's flamboyant Chelsea team were on a fantastic run of just one defeat in 24 matches and looked set to continue their good form when they went two goals up at Orient thanks to towering headers by David Webb and Peter Osgood. However, the Second Division outfit were encouraged by a 25-yard piledriver by Phil Hoadley just before half-time and, when Mickey Bullock equalised early in the second half after a mix-up in the Blues defence, the home side smelt blood. However, they had to wait until four minutes from the end to get the winner, Barrie Fairbrother capitalising on more defensive chaos on a mud-clogged pitch to shoot into an empty net.

6) Chelsea 2 Millwall 3, FA Cup fourth round, 4 February 1985

Whisper it, but Chelsea have been knocked out of the FA Cup by Millwall on all four occasions that the two clubs have been drawn together. However, the Blues had a bit of an excuse when losing to George Graham's Lions in 1985 as this was their fifth game in ten days and they were without prolific striker Kerry Dixon. Taking their lead from bullish centre-forward John Fashanu, who scored once and rattled the Chelsea defence throughout the evening, the promotion-hunting Third Division outfit were good value for their win – although the Blues would have salvaged a replay if David Speedie hadn't missed a last-minute penalty.

7) Bristol City 3 Chelsea 1, FA Cup fourth round, 27 January 1990

On a run of one defeat in nine games, the Blues should have approached a trip to third-tier Bristol City with some confidence. However, they got off to a terrible start when goalkeeper Dave Beasant fumbled a long-range effort, allowing Robbie Turner to score. Turner added a second in the second half, possibly from an offside position, and although a header from Kevin Wilson halved the arrears, it was all over for the Blues when the Robins scored a third in the dying seconds through Mark Gavin.

8) Chelsea 0 Wigan Athletic 1, FA Cup third round, 14 January 1980

Two days after thrashing Newcastle 4-0, the Blues found Fourth Division Wigan a much tougher nut to crack on an icy pitch at Stamford Bridge. The key moment came five minutes before half-time when midfielder Tommy Gore fired home for the Latics from the edge of the box and, despite piling on the pressure after the break, the Londoners were denied an equaliser and left to concentrate on their ultimately fruitless quest to gain promotion back to the top flight.

9) Luton Town 2 Chelsea 0, FA Cup third-round replay, 16 January 1935

Luton were one of three lucky third-tier clubs to get a bye to the third round, and took advantage of their good fortune to claim a 1-1 draw at the Bridge in the original fixture. Four days later, second-half goals from forwards Jack Ball and Fred Roberts saw off the Blues in front of over 23,000 delighted fans at Kenilworth Road.

10) Brighton & Hove Albion 2 Chelsea 1, FA Cup third round, 14 January 1933

In the first-ever match between the clubs, Brighton got off to a great start when striker Arthur Attwood scored in the opening minute. Veteran winger Ernie 'Tug' Wilson added a second for the Seagulls midway through the second half and although George Barber scored a late goal for the Blues, it proved to be a mere consolation. On a more positive note, this remains Brighton's sole success against Chelsea in 16 meetings.

TOP 10 PLAYER QUOTES

Past and present players on what makes Chelsea so special:

1) 'You have given me everything. From the age of 14 when I signed, you picked me up when I was down, you sung my name when I had bad games and disappointed you. Thank you will never ever be enough.'
John Terry, thanking the Chelsea fans after his final game for the Blues in 2017

2) 'The ideal thing would be to be manager of Chelsea, but it doesn't always work out like that.'
Frank Lampard, contemplating his future in 2009. Ten years later, he got his wish

3) 'In that moment, there was only Tottenham to go to but I didn't sign. When at the last moment Chelsea came in, I said "I'm sorry, but I go to Chelsea – that's my dream and I have to go there. I don't care. I go there." I think it was the best day of my life when I signed with Chelsea.'
Willian, reflecting on snubbing Spurs for Chelsea in 2013

4) 'I would come back and cut the grass if they asked me. My blood is blue.'
Didier Drogba, before he returned to Chelsea in 2014

5) 'Chelsea gave me what I was looking for when I left Liverpool – trophies. I'll always see it as a success.'

Fernando Torres

6) 'I gave Chelsea fans what they wanted, a dream. And they gave me what I was dreaming of too.'

Gianfranco Zola

7) 'I've always said I wanted to play in England. There was a struggle between Chelsea and United, but according to me, Chelsea has the best project.'

Eden Hazard in 2012, on why he chose to sign for Chelsea ahead of Manchester United

8) 'I miss our fans clapping along to the Liquidator when we walk out. That means a lot to me.'

Mason Mount, on playing behind closed doors during the Covid-19 pandemic

9) 'In the end, my decision went Chelsea's way. Not because there was anything wrong with Liverpool. But at Chelsea, the whole package was a better fit for me.'

Timo Werner, explaining why he chose to move to west London rather than Merseyside in 2020

10) 'I'd rather sell groundnuts in my village than play for a pathetic club like Chelsea.'

Barcelona's Samuel Eto'o in 2005. Eight years later, he signed for Chelsea!

TOP 10 TON-UP GOALSCORERS

The players who have scored a century or more goals for the Blues:

1) Jimmy Greaves

After scoring a phenomenal 114 goals in a single youth-team season, 17-year-old Jimmy Greaves made his Chelsea debut in August 1957, opening his account in a 1-1 draw at White Hart Lane. Despite never winning major honours at the Bridge, the quicksilver striker carried on finding the net at a sensational rate, hitting 132 goals in just 169 appearances while notching a club record 13 hat-tricks in the process. After signing off with all four goals in a 4-3 defeat of Nottingham Forest at the Bridge in April 1961, he joined Italian giants AC Milan.

2) Frank Lampard

When Frank Lampard joined Chelsea from West Ham in the summer of 2001, few would have bet on him becoming the club's all-time top scorer. However, that's precisely what happened as the promising 23-year-old matured into one of the greatest goalscoring midfielders of all time while helping the Blues win enough silverware to fill a vault at Fort Knox over the next 11 years. By the time he left the Bridge in 2014, he had taken his Chelsea goals tally to 211 (including an incredible 49 from the penalty spot), smashing Bobby Tambling's long-standing club record and setting a new benchmark that will take some beating.

3) Didier Drogba

Always a player for the big occasion, Didier Drogba scored in all eight of the finals he appeared in for Chelsea in his first spell at the Bridge, most famously heading the equaliser against Bayern Munich in the 2012 Champions League Final before calmly slotting home the winning spot kick in the penalty shoot-out. In total, he banged in 164 goals for the Blues, including a club-record 36 in European competitions, to make him easily the most prolific of Chelsea's foreign legion.

4) Peter Osgood

The flamboyant frontman in the exciting Chelsea team of the late 1960s and early 1970s, Peter Osgood hit 150 goals in his two spells with the Blues, including vital strikes that helped bring domestic and European silverware to the Bridge. Two-footed and a superb header of the ball, Ossie's most prolific season was in 1969/70 when he notched 31 goals in all competitions, finding the net in every round of the FA Cup, including in the 2-1 win in the replayed final against Leeds at Old Trafford.

5) Bobby Tambling

Spotted playing for Hampshire by legendary Chelsea scout Jimmy Thompson, Bobby Tambling opted to sign for the Blues ahead of a host of other clubs chasing his signature, including Arsenal and Wolves. Aged just 17, Tambling scored on his debut against West Ham in February 1959 and never looked back. Over the next decade, the fleet-footed striker banged in 202 goals for the club – a tally surpassed only by Frank Lampard – before joining Crystal Palace in 1970.

6) Kerry Dixon

A tall, powerful striker who packed a fearsome shot with both feet and was deadly in the air, Kerry Dixon arrived at the Bridge from Reading in 1983 for £175,000. The fee turned out to be a snip, as 'Kerrygoal' scored 70 goals in his first two seasons with the Blues before earning his first England cap in 1985. By the time he left Chelsea in 1992 for Southampton, his total of 193 goals for the Blues left Dixon just nine short of Bobby Tambling's then-club goalscoring record.

7) Roy Bentley

Bristol-born Bentley was signed by the Blues from Newcastle in January 1948 and went on to serve the club with distinction for the next eight years, scoring 150 goals in total, before joining Fulham in 1956. An intelligent striker who liked to roam around the front line and was a strong finisher in the air and on the ground, he famously skippered Chelsea to the league title in 1955, topping the club's scoring charts with 21 goals.

8) Eden Hazard

An attacking midfielder whose darting runs into the penalty area often left a trail of defenders in his wake, Eden Hazard joined Chelsea from Lille for £32m in the summer of 2012. A regular matchwinner for the Blues before his departure to Real Madrid in 2019, his 110 goals for the club included the winner in the 2018 FA Cup Final against Manchester United and a brace in the Europa League Final against Arsenal the following year.

9) George Mills

The first Chelsea player to score 100 league goals, George Mills signed for the Blues from non-league Bromley in 1929. He went on to serve the club for a decade and, despite sometimes playing second fiddle to the likes of Hughie Gallacher and Joe Bambrick, notched an impressive 125 goals in 239 games, with a personal best of 23 in the 1936/37 campaign.

10) George Hilsdon

After joining Chelsea from West Ham in 1906, George Hilsdon enjoyed a terrific debut with five goals in a 9-2 thrashing of Glossop North End. Nicknamed 'Gatling Gun' for his high-speed shooting, Hilsdon secured his place in the club's record books by becoming the first Chelsea player to score 100 goals, finishing with 108 before he rejoined West Ham in 1912.

TOP 10 OWN GOALS

Celebrating the opposition players who helped the Chelsea cause by generously putting the ball in their own net:

1) Steven Gerrard

With the Blues losing 1-0 to Liverpool in Cardiff in the 2005 League Cup Final and only 11 minutes to play, it seemed as though the trophy would be heading to Merseyside. However, Reds skipper Steven Gerrard came to Chelsea's aid by heading Paulo Ferreira's deep free kick on to a post and into his own net to send the match into extra time. The Blues came out on top in the additional 30 minutes play, winning 3-2 and leaving Gerrard to reflect on his costly error. 'Losing any game of football is painful, but to lose a cup final and to score an own goal makes it a really bad day for me,' he lamented afterwards. At least the kindly Chelsea fans at the Millennium Stadium tried to cheer him up, chanting, 'There's only one Steven Gerrard!' as he trudged off the pitch at the end.

2) John Arne Riise

Trailing 1-0 to Liverpool in the first leg of the Champions League semi-final at Anfield in April 2008, Chelsea were handed a late equaliser when Norwegian defender John Arne Riise stooped low to head clear a Salomon Kalou cross but could only watch in horror as it flew past Reds goalkeeper Pepe Reina and high into the net. The Blues took full advantage of this unexpected gift, beating Liverpool 3-2 in the return at the Bridge to go through to the final in Moscow.

3) Stan Milburn and Jack Froggatt

When Chelsea met Leicester at the Bridge on 18 December 1954, the Foxes kindly donated the Blues an early Christmas present in the form of the most bizarre own goal in football history. After Chelsea midfielder Johnny McNichol shot against the bar, Leicester defenders Stan Milburn and Jack Froggatt attempted to clear but only succeeded in sending the ball spinning into their own net as they both kicked it at precisely the same time. The freakish goal, Chelsea's second in a 3-1 win, was recorded as a 'shared own goal' – the first and only one of its kind.

4) Sam Allardyce

In an incredibly exciting First Division match at Stamford Bridge in October 1978, Chelsea had come back from 3-0 down against Bolton with three goals in the last 15 minutes and were searching for another as the clock ticked into injury time. The dramatic turnaround had been sparked by substitute Clive Walker, and it was the blond winger's cross that struck Trotters defender Sam Allardyce and flew into the net for an unlikely winner.

5) Harry Maguire

Already two goals to the good against Manchester United in the FA Cup semi-final at Wembley in July 2020, the Blues launched yet another attack down the left wing, Marcos Alonso firing in a cross towards Antonio Rudiger. However, United centre-back Harry Maguire got there first, sticking out a foot to send the ball shooting past goalkeeper David de Gea at the near post. Nice one, Harry!

6) Ron Healy

Chelsea were leading Manchester City 1-0 from the first leg of the European Cup Winners' Cup semi-final in April 1971 and knew they would be in for a tough game in the return at Maine Road. However, City goalkeeper Ron Healy, deputising for Joe Corrigan, who had dropped out just an hour before kick-off with a painful boil on his knee, made the Blues' task that much easier by palming an indirect free kick by Keith Weller over his own goal line. It proved to be the only goal of the evening, ensuring the Londoners marched on to their first-ever European final.

7) Kieran Trippier

Chelsea were holding on to a 1-0 lead in their Premier League derby with Tottenham in February 2019 when the ball fell to Spurs right-back Kieran Trippier just outside his own penalty area. Without looking, he passed back to Hugo Lloris, but the Tottenham goalkeeper had advanced some way from his line and the ball rolled past the stranded Frenchman and into an empty net to seal a 2-0 win for the Blues.

8) Frank Sinclair

Although he served Chelsea well for most of the 1990s, defender Frank Sinclair was prone to the occasional howler and his mishaps continued after he moved to Leicester in 1998. The following year he started the season in calamitous fashion, scoring an own goal on the opening day to gift Arsenal a 2-1 win. The next week he was at it again, against his old team, heading in past Foxes goalkeeper Tim Flowers in injury time to give the Blues a point in a 2-2 draw. Frank Sinclair? No, this was more like the accident-prone Frank Spencer!

9) Fernando Meira

Chelsea's hopes of reaching the quarter-finals of the Champions League in 2004 were boosted by the Portuguese defender, who diverted a Glen Johnson cross into his own net to give the Blues a 1-0 victory in Stuttgart in the first leg of the clubs' last 16 tie. With the return at Stamford Bridge finishing goalless, Meira's inadvertent intervention proved to be the decisive moment of the 180 minutes of action.

10) Joleon Lescott

Despite being reduced to ten men following a red card for midfielder John Obi Mikel, Chelsea were pressing for a late winner in the first leg of their League Cup semi-final against Everton at Stamford Bridge in January 2008. It eventually came from an unexpected source, Toffees defender Joleon Lescott heading Michael Ballack's cross into his own net. 'It hit me straight in the face,' the Everton man said afterwards. 'I know I should have got it away. It's a horrible feeling knowing you've let your team-mates down.' Never mind, Joleon, just think how happy you made the Chelsea players!

TOP 10 CHELSEA FC WOMEN VICTORIES

Chelsea Women have enjoyed some great moments in recent years, with these matches being especially memorable:

1) Chelsea 3 Arsenal 1, FA Cup Final, 5 May 2018

In front of an FA Cup Final record crowd of 45,423, Swiss international Ramona Bachmann put the Blues on the road to victory with two superb goals after half-time. Chelsea nerves were jangling when Arsenal's Dutch striker Vivianne Miedema pulled a goal back on 73 minutes, but shortly afterwards Fran Kirby settled the contest in the Blues' favour with a beautiful left-foot curler.

2) Chelsea 4 Bayern Munich 1, Champions League semi-final second leg, 2 May 2021

Trailing 2-1 from the first leg, the Blues levelled the aggregate scores after ten minutes when Fran Kirby shot home after a neat one-two with strike partner Sam Kerr. Bayern hit back with a 25-yard wonder goal but midfielder Ji So-Yun responded for the Blues just before half-time, lashing in from the edge of the box after her free kick had been blocked. Seven minutes from time Pernille Harder put Chelsea ahead in the tie, heading in Jess Carter's pinpoint free kick. In a frenetic finale, Bayern missed two great chances before Fran Kirby clinched Chelsea's place in the final, side-footing into an empty net with the German goalkeeper stranded upfield.

3) Chelsea 1 Notts County 0, FA Cup Final, 1 August 2015

In the first-ever Women's FA Cup Final played at Wembley, the Blues triumphed in a tight match to lift the cup for the first time in their history in front of a crowd of 30,710. The key moment came in the first half when 'Player of the Match' Eniola Aluko set up midfielder Ji So-Yun for the only goal of the game.

4) Arsenal 1 Chelsea 4, Women's Super League, 19 January 2020

Thanks to some superb finishing, the Blues destroyed reigning Women's Super League champions Arsenal, with Sophie Ingle's rising left-foot shot from outside the box the pick of the visitors' four goals. 'It's a Champions League-level performance, everybody was outstanding,' beamed Chelsea boss Emma Hayes afterwards.

5) Wolfsburg 0 Chelsea 3, Champions League quarter-final second leg, 31 March 2021

Leading 2-1 after the first leg in Budapest, the Blues returned to the Hungarian capital to face bogey side Wolfsburg with a place in the Champions League last four up for grabs. After surviving some early German pressure, Pernille Harder gave Chelsea the lead from the spot before Sam Kerr scored from close range just four minutes later. When Fran Kirby finished off a quick counter-attack late on it was all over, with delighted boss Emma Hayes saying afterwards, 'I think this probably ranks as my most favourite win in charge.'

6) Chelsea 1 Tottenham 0, Women's Super League, 8 September 2019

A crowd of 24,564 – more than five times the women's team's previous best home attendance at Kingsmeadow – turned up at Stamford Bridge to see Chelsea secure a deserved win against WSL newcomers Tottenham. The only goal of the game came after just four minutes when Beth England belted in a superb shot from 25 yards that sped like a rocket into the top corner.

7) Chelsea 2 Paris St-Germain 0, Champions League quarter-final first leg, 21 March 2019

In a match of few chances, two fine goals in the last 20 minutes from defender Hannah Blundell and midfielder Erin Cuthbert gave the Blues a useful first-leg lead before the return in Paris, where a 2-1 defeat was enough to take Emma Hayes' side through to the semi-finals for a second consecutive season.

8) Chelsea 2 Arsenal 1, League Cup Final, 29 February 2020

In front of a crowd of 6,743 at the City Ground, Nottingham, the Blues got their hands on the League Cup for the first time in their history thanks to two goals from striker Beth England, with the winner coming deep into injury time after Arsenal had equalised with just five minutes left on the clock.

9) Fiorentina 0 Chelsea 6, Champions League Round of 16 second leg, 31 October 2018

After a narrow 1-0 win in the first leg, the Blues might have expected a tough night in Florence but a magnificent team performance saw them massacre the Italians on their own patch. Fran Kirby was the star of the show with a hat-trick, including a first-half penalty, while Drew Spence, Erin Cuthbert and Ramona Bachmann also got on the scoresheet.

10) Chelsea 9 Bristol City 0, Women's Super League, 13 September 2020

The Blues recorded the biggest-ever win in the history of the WSL with a 9-0 hammering of Bristol City at Kingsmeadow. Incredibly, nine different players were on target for Emma Hayes' side, including Fran Kirby, who opened the scoring with her first goal after a year-long lay-off, and Pernille Harder, who notched her first goal for the Blues after her £250,000 move from Wolfsburg, with a cheeky backheel.

TOP 10 FAMOUS FACES AT THE BRIDGE

Numerous A-list celebs have been spotted at the home of the Blues over the years, including these well-known names:

1) Madonna

'The Queen of Pop' went along to the Blues' Champions League quarter-final clash with Manchester United in April 2011, accompanied by French dancer Brahim Zaibat, her then boyfriend, and her adopted daughter Mercy. Sadly, Chelsea didn't really 'get into the groove' and went down to a 1-0 defeat.

2) Raquel Welch

The Hollywood pin-up attracted newspaper headlines when she was taken along to Chelsea's 1-1 draw with Leicester in November 1972 by Blues-supporting photographer Terry O'Neill and football pundit Jimmy Hill. To the delight of fans at the Bridge, Raquel walked along the side of the pitch when she left before the game finished and waved goodbye to her favourite player, Blues striker Peter Osgood.

3) Ed Sheeran
The ginger-haired singer enjoyed a Christmas visit to the Bridge in 2013 to see Jose Mourinho's Blues beat Liverpool 2-1. After the match, he tweeted that he had been 'finally converted' by his father, John, to the Chelsea cause.

4) Steve McQueen
One of a number of top Hollywood actors to be brought along to the Bridge by Chelsea director Dickie Attenborough, *The Great Escape* star saw the Blues beat Everton 3-1 in November 1973 and afterwards enjoyed a crafty cigarette in the home dressing room with fellow smoker Eddie McCreadie.

5) Geri Halliwell
The one-time Spice Girl has visited the Bridge on a number of occasions, notably in September 2010 when she watched the Blues thrash new boys Blackpool 4-0 with then-boyfriend Henry Beckwith. Sadly, it was a case of '2 Become 1' the next year when the pair split up.

6) Boy George
The Culture Club singer was famously photographed with Stamford the Lion when his band filmed part of the video for their new single, 'The Medal Song', at Stamford Bridge during half-time of the Blues' 3-2 defeat to Watford in October 1984. After the match, the band shared a drink with the Chelsea team in the players' bar. 'I thought one or two were a bit macho,' Boy George later told reporters, 'especially the pretty one who asked me about my hair.' He probably won't wish to be reminded, but 'the pretty one' was later revealed to be midfielder John Bumstead.

7) Benedict Cumberbatch

The *Sherlock* actor was spotted wearing a black cap at the Blues' Champions League home game with Schalke in November 2013. After Chelsea's 3-0 win, he admitted: 'I'm an Arsenal fan but I haven't made it to the Emirates this season.' Never mind, Benny, you probably didn't miss much!

8) Prince Harry

Arsenal fan Harry went along to the Blues' 1-0 defeat of Liverpool in the Champions League semi-final at the Bridge with then-girlfriend Chelsy Davy in April 2007. Presumably, he now regularly gets the mickey taken out of him by nephew George, who has wisely decided to support Chelsea rather than follow his father's team, Aston Villa.

9) Samuel L. Jackson

The *Pulp Fiction* actor supports Liverpool, but didn't refuse a freebie to watch Chelsea play Aston Villa in an executive box at the Bridge alongside comedian David Walliams in September 2014. Appropriately enough, the Blues pulped the Villans 3-0.

10) King George V

A 40,000 crowd at Stamford Bridge were surprised to see the reigning monarch out on the pitch meeting the teams alongside war veterans when Chelsea hosted Leicester in the FA Cup third round in February 1920. The Blues put on a performance fit for a king, winning 3-0.

TOP 10 MATCHES AGAINST NATIONAL TEAMS

A number of countries, big and small, have taken on Chelsea over the years in high-profile friendlies and, as this list reveals, the Blues have generally come out on top:

1) West Germany 0 Chelsea 1, 16 February 1965

Tommy Docherty's Treble-chasers were invited to play a prestigious friendly against West Germany in Duisburg by national team manager Helmut Schoen, who was impressed by the Blues' South American-influenced attacking style of play. The Londoners lived up to their star billing, John Hollins supplying Barry Bridges for the only goal of the game late on. 'Considering their average age is under 22, Chelsea are a marvellous team,' a gracious Schoen conceded afterwards. 'They are the best English side I have seen for a long time.'

2) Chelsea 3 China 1, 13 August 1979

It was Ray Wilkins' last game as a Chelsea player before the iconic midfielder joined Manchester United; the Blues took on the might of the People's Republic of China in a pre-season friendly at Stamford Bridge. Fittingly, 'Butch' was on target for the home side in a 3-1 win, with strikers Tommy Langley and Trevor Aylott also getting their names on the scoresheet.

3) Iraq 1 Chelsea 1, 4 March 1986

Chelsea interrupted their ultimately unsuccessful quest for the First Division title by heading out to Baghdad to play the Iraqi national team at the height of the Iran-Iraq war. 'On every street corner there were blokes in army uniform carrying machine guns,' recalled midfielder John Bumstead. 'They all had black moustaches and looked like Saddam Hussein.' The Iraqi dictator was expected to be guest of honour at the match, but arrived an hour and a half late, leaving the players to wait around in the baking sun. When the match eventually kicked off, defender Joe McLaughlin netted for the Blues in a diplomatic 1-1 draw.

4) Israel 0 Chelsea 2, 4 May 1961

After warming up with a 1-0 win against Hapoel Tel Aviv, Ted Drake's Blues stayed on in the city to play the

Israeli national team and won 2-0 thanks to goals from midfielder Johnny Brooks and striker Bobby Tambling. The locals, though, were disappointed not to catch a glimpse of goalscoring phenomenon Jimmy Greaves, who was in the process of sorting out his move from Chelsea to AC Milan.

5) El Salvador 0 Chelsea 1, 1 June 1971

A few days after winning the European Cup Winners' Cup in Athens, Chelsea headed off to central America, starting a ten-day trip with an 8-3 thrashing of fellow tourists Southampton before taking on El Salvador in the capital, San Salvador. A single goal by Tommy Baldwin was enough to beat a team that had featured at the 1970 World Cup in Mexico, in a match watched by 18,000 local fans and hundreds of menacing gun-toting soldiers.

6) Jamaica 1 Chelsea 4, 4 June 1964

The Blues' 17-day post-season tour of the Caribbean saw them play a number of games against local sides plus an incredible five matches with Wolves (Chelsea winning the series 3-2). After stops in Barbados and Trinidad, the squad moved on to Jamaica, where they beat the national side 4-1 in Kingston, Bobby Tambling grabbing a brace. The tour ended in Port-au-Prince, where a match against the Haiti national team had to be abandoned after an hour because of torrential rain.

7) Australia 1 Chelsea 1, 30 May 1965

A young Peter Osgood took his chance to shine on a month-long post-season tour Down Under, scoring 11 goals in total against a variety of state teams. However, he failed to get on the scoresheet in the biggest game of the lot, Barry Bridges netting against the Australian national side in a 1-1 draw in Melbourne.

8) Mozambique 3 Chelsea 9, 5 June 1969

Having toured Bermuda two years earlier, the Chelsea players were a tad disappointed to be going to southern Africa after the end of the 1968/69 season. 'Mozambique was a very sinister place back then,' recalled striker Alan Birchenall. 'There was a civil war going on, you saw soldiers and tanks on the street and it was quite scary.' Still, the team put on a decent show against the national side in Maputo, Bobby Tambling scoring four and 'The Birch' nabbing a brace in a Sunday League-style 9-3 rout.

9) Gibraltar 1 Chelsea 4, 6 May 1991

The Blues have always been a popular team on 'The Rock' so the locals were delighted when Bobby Campbell's boys flew over for a game just before the end of the 1990/91 season. The minnows put up a brave fight, but eventually went down 4-1, with Gareth Hall, Alan Dickens, Kevin Wilson and Kerry Dixon getting the goals for the visitors.

10) Chelsea 1 Bahrain 0, 31 August 1983

A day after the Blues beat Gillingham 2-1 in the first round of the League Cup, a Chelsea reserve side featuring the likes of Joey Jones, Micky Droy and David Speedie met Bahrain in a friendly at Harlow Town. Pat Nevin, still to make his first-team debut after a summer move from Clyde, scored the only goal of the game in the first half.

TOP 10 BLUE BLOOPERS

The 'head in hands' Chelsea moments that Homer Simpson would sum up with one word … 'D'oh!'

1) Fernando Torres, Manchester United 3 Chelsea 1, Premier League, 18 September 2011

Having scored an excellent goal earlier in the second half, Blues striker Fernando Torres looked set to add another when he collected a Ramires pass and raced into the Manchester United penalty area. Expertly sidestepping United goalkeeper David de Gea, Torres only had to stick the ball into the open net from six yards but he somehow shanked his shot with his weaker left foot and missed the target by some distance. 'Ground open up and swallow him!' screeched Sky commentator Peter Drury, after one of the worst misses in Premier League history.

2) Ed de Goey, Chelsea 6 Coventry City 1, Premier League, 21 October 2000

Thanks largely to four goals by Jimmy Floyd Hasselbaink, Chelsea were cruising to an emphatic victory against strugglers Coventry when Blues defender Frank Leboeuf played a back pass to goalkeeper Ed de Goey. Instead of clearing the ball, the Dutchman bizarrely decided to show off his keepy-uppy skills on the goal line before kicking the ball straight at City substitute Cedric Roussel, who tapped in from close range. Arguably, the most ludicrous and unnecessary goal Chelsea have ever conceded.

3) Craig Burley, Chelsea 1 Manchester United 2, FA Cup semi-final, 31 March 1996

In a tense FA Cup semi-final at Villa Park, Chelsea and Manchester United were drawing 1-1 approaching the hour mark. Struggling to deal with a bouncing ball on the sandy pitch, Blues midfielder Craig Burley whacked it from the halfway line back towards goalkeeper Kevin Hitchcock, only to send his misdirected pass into the path of young United winger David Beckham. Coolly accepting the unexpected gift, Beckham slid the ball past Hitchcock for what proved to be the winner.

4) Kepa Arrizabalaga, Chelsea 0 Liverpool 2, Premier League, 20 September 2020

Trailing 1-0 and down to ten men, Chelsea's hopes of getting a result against the reigning champions were already slim when goalkeeper Kepa Arrizabalaga dallied on a back pass from Fikayo Tomori before trying to play out to Jorginho. However, he only succeeded in passing the ball straight to Reds striker Sadio Mane, who easily converted from eight yards. 'It's totally gift-wrapped by the goalkeeper,' was the verdict of Sky commentator Martin Tyler. Chelsea boss Frank Lampard agreed, consigning Arrizabalaga to the bench for the Blues' next Premier League match at West Brom.

5) Salomon Kalou, Chelsea 1 Portsmouth 0, FA Cup Final, 15 May 2010

After completely dominating the opening stages of the 2010 FA Cup Final against Portsmouth, Chelsea looked set to take the lead when Ashley Cole crossed from the left to the unmarked Salomon Kalou. Just five yards out and facing an unguarded goal, the Ivorian striker seemed bound to score but he somehow hit his shot against the bar. Fortunately, a goal from Didier Drogba in the second half clinched the cup for the Blues and spared Kalou's blushes.

6) Pat Nevin, Chelsea 4 Manchester City 1, League Cup fourth round, 21 November 1984

Numerous Chelsea players have missed penalties over the years, but Pat Nevin's woeful spot kick in a League Cup tie against Manchester City in 1984 has to rate as the worst ever. On a heavy Stamford Bridge pitch, the little Scottish winger took just a single-step run-up before slowly side-footing the ball along the muddy surface into the grateful arms of City keeper Alex Williams. 'Oh dear, oh dear, that has to be the worst penalty I have ever seen at this level of football!' wailed BBC commentator Barry Davies, although with Chelsea leading 4-0 at the time even Nevin himself managed to crack a smile at his laughable effort.

7) Dave Beasant, Chelsea 2 Norwich City 3, Premier League, 12 September 1992

Two goals up against Norwich, the Blues ended up losing to the Canaries after goalkeeper Dave Beasant endured a nightmare second half. First, he fumbled a tame Mark Robins shot over the line; then, soon after the visitors had levelled, he let a trundling 20-yard daisycutter from Norwich midfielder David Phillips slip through his grasp and trickle into the net for the winner. Afterwards, Chelsea boss Ian Porterfield told reporters that Beasant would never play for the club again, but the former Wimbledon keeper briefly returned to the first team six months later after Porterfield had been axed.

8) Marvin Hinton, Chelsea 1 Liverpool 2, First Division, 24 December 1966

A visit from reigning champions Liverpool was always going to test a Blues side without a win in their previous five matches and they made life considerably more difficult for themselves by conceding a needless own goal after 20 minutes. Defender Marvin Hinton was the culprit, diving full length on the edge of the six-yard box to powerfully head in Peter Thompson's corner at the near post. The mistake was a costly one as Liverpool went on to win the match 2-1.

9) Antonio Rudiger, Sheffield United 1 Chelsea 2, Premier League, 7 February 2021

Leading at Premier League no-hopers Sheffield United through a Mason Mount goal, a rare Blades foray into the Chelsea penalty area ten minutes into the second half didn't seem to carry much threat, with Blues defender Antonio Rudiger in position to clear the danger. However, instead of booting the ball away, the normally reliable German stopper tried to pass back to goalkeeper Edouard Mendy, who was already advancing from his line. It proved to be a calamitous decision, as the ball dribbled agonisingly past the stranded Mendy and into the net for one of the most avoidable own goals in Chelsea's history. Fortunately, the Blues still went on to win the match when Jorginho converted a penalty just three minutes later.

10) Ron Harris and Eddie McCreadie, Chelsea 2 Leeds United 2, FA Cup Final, 11 April 1970

One of the worries for the Blues ahead of the 1970 FA Cup Final was the threat posed by gangly Leeds defender Jack Charlton at set pieces, but when the England international outjumped Chelsea goalkeeper Peter Bonetti his header from Eddie Gray's inswinging corner carried no real power. Either Eddie McCreadie or Ron Harris, both stationed on the goal line, seemed well-placed to clear but the ball bounced lower than they expected on the sandy Wembley pitch and trickled over the line as they kicked thin air for the opening goal of the game. Happily, the Blues fought back to draw 2-2 and then won the replay at Old Trafford.

TOP 10 FOREIGN PLAYERS SIGNED FROM ENGLISH CLUBS

These overseas players were already settled in England but jumped at the chance to up sticks again for west London.

1) N'Golo Kante

After starring for Leicester in the Foxes' surprise 2016 Premier League title win, dynamic midfielder N'Golo Kante moved to Chelsea for £32m that summer. The Frenchman slotted seamlessly into Antonio Conte's side, breaking up opposition attacks with timely interceptions before launching swift counters with a simple pass. He won the league again in his first season at the Bridge, becoming the first player to achieve back-to-back Premier League titles with different clubs and also picking up both Footballer of the Year awards. Over the next three seasons he added the FA Cup, the World Cup, the Europa League and the Champions League to his impressive collection of honours.

2) Dan Petrescu

Chelsea boss Glenn Hoddle's attractive 3-5-2 system finally began to pay dividends when he signed Dan Petrescu from Sheffield Wednesday for £2.3m in November 1995. With his skill on the ball, eye for a goal and excellent crossing ability, the Romanian was made for the right wing-back position and over the next five years became a firm fans' favourite at the Bridge while helping the Blues win an armful of silverware. However, a falling-out with Chelsea manager Gianluca Vialli led to 'Super Dan' moving on to Bradford City in the summer of 2000.

3) Eidur Gudjohnsen

Signed from Bolton in the summer of 2000 for £4m after scoring an impressive 21 goals for the Trotters the previous season, Eidur Gudjohnsen was eased into the first team by Blues boss Claudio Ranieri before forming a prolific striking partnership with Jimmy Floyd Hasselbaink during the 2001/02 campaign. Jose Mourinho used the skilful Icelandic forward in a slightly more withdrawn role, but he still chipped in with 12 goals when the Blues won the Premier League title in 2005. The following season Gudjohnsen was more of a squad player, and in 2006 he joined Barcelona for £8m.

4) Nicolas Anelka

The much-travelled Anelka arrived at the Bridge from Bolton in the January transfer window in 2008. At first, the French striker failed to live up to his £15m fee, suffering a personal nightmare in the Champions League Final when his penalty miss in Moscow handed the trophy to Manchester United. The following campaign, though, he was much improved, his 19 league goals earning him the Golden Boot, and his good form continued throughout the Blues' 2009/10 Double season. After four years at the club, he joined Chinese outfit Shanghai Shenhua in January 2012.

5) Olivier Giroud

Signed from Arsenal for £18m in the 2018 January transfer window, Olivier Giroud went on to help the Blues win the FA Cup later that year – the French striker's fourth success in the competition. The following year, he hit a Chelsea record 11 goals in the Europa League, including one in the final in Baku against the Gunners. A superb leader of the line and a brilliant header of the ball, he also won a World Cup winner's medal with France in 2018.

6) Victor Moses

The Blues signed the Nigerian international midfielder from Wigan for £7m in August 2012, but after a mediocre first season at the Bridge he was loaned out to Liverpool, Stoke and West Ham. New Chelsea boss Antonio Conte recalled him to first-team action in 2016, converting Moses to an attacking right-sided wing-back. He excelled in the role as the Blues won the Premier League, but then blotted his copybook by stupidly getting sent off in the 2017 FA Cup Final against Arsenal for diving. Since then, he has had further loan spells at Fenerbahce, Inter Milan and Spartak Moscow.

7) Fernando Torres

The Blues splashed out a then-British record £50m to bring Fernando Torres to the Bridge from Liverpool in January 2011, but the Spanish striker struggled to recapture the form that had electrified Anfield over the previous three and a half seasons. He did, though, provide some memorable moments for Blues fans, notably goals against Barcelona in the Champions League semi-final in 2012 and against Benfica in the Europa League Final the following year before joining AC Milan in 2014.

8) Demba Ba

Signed from Newcastle in January 2013 for £7m, the Senegal striker scored twice on his Chelsea debut in a 5-1 win at Southampton in the FA Cup. The goals did not flow so easily after that, but he did nab the winner the following year against PSG in the Champions League quarter-final and the opener in Chelsea's 2-0 famous victory at Liverpool in May 2014 after Steven Gerrard's notorious slip. However, that summer he joined Besiktas for around £5.5m.

9) Raul Meireles

The heavily tattooed Portuguese midfielder was a £12m signing from Liverpool in August 2011, having previously played under then-Chelsea boss Andre Villas-Boas at Porto. Fiery and combative, he proved to be a useful acquisition to the squad, helping the Blues triumph in the FA Cup and Champions League – although he missed the final of the latter competition through suspension. In September 2012, he moved on to Turkish outfit Fenerbahce for £8m.

10) Loic Remy

Signed from QPR for £10.5m in August 2014 after impressing while on loan at Newcastle the previous season, Loic Remy's Chelsea career got off to a great start when he scored ten minutes into his debut in a 4-2 win against Swansea at the Bridge after coming off the bench. Despite being mainly used as a sub, the French striker made a useful contribution to the Blues' 2015 title win before being loaned out to Crystal Palace and then moving on a free to Las Palmas in 2017.

TOP 10 OPENING-DAY WINS

There's nothing like getting the season off to a great start with a confidence-boosting win – as the Blues did on these occasions:

1) Chelsea 9 Glossop North End 2, Second Division, 1 September 1906

Five months earlier, Glossop had come away from Stamford Bridge with a plucky 0-0 draw – but there would be no repeat on this occasion. Chelsea's new striker George 'Gatling Gun' Hilsdon, a summer signing from West Ham, lived up to his nickname by rattling in five goals on his debut, and was also involved in the Blues' four other goals. A stunning victory raised expectations that Chelsea would mount a significant promotion challenge and, sure enough, at the end of the campaign the Londoners secured top-flight status after just two seasons in the Football League.

2) Chelsea 4 Sunderland 0, Premier League, 7 August 1999

A marvellous all-round team performance saw the Blues blow newly promoted Sunderland away on a gloriously sunny west London afternoon. After 20 minutes of unceasing Chelsea pressure, Gus Poyet opened the scoring with a header from Dennis Wise's corner. Then, ten minutes later, Gianfranco Zola fired a low shot into the corner. A succession of poor misses by new £10m striker Chris Sutton prevented the Blues increasing the lead until the final quarter of the match, when Tore Andre Flo headed in Dan Petrescu's cross. The home side, though, saved the best till last, Poyet dashing forward to volley home Zola's impudent scooped pass.

3) Chelsea 6 Liverpool 1, First Division, 28 August 1937

The Blues got their season off to a cracking start, scoring twice through George Mills and Billy Mitchell in the opening ten minutes. Although Liverpool soon pulled a goal back, Mills restored the Londoners' two-goal advantage before half-time. He then completed his hat-trick after the break, and with Jimmy Argue and Harry Burgess also finding the net the Blues recorded their biggest-ever win against the Reds.

4) Chelsea 4 Leeds United 0, First Division, 12 August 1972

An opening-day clash between old rivals Chelsea and Leeds attracted a capacity crowd of 51,102 to the Bridge, with another 9,000 fans locked out. The match swung the Blues' way early on when injuries to Leeds striker Mick Jones and goalkeeper David Harvey reduced the Yorkshiremen to ten men, with winger Peter Lorimer taking over the gloves. The Scottish international kept the home side at bay until just before half-time, when Peter Osgood scored. In the second half, the Blues capitalised on their numerical advantage in some style, Charlie Cooke firing in from Alan Hudson's defence-splitting pass before Chris Garland added two more to complete a convincing victory.

5) Liverpool 1 Chelsea 2, Premier League, 17 August 2003

With new owner Roman Abramovich watching on, Chelsea produced a superb performance to record their first-ever Premier League victory at Anfield. Midfielder Juan Sebastian Veron, a £15m summer recruit from Manchester United, opened the scoring after 25 minutes with a low drive, and the Blues remained in control until Liverpool equalised with a twice-taken penalty by Michael Owen. However, three minutes from the end, Jimmy Floyd Hasselbaink controlled Frank Lampard's lofted pass, held off a Liverpool defender and drilled a shot into the bottom corner for the winner.

6) Chelsea 6 West Bromwich Albion 0, Premier League, 14 August 2010

Former Blue Roberto Di Matteo returned to the Bridge for his first match as a Premier League manager only to see his West Brom side torn apart by the reigning Premier League champions. Florent Malouda started and finished the rout, while the meat in the sandwich was provided by Didier Drogba, who helped himself to a 23-minute hat-trick either side of half-time, while Frank Lampard also got on the scoresheet. Incredibly, a week later the Blues travelled up to Wigan and again won 6-0.

7) Chelsea 5 Derby County 0, Second Division, 27 August 1983

After narrowly avoiding relegation to the third tier the previous season, a Blues side featuring five new signings made light work of Derby at the Bridge. One of the new faces, Nigel Spackman, opened the scoring after just four minutes when he drilled in from the edge of the area. Two goals early in the second half by Chris Hutchings and Clive Walker effectively settled the contest, before another debutant, Kerry Dixon, scored two more after assists by his strike partner Colin Lee. The bright start set the tone for the rest of the campaign, which ended with Chelsea topping the table.

8) Chelsea 4 Sheffield Wednesday 0, First Division, 19 August 1950

'Will this at last be Chelsea's year?' wondered *The Times* in its preview of the 1950/51 season. The 48,468 fans at the Bridge must have been having similar positive thoughts after watching the Blues hammer Sheffield Wednesday on the opening day, centre-forward Roy Bentley grabbing two of the goals in a resounding 4-0 win. Yet, by the end of the campaign, Chelsea only managed to avoid relegation on goal average ahead of Everton and the Owls – making this emphatic win even more significant than it appeared at the time.

9) Chelsea 4 Portsmouth 0, Premier League, 17 August 2008

In Luiz Felipe Scolari's first match as Chelsea manager, the Blues were completely dominant throughout, roaring into a 3-0 half-time lead following goals by Joe Cole, Nicolas Anelka and a Frank Lampard penalty. The best moment, though, came right at the end when Portuguese midfielder Deco capped an excellent debut by smashing a 25-yarder beyond Portsmouth goalkeeper David James to round off an excellent first day's work by the Blues.

10) Chelsea 4 Bolton Wanderers 3, First Division, 31 August 1946

After the small matter of World War II put an end to league football for seven long years, Chelsea fans were eager to see their heroes back in meaningful action, a massive crowd of 62,850 packing out the Bridge for the visit of Bolton. The home supporters were rewarded with a thrilling victory, the Blues overcoming their opponents thanks to a brace apiece by striker Tommy Lawton and winger Dickie Spence, the only survivor in the Blues' line-up from the first game of the aborted 1939/40 season.

TOP 10 IRISH BLUES

Players from both sides of the border of the Emerald Isle who starred for Chelsea:

1) Damien Duff

Briefly Chelsea's record signing following his £17m move from Blackburn Rovers in July 2003, Republic of Ireland international Damien Duff more than justified his fee with some thrilling wing play over the next three seasons while picking up back-to-back Premier League titles with the Blues in 2005 and 2006. When he left for Newcastle after the second of those triumphs, Chelsea boss Jose Mourinho admitted, 'He is a player I really miss. Damien Duff is a top man, a top character and a great team player.'

2) John Dempsey

Signed from neighbours Fulham for £70,000 in January 1969, John Dempsey was a tough centre-back who was especially commanding in the air. Perhaps, though, his nine years at the Bridge are best remembered for a cracking volley he scored in the replayed final of the European Cup Winners' Cup against Real Madrid in May 1971. 'It was not only the most important goal I scored but also the best,' he later recalled. Capped 19 times by the Republic of Ireland, Dempsey joined American side Philadelphia Fury in 1978 and was voted the league's best defender the following year ahead of German legend Franz Beckenbauer.

3) Joe Bambrick

A prolific goalscorer in Irish football, Joe Bambrick joined the Blues from Linfield on Christmas Eve 1934. The 29-year-old proved to be an instant hit at the Bridge, scoring 15 goals in the remainder of the season, including four-goal hauls against both Leeds and Manchester City. The following season, he was top scorer for the Londoners with 19 goals but after that he only made occasional appearances before joining Walsall in 1938. Capped 11 times at international level, Bambrick scored an impressive 12 goals for Ireland, including six in a 7-0 thrashing of Wales in 1930.

4) Andy Townsend

Chelsea paid Norwich City £1.2m for Andy Townsend shortly after the dynamic midfielder had starred for the

Republic of Ireland at the 1990 World Cup in Italy. After an outstanding first season with the Blues, during which he took on the additional responsibility of captaining the side, Townsend was named the club's Player of the Year. However, he grew increasingly frustrated with the Blues' lack of success and in 1993 moved on to Aston Villa, with whom he twice won the League Cup. He later played for Middlesbrough and West Brom before becoming a pundit on TV and radio.

5) Kevin Wilson

A £335,000 recruit from Ipswich Town in June 1987, Northern Ireland international Kevin Wilson formed a potent attacking trident with fellow strikers Kerry Dixon and Gordon Durie, hitting double figures in the league when the Blues won the Second Division Championship in 1989 and again the following season back in the top flight. However, his goals rather dried up afterwards and on transfer deadline day in 1992 he was offloaded to Notts County for £225,000. He later played for Walsall and Northampton, taking on the Cobblers' managerial role between 1999 and 2001.

6) John Kirwan

An FA Cup winner with Tottenham in 1901, tricky left-winger John Kirwan joined the Blues four years later, shortly after the club's foundation. In 1906, he became the first Chelsea player to be capped internationally when he played for Ireland against England, and the following year helped the Londoners earn promotion from the Second Division, finishing the campaign as the club's third-highest goalscorer with nine goals. However, he only played twice in the top flight before joining Clyde. He later moved to Holland, where he became the first professional manager of Ajax.

7) Paddy Mulligan

An attacking full-back, Paddy Mulligan joined the Blues from Shamrock Rovers for a bargain £17,500 in October 1969. He gradually forced himself into the first-team picture, featuring as a late substitute in the European Cup Winners' Cup Final against Real Madrid in 1971 and as a starter in the League Cup Final defeat against Stoke City the following year. In the autumn of 1972 he was surprisingly sold to Crystal Palace, and later played for West Brom before finishing his career back at Shamrock. A regular for the Republic of Ireland throughout the 1970s, he won 50 caps at international level.

8) Billy Mitchell

Signed from Belfast club Distillery in the summer of 1933, Billy Mitchell was a pint-sized half-back who excelled at tackling. After a couple of seasons adapting to a higher standard of football, he became a first-team regular in the mid-1930s while also playing for Northern Ireland, for whom he won 15 caps. After making over 100 appearances for the Blues, his career was effectively ended by the outbreak of World War II, although he did turn out occasionally for both Chelsea and Bristol City during the conflict.

9) Mal Donaghy

Blues fans probably expected veteran defender Mal Donaghy to be no more than a back-up option when he signed from Manchester United for £100,000 in the summer of 1992. However, the 34-year-old's form was so consistent that he was a near ever-present in the inaugural Premier League campaign. The following season, new manager Glenn Hoddle moved Donaghy into the midfield holding role, a position he performed well in before losing his place to the more mobile Eddie Newton. He hung up his boots in the summer of 1994, having won 91 caps for Northern Ireland – a total only surpassed by five other players.

10) Billy Dickson

In a transfer that stunned the football world, Chelsea surprisingly sold England centre-forward Tommy Lawton to Third Division Notts County in November 1947 for a British-record £20,000. Moving in the opposite direction as part of the deal was wing-half Billy Dickson, a 24-year-old Northern Ireland international with a growing reputation. Although lacking Lawton's charisma and goalscoring ability, Dickson gave the club good service over the next six years, making well over 100 appearances before joining Arsenal in 1953.

TOP 10 OPPOSITION QUOTES

Opposing players, managers, directors and fans reveal their innermost thoughts about the Blues:

1) 'There are players here who hate Chelsea more than Real Madrid.'

Barcelona star Lionel Messi, 2006

2) 'Roman Abramovich has parked his Russian tank in our front garden and is firing £50 notes at us.'

Arsenal vice-chairman David Dein, 2003

3) 'Chelsea definitely excited me. I can't deny that.'

Liverpool's Steven Gerrard on his rumoured move to Stamford Bridge in 2005
(Gerrard: *My Autobiography*, 2006)

4) 'He's out of order, disconnected with reality and disrespectful. When you give success to stupid

people, it makes them more stupid sometimes and not more intelligent.'
Arsenal manager Arsene Wenger responds to Blues boss Jose Mourinho's 'voyeur' comments, 2005

5) 'If Chelsea drop points, the cat's out in the open. And you know what cats are like – sometimes they don't come home.'
Manchester United manager Sir Alex Ferguson, trying his famous 'mind games' during the 2006/07 title race – but isn't the usual expression 'the cat's out of the bag', Fergie?

6) 'Games at Chelsea are inevitably dismal. You stand there on the huge crumbling terrace, your feet stiffening and then actually burning in the cold, with the Chelsea fans jeering and gesturing at you, and you wondered why you bothered.'
Arsenal fan Nick Hornby (*Fever Pitch*, 1992)

7) 'He's not my cup of tea. I've found him really irritating when I've coached against him.'
Roy Keane reveals he is not a fan of former Blues boss Jose Mourinho, 2016

8) 'That's seven goals we've given Chelsea. We'll have to stop coming here.'
Liverpool boss Bob Paisley after Chelsea beat the Reds 3-1 in the league at Stamford Bridge in March 1978, two months after defeating them 4-2 in the FA Cup third round

9) 'How can they talk about the First Division when we are sitting in a pig-hole of a dressing-room? It's criminal.'
Nottingham Forest manager Brian Clough is unimpressed with the Stamford Bridge facilities after a 2-1 defeat in 1977

10) 'I hate Chelsea, they stand for everything I hate in football with their showbiz supporters!'
Newcastle fan Terry Collier, in 1970s sitcom *Whatever Happened to the Likely Lads?*

TOP 10 CAPTAINS

The best of the Blues having the honour of wearing the armband:

1) John Terry

The Blues' most successful-ever captain, John Terry was first given the armband by then-boss Claudio Ranieri in December 2001 – just two years after his Chelsea debut. However, it was Jose Mourinho who made the commanding centre-half the team's captain on a permanent basis in 2004, and it proved to be an inspirational choice. Terry went on to skipper the Blues in a record 580 games, collecting an Aladdin's Cave-worth of silverware along the way, including the Double in 2010. A true club icon for the ages, his place in the hearts of the Chelsea faithful is summed up by the banner that hangs from the Bridge stands at every home game, 'JT Captain, Leader, Legend'.

2) Dennis Wise

The impish and spiky midfielder was first made Chelsea skipper in 1993 by new boss Glenn Hoddle, but the following year lost the armband as a punishment after an unsavoury incident with a London taxi driver. However, he eventually regained the captaincy and became the pivotal player at the club, helping a legion of overseas stars adapt to the English game and leading the Blues to five major honours, including the FA Cup in 1997 and the European Cup Winners' Cup the following year, when his astute pass set up Gianfranco Zola for the winner in the final against Stuttgart.

3) Ron Harris

Appointed Chelsea captain in 1965 by Tommy Docherty, Ron Harris became the first Blues skipper to lift the FA Cup following victory over Leeds five years later. The next year, he paraded the European Cup Winners' Cup around west London after the Blues beat Real Madrid in a dramatic replayed final in Athens. Not the loudest of skippers, 'Chopper' led more by example, his committed defensive displays earning the respect of his team-mates while chilling the bones of opponents. Surprisingly, boss Dave Sexton decided to relieve him of the armband in 1972. Was it purely a coincidence that Chelsea's fortunes began to decline from that point?

4) Roy Bentley

One of Ted Drake's first decisions when he became Chelsea manager in the summer of 1952 was to appoint Roy Bentley as captain. It was a bold choice as, although Bentley had skippered the Blues before on various occasions, he was also the team's main source of goals and some fans feared the responsibilities that came with the armband might affect his form. They needn't have worried. Bentley remained a prolific striker and in 1955 led the Blues to their first-ever league title.

5) Cesar Azpilicueta

Signed from Marseille for a bargain £7m in 2012, Spanish right-back Cesar Azpilicueta became Chelsea vice-captain in 2017 while Gary Cahill had possession of the armband. However, with Cahill barely featuring under then-boss Maurizio Sarri, it was the reliable Azpi who led the Blues to victory over Arsenal in the 2019 Europa League Final and lifted the trophy in faraway Baku. The following season, he was made the regular skipper by new boss Frank Lampard and was retained in the role by Lampard's successor, Thomas

Tuchel. At the end of the campaign, he skippered the side to glory in the Champions League following a superb 1-0 win against Manchester City in the final in Porto.

6) Terry Venables

A clever and astute midfield general with a bubbly personality, Terry Venables was made Chelsea skipper by boss Tommy Docherty in 1963 when he was only 20. He led the Blues to triumph in the League Cup two years later after a two-legged final win against Leicester but clashes with 'The Doc' over tactics and disciplinary matters led to him being replaced as captain by Ron Harris, and in 1966 he was sold to Tottenham.

7) Ray Wilkins

'Butch' was appointed Chelsea's captain in April 1975 by new boss Eddie McCreadie when he was just 18, making him the Blues' youngest-ever skipper. Showing maturity beyond his years, the creative midfielder led a mainly young team through shining example and was the standout player in the Blues' promotion-winning team of 1977. Chelsea Player of the Year on two occasions, he retained the armband until signing for Manchester United in 1979.

8) Jack Harrow

A loyal servant to Chelsea for 15 years, full-back Jack Harrow skippered the Blues both before and after World War I. In 1915, he became the first Chelsea captain to lead out his team at the FA Cup Final, although a 3-0 defeat to Sheffield United at Old Trafford meant he was unable to bring the trophy back to west London. His devotion to the Chelsea cause, though, was perhaps best illustrated during the war when he would frequently sneak out of his Royal Flying Corps camp without permission to play for his beloved Blues.

9) Marcel Desailly

The first non-Brit to be awarded the captaincy on a permanent basis, Marcel Desailly took over the armband in 2001 from Dennis Wise when the veteran midfielder moved on to Leicester City. Over the next three years, the Frenchman didn't quite manage to lift any silverware with the Blues, but his dependably solid performances at the back were an inspiration to his multinational team-mates.

10) Colin Pates

The first Chelsea skipper to have a regular 'Captain's Column' in the matchday programme, the ball-playing centre-half led the Blues to the Second Division title in 1984 and victory in the Full Members Cup Final at Wembley two years later. A bit of a quirky character, Pates decided that the traditional black armband was 'morbid' and instead wore a red one – a tatty affair, made out of an old sock!

TOP 10 EXPENSIVE FLOPS

Chelsea striker Fernando Torres never really justified his £50m fee, but compared to this lot he was an absolute bargain:

1) Danny Drinkwater

The Blues hoped that Danny Drinkwater could reprise his supremely effective midfield partnership with N'Golo Kante when they signed him from Leicester for £35m, but he showed virtually nothing of his Foxes form in his occasional appearances for his new club in the 2017/18 season. Since then, his career has gone into complete free fall: unsuccessful loan spells at Burnley and Aston Villa coinciding with off-the-pitch problems that saw him plead guilty to a drink-driving offence and injure himself in an incident outside a Manchester nightclub. In January 2021, he further alienated

*Jose Mourinho,
Chelsea's most
successful manager,
shows off the
Premier League
trophy in 2005.*

*Alan Hudson
shoots for goal in
Chelsea's biggest
ever win, a 13-0
thrashing of Jeunesse
Hautcharage at
Stamford Bridge in
1971.*

There's some stiff competition, but is Eden Hazard Chelsea's greatest ever European player?

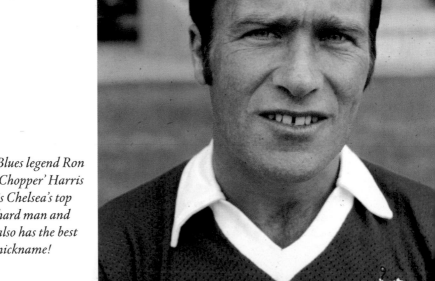

Blues legend Ron 'Chopper' Harris is Chelsea's top hard man and also has the best nickname!

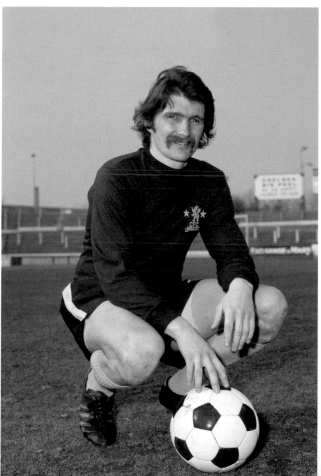

Was Dennis Wise's famous equaliser against AC Milan in the San Siro in 1999 the Blues' best ever European goal?

Chelsea have had many brilliant Scottish players but none better than the stylish Charlie Cooke.

Didier Drogba, Chelsea's greatest ever African player, celebrates winning the Premier League for a fourth time in 2015.

Fran Kirby in action during Chelsea Women's greatest triumph, a 3-1 defeat of Arsenal in the 2018 FA Cup Final.

John Terry, Chelsea's most successful captain, ended his Blues career by winning the Premier League for a fifth time in 2017.

£35m flop Danny Drinkwater might just well be the worst bit of transfer business the Blues have ever done.

The Blues celebrate a goal in their 4-1 thrashing of Arsenal in the 2019 Europa League Final, their best 'derby' win ever.

Chelsea players celebrate after beating Bayern Munich in the 2012 Champions League Final, the Blues' greatest triumph ever.

Is Brazilian winger Willian the best Chelsea player to hail from North or South America?

The Blues have picked up some real gems from non-league football, including 1930s goalkeeper Vic Woodley.

Frank Lampard won more caps for England while at Chelsea than any other Blues player.

Blues skipper Cesar Azpilicueta models what will surely go down as the worst Chelsea kit ever during the 2020/21 season.

himself from Chelsea fans by appearing to celebrate the departure of Blues boss Frank Lampard on social media.

2) Adrian Mutu

Signed from Parma for £15.8m as part of Roman Abramovich's initial £111m spending spree when he bought Chelsea in 2003, the Romanian striker scored on his debut against Leicester and then added two more in a 4-2 win against Tottenham. The goals rather dried up after that, but worse followed when Mutu tested positive for cocaine in September 2004. Banned from football for seven months, he was promptly sacked by the Blues, who then pursued him in the courts for damages. While reviving his career with Juventus and Fiorentina, Mutu was ordered by FIFA to pay Chelsea £15.2m – a sum that, after making numerous unsuccessful appeals, he is still to stump up.

3) Tiemoue Bakayoko

France manager Didier Deschamps once described Bakayoko as 'a complete midfielder' but, given his often-woeful performances for the Blues, Chelsea fans could be forgiven for thinking something was lost in translation. Signed from French champions Monaco for a cool £40m in July 2017 as a replacement for Nemanja Matic in the holding role, the clumsy-looking Frenchman had a poor first season at the Bridge, the nadir coming in a grisly 4-1 defeat at Watford when he was sent off for two rash challenges inside the first 30 minutes. Swiftly ushered out of the club, he has since been loaned to Milan, Monaco and Napoli.

4) Kepa Arrizabalaga

Arrizabalaga's £71.6m move from Athletic Bilbao to Chelsea in August 2018 made him the most expensive goalkeeper in the world – a tag that, at times, has appeared to weigh heavily on the Spaniard. Although he helped the Blues win the Europa League in his first season at the Bridge, he also showed his temperamental side in the League Cup Final against Manchester City, when he refused to be substituted. Poor form in the 2019/20 season saw him dropped by Frank Lampard, and further blunders at the start of the following campaign prompted the Blues to sign a new keeper, Edouard Mendy, leaving Kepa's future looking extremely uncertain.

5) Andriy Shevchenko

Chelsea broke the British transfer record to buy the Ukrainian striker from AC Milan, shelling out £30.8m in May 2006. However, it was soon clear that the 29-year-old's best days were behind him, the lightning pace and quick reflexes that had terrified defences all over Europe a thing of the past. In two seasons with the Blues, Shevchenko only scored nine goals in the Premier League, often giving the impression that he would rather be improving his golf handicap at Wentworth than running around in the cold at the Bridge. Few fans were disappointed when he moved back to Milan on loan, after which he joined Dynamo Kiev on a free transfer.

6) Juan Sebastian Veron

A midfielder with a reputation as one of the finest playmakers of his generation, the Argentinian signed for the Blues from Manchester United for £15m in August 2003. He got off to a superb start, scoring a fine goal and dictating proceedings in an opening-day win at Liverpool, but it was a performance he failed to repeat as he fell victim to a string of niggling injuries. After playing just 15 times for the Blues, 'La Brujita' ('The Little Witch') moved to Inter Milan on loan before returning to Argentina with Estudiantes on a free transfer.

7) Chris Sutton

Gianluca Vialli forked out a then-club record £10m for the Blackburn striker in the summer of 1999, but his one season at the Bridge was nothing short of a disaster. After missing a host of easy chances on his debut against Sunderland, Sutton finally broke his Premier League duck with a header in the famous 5-0 demolition of Manchester United. That, however, proved to be his only league goal of the campaign and, with no sign that his scoring form would return, it made sense to sell him to Celtic in the summer of 2000 – albeit for a 40 per cent loss.

8) Juan Cuadrado

The Blues shelled out £23.3m to bring the Fiorentina winger to the Bridge in January 2015 but the Colombian's occasional performances in the second half of a title-winning season were so anonymous he might as well have been auditioning for the role of 'The Invisible Man'. Fortunately, his stock back in Italy was still high and Chelsea were able to recoup most of their outlay in a 'loan then buy' deal with Juventus.

9) Baba Rahman

The Ghanaian left-back arrived in west London from Germany after the Blues wrote out a hefty £14m cheque to Augsburg in August 2015. Rahman went on to start 19 games that season, his most memorable contribution in a Chelsea shirt coming when he gifted a goal to Southampton's Shane Long, after which he was promptly substituted at half-time. Since then, he has spent time on loan at Schalke, Reims, Mallorca and PAOK without noticeable success and, presumably, he won't be seen back at the Bridge any time soon.

10) Davide Zappacosta

Maybe in the weird world of modern football, £23m is the going rate for a back-up defender, but it does seem an awful lot to cough up for a reserve right-back. Anyway, that's how much the Blues paid Torino in August 2017 for Zappacosta, and although he never let the team down when called upon, he hardly set west London alight either – apart from one spectacular, if slightly flukey, goal in the Champions League against minnows Qarabag. Subsequent loans to Roma and Genoa have largely seen him stuck on the subs' bench.

TOP 10 SEASONS TO REMEMBER

The campaigns which had Blues fans popping champagne corks:

1) 2004/05
In Jose Mourinho's first season at the Bridge, the Blues won their first-ever Premier League title with something to spare, losing just one match and conceding only 15 goals in 38 matches – a record that still stands to this day. For good measure, the west Londoners also won the League Cup, beating Manchester United over two legs in the semifinal and then defeating Liverpool 3-2 in the final at the Millennium Stadium, Cardiff.

2) 2009/10
In his first season in charge, Italian boss Carlo Ancelotti led the Blues to a glorious Double. On the final day of the season, Chelsea pipped Manchester United to the Premier League title, thrashing Wigan 8-0 at the Bridge to top the table by a single point. The following week, a free kick by Didier Drogba was enough to see off Portsmouth in the FA Cup Final at Wembley, ensuring that the Blues won the two main English trophies in the same season for the first time.

3) 2011/12
A season that appeared to be going nowhere was transformed when manager Andre Villas-Boas was sacked in March

and replaced with his assistant, Blues legend Roberto Di Matteo. Finding their best form at just the right moment, the Blues made it through to the FA Cup Final, where they beat Liverpool 2-1 at Wembley. Two weeks later, on a never-to-be-forgotten night in Bavaria, Didier Drogba and co. beat Bayern Munich on penalties to claim the Champions League for the first time after numerous near misses in the recent past.

4) 1954/55

When Ted Drake's Blues lost four consecutive matches in October 1954, nobody was talking about them as title challengers. However, a stunning turnaround in form saw Chelsea steadily climb the table until they reached the summit six months later. A tense 1-0 home win against Wolves at Easter virtually clinched the trophy before a 3-0 victory against Sheffield Wednesday at the Bridge ensured that the fans could celebrate a first-ever title triumph.

5) 2014/15

In his second spell as Chelsea manager Jose Mourinho delivered two more trophies, starting with the League Cup after a 2-0 win against London rivals Tottenham at Wembley. The focus then switched to the league, the Blues clinching the title with a 1-0 win at the Bridge against Crystal Palace.

6) 2016/17

Free from European distractions after a mid-table finish the previous season, Chelsea were able to concentrate on the league under new manager Antonio Conte and raced to the title with a then-record 30 wins in 38 games. It might well have been a second Double too, but the Blues were surprisingly beaten 2-1 in the FA Cup Final by Arsenal at Wembley.

7) 2020/21

In a campaign largely played behind closed doors because of the Covid-19 pandemic, the Blues got off to a good start before a dip in form resulted in club legend Frank Lampard being replaced as manager by Thomas Tuchel. The German led the Blues to two major finals, losing out to Leicester in the FA Cup before lifting the Champions League following an impressive 1-0 win against favourites Manchester City in Porto.

8) 1997/98

Despite making a controversial managerial change mid-campaign – Gianluca Vialli replacing Ruud Gullit as player-manager – the Blues won two major trophies in the same season for the first time. First up was the League Cup, the west Londoners beating Middlesbrough 2-0 after extra time in the final at Wembley. Six weeks later, skipper Dennis Wise got his hands on the European Cup Winners' Cup as well after the Blues beat Stuttgart 1-0 in the final in Stockholm.

9) 2005/06

The Blues became only the second club to claim back-to-back Premier League titles after a glorious campaign they dominated from start to finish. Jose Mourinho's men clinched the title in fine style too, destroying nearest challengers Manchester United 3-0 at a sun-soaked Bridge thanks to goals by William Gallas, Joe Cole and Ricardo Carvalho.

10) 1969/70

After a number of near misses in the 1960s, the Blues finally won the FA Cup after a dramatic 2-1 victory against Leeds in a replayed final at Old Trafford. Dave Sexton's men also enjoyed an excellent league campaign, finishing third behind Leeds and champions Everton. The only disappointment came in the League Cup, the Blues surprisingly going out in the fourth round to Second Division Carlisle United.

TOP 10 LONDON DERBIES

The matches that had Blues fans singing, 'One team in London, there's only one team in London ...'

1) Chelsea 4 Arsenal 1, Europa League Final, 24 May 2019

The Chelsea fans who made the laborious 3,000-mile journey to Azerbaijan for the Europa League Final were rewarded with a scintillating display by their team in what turned out to be boss Maurizio Sarri's last match in charge. Olivier Giroud, playing against his old club, got the ball rolling shortly after half-time with a superbly guided header from Emerson's cross and ten minutes later Pedro doubled the Blues' lead, crisply converting Eden Hazard's pass. The Belgian playmaker then made it three from the spot after a foul on Giroud, before Alex Iwobi pulled one back for the Gunners with a piledriver from outside the box. However, this was most definitely a Blue day in Baku, and after Hazard volleyed in Giroud's pass with 15 minutes to go there was no coming back for the north Londoners.

2) Tottenham 1 Chelsea 6, Premier League, 6 December 1997

The Blues recorded their biggest-ever win against Spurs in extraordinary fashion, scoring five goals after the break following an even first half. Roberto Di Matteo began the rout on 47 minutes before Dan Petrescu scored the goal of the game with a delicate lob over Tottenham goalkeeper Ian Walker. It was all over as a contest when Tore Andre Flo, who had headed the Blues' opener, scored with a right-foot cross shot, but there was still time for sub Mark Nicholls and Flo, completing his first Chelsea hat-trick with a looping shot, to really rub Spurs noses in the dirt. 'I have never lost 6-1 in my life,' lamented Tottenham boss Christian Gross afterwards. 'It was hard to take.'

3) Arsenal 1 Chelsea 2, Champions League quarter-final second leg, 6 April 2004

It's hard to imagine now, but back in the spring of 2004 Arsenal were a real force in the land, heading for the Premier League title without losing a single match. The Blues, then, were really up against it when they arrived at Highbury after a 1-1 draw at the Bridge and their prospects of reaching the last four of the Champions League looked bleak when Jose Antonio Reyes poked the Gunners ahead on the stroke of half-time. However, Chelsea hit back with a close-range goal from Frank Lampard early in the second half and then began to gain the upper hand. The Blues' winning goal near the end of a thrilling encounter was a beauty, Wayne Bridge and Eidur Gudjohnsen combining before the left-back fired in a low-angled drive to leave the so-called 'Invincibles' looking not so unbeatable after all.

4) Chelsea 6 Arsenal 0, Premier League, 22 March 2014

Arsene Wenger's 1,000th game in charge of Arsenal proved to be a memorable one, but not quite in the way the Frenchman would have hoped. After Samuel Eto'o opened the scoring with a well-placed shot, the Blues simply tore a limp Gunners side apart, Andre Schurrle quickly adding a second and then Eden Hazard scoring from a penalty awarded for a handball that resulted in Kieran Gibbs being sent off (although Alex Oxlade-Chamberlain was the real culprit). Three goals up after just 15 minutes, the Blues could have taken their foot off the gas; instead, they continued to push the knife in, doubling their tally through further strikes by Oscar (2) and substitute Mohamed Salah to achieve their biggest-ever win against their north London rivals.

5) Chelsea 2 Tottenham 0, League Cup Final, 1 March 2015

After surviving an early scare when Christian Eriksen rattled the bar with a 25-yard free kick, Chelsea gradually gained the upper hand and took the lead right on half-time when skipper John Terry lashed a shot past Hugo Lloris after the Spurs defence failed to clear Willian's floated free kick. Ten minutes after the break, Diego Costa doubled the Blues' lead with a fierce drive that deflected in off Kyle Walker, and from then on it was only a matter of time before JT and co. got their hands on the trophy.

6) Chelsea 2 Arsenal 1, League Cup Final, 25 February 2007

In the last domestic cup final held at the Millennium Stadium in Cardiff, Chelsea fell behind early on when Theo Walcott scored with a well-taken shot – his first-ever goal for the Gunners. However, the Blues soon hit back with a goal from Didier Drogba, who beat the Arsenal offside trap to shoot past Manuel Almunia. The west Londoners controlled the game in the second half and deservedly found a winner in the 84th minute when Drogba met substitute Arjen Robben's pinpoint cross with a trademark power header. In the final minute, John Obi Mikel and Kolo Toure were the instigators of a mass fracas and, once order was restored, were both shown the red card.

7) Chelsea 5 Tottenham 1, FA Cup semi-final, 15 April 2012

The Blues eventually battered Spurs in this Wembley semi-final but had to wait until just before half-time to take the lead, Didier Drogba firing an unstoppable left-foot shot past former Chelsea goalkeeper Carlo Cudicini. Four minutes after half-time, Juan Mata scored a controversial second, his low shot appearing not to cross the line in a crowded goalmouth. Spurs quickly hit back through Gareth Bale, but 13 minutes from the end Ramires made the match safe for the Blues with a clever flicked finish. With Spurs on the ropes, Frank Lampard compounded their misery with a spectacular 30-yard free kick before Florent Malouda completed the drubbing in the final minute.

8) Chelsea 4 Tottenham 2, FA Cup semi-final, 22 April 2017

In a Wembley semi-final of high quality and spellbinding drama, Willian gave the Blues an early lead with a beautifully struck free kick. Spurs soon equalised through Harry Kane, but Willian restored Chelsea's advantage from the spot two minutes before half-time. On 52 minutes, Dele Alli levelled the scores again, but the west Londoners had an ace to play in sub Eden Hazard and it was the little Belgian who put the Blues ahead for the third time with a low shot from just inside the area. Then, ten minutes from the end, Nemanja Matic settled a pulsating tie with a blistering 25-yard left-footer that almost tore the net off.

9) Chelsea 2 Arsenal 1, FA Cup semi-final, 18 April 2009

Arsenal had knocked Chelsea out of the FA Cup in four consecutive seasons earlier in the decade – including victory in the 2002 final – so the Blues were delighted to exact a semblance of revenge in this Wembley semi-final. However, they had to come from behind after Theo Walcott put the Gunners ahead in the 18th minute with a shot that deflected in off Ashley Cole. The equaliser came 15 minutes later when Florent Malouda collected a long crossfield pass from Frank Lampard, cut inside and drilled a low shot in at the near post.

Lampard also set up the Blues' winner six minutes from time, Didier Drogba controlling his long pass before rounding Gunners goalie Lukasz Fabianski and planting the ball into the empty net.

10) QPR 2 Chelsea 4, FA Cup sixth round, 21 February 1970

The first-ever cup tie between the two west London neighbours was a fantastic spectacle despite being played on an old-fashioned mud heap at Loftus Road. The Blues went ahead early on when David Webb volleyed in a cross by John Hollins and, just a minute later, doubled their lead with a lovely goal, Charlie Cooke's beautifully weighted pass setting up Peter Osgood for an emphatic left-foot finish. Rangers hit back with a twice-taken Terry Venables penalty, but Ossie restored the Blues' two-goal advantage when QPR keeper Mike Kelly spilled Hollins' long-range shot. In the second half, Osgood completed his hat-trick with a bobbling shot into the corner, making Barry Bridges' late goal for the home side no more than a consolation.

TOP 10 CHELSEA RACEHORSES

Chelsea fans may fancy a flutter on these Blues-related racehorses, but should be warned: none of them are exactly Red Rum or Frankel out on the turf.

1) Chelsea Flyer

Now a veteran, the nine-year-old Irish bay gelding has won over £10,000 during its career. Not bad at all.

2) Harry Hazard

If the six-year-old bay gelding combines the speed of Eden Hazard with the clear-eyed focus of England skipper Harry Kane, it should be some horse.

3) Blue Cup

The Blues have won numerous cups in their time, suggesting you could be on to a winner backing the four-year-old grey gelding.

4) Big-Time Frank

Frank Lampard has been in the big time as a player and manager for well over 20 years, but will this nag deliver as consistently as he has done?

5) Stamford Bridge

A name to stick out on the list of runners for all Chelsea fans, but this two-year-old bay gelding is still waiting for a first win.

6) Chelsea's Boy

The seven-year-old grey gelding has won over £9,000 in prize money during its career. Not a fortune, true, but better than some of the also-rans on this list.

7) Wise Words

Former Chelsea skipper Dennis Wise was known for his clenched-fist pre-match team talks. But will 'Wise Words' show the same commitment out on the track?

8) N'Golo

If the Irish grey gelding shows the same energy, stamina and acceleration as Blues midfielder N'Golo Kante, it will be in with a chance in our sweepstakes.

9) Singing the Blues

CFC fans feel like singing the Blues 'when Chelsea win and Tottenham lose', but will this five-year-old bay gelding get punters cheering?

10) Electric Blue

Presumably, this two-year-old chestnut filly's name references the time in the mid-1980s when kindly Chelsea chairman Ken Bates threatened to erect electric fences at the Bridge to stop fans running onto the pitch. Ah, those were the days.

TOP 10 BLUE PUNDITS

Thankfully, the days are long gone when the only footy pundits on TV were former Manchester United or Liverpool players. Indeed, it's quite likely that if you watch a pre or post-match discussion these days, at least one of the talking heads in the studio will have worn the famous blue shirt in the recent or dim-and-distant past.

1) Pat Nevin

Insightful, thoughtful, articulate and slightly quirky, the popular Blues winger from the mid-1980s is always worth listening to in his role as a regular co-commentator and analyst on Radio 5 Live. He also has a weekly column on the official Chelsea website that invariably makes for illuminating reading.

2) Chris Sutton

Sutton's over-the-top rants, deadpan humour and barbed comments may not be to everyone's taste, but he's certainly a more impressive communicator than he ever was a striker for Chelsea. Paired with Robbie Savage on Radio 5 Live's popular *606* phone-in, he usually gets the better of the gibbering Welshman in their weekly debates. Admittedly, getting one over a man once voted Britain's worst pundit is not that hard!

3) Joe Cole

A fairly new addition to BT Sport's punditry team, the former Chelsea midfielder has already made something of a mark on the small screen and is one to watch in the future. His simple, boyish enthusiasm for the game is endearing, but is accompanied by genuine insight and occasional golden nuggets of football wisdom. A true Chelsea fan, Cole showed his love for the club by leaping for joy on camera at the final whistle of the Blues' 2021 Champions League Final victory over Manchester City in Porto.

4) Glenn Hoddle

Happily recovered from a near-fatal heart attack in October 2018, the former Chelsea player-manager is back in the BT studio, where he exudes a relaxed, amiable and authoritative presence. A true football purist, he can be relied upon to wax lyrical if he spots a central defender who declines to simply boot the ball into Row Z and is comfortable 'stepping out from the back'.

5) Jimmy Floyd Hasselbaink

After cutting his punditry teeth covering Championship matches, the former Blues striker has recently been promoted to the top table by Sky, despite being back in management with Burton Albion. Just as he did so many times for the Blues, the Dutchman has snapped up the opportunity, his forthright opinions making him especially watchable when he is paired with an antagonist such as ex-Manchester United defender Patrice Evra.

6) Ashley Cole

As a player, Ashley Cole rather shied away from media interviews – understandably, perhaps, given the prurient tabloid interest in his personal life. So it has been something of a surprise to see him emerge as a more-than-decent pundit on Sky and the BBC in recent seasons. His analysis of defensive situations, in particular, is always top-notch and usually communicated extremely effectively in a jargon-free manner.

7) Jason Cundy

A pundit and presenter on TalkSPORT for many years, the former Blues defender never shies away from an argument – usually with his regular co-presenter, Manchester United fan Andy Goldstein – and often goes in feet first, delivering his opinions in incendiary language. In 2014, for example, he described Liverpool fans as 'bitter, twisted, bitchy and spiteful', with predictable results on social media.

8) Karen Carney

Equally comfortable whether covering men's or women's football for BT or the BBC, the former Chelsea Women winger has built up an impressive media CV since retiring from the game in 2019. Likeable, knowledgeable and perceptive, she is certainly the hardest-working female pundit in the business, appearing on screen or across the airwaves most days of the week. In January 2021, she was forced to close her Twitter account after receiving a torrent of sexist abuse from Leeds fans who took exception to a comment she had made about their team.

9) Mark Schwarzer

The former Blues back-up goalkeeper is not the most visible pundit as a lot of his work is for Australian media companies. However, his occasional contributions on Radio 5 Live and TalkSPORT are always astute and to the point. He is not afraid, either, to break the omerta of the 'goalkeepers' union' and criticise underperforming glove-wearers such as Manchester United's David de Gea and Chelsea flop Kepa Arrizabalaga.

10) Glen Johnson

The one-time Blues right-back was quite outspoken as a player, once describing Paul Merson as an 'alcoholic drug abuser' who 'was average at the best of times' after the Sky

Sports pundit criticised Johnson's performances for Liverpool. Slightly awkward, then, that Jonno is now sharing a desk with 'the Magic Man' on Sky's revamped *Soccer Saturday* show. There's clearly no love lost between the pair but, for the moment at least, anchor Jeff Stelling has not had to step in to separate them.

TOP 10 CHELSEA FC WOMEN GOALS

The girls have scored some crackers over the years, including these beauties:

1) Millie Bright, Chelsea 2 Manchester City 0, Community Shield, 29 August 2020

Stepping into midfield, the tall Chelsea centre-back carried the ball forward, looked up and then unleashed a fearsome swerving shot from fully 35 yards that gave the City goalkeeper no chance. A Wembley strike worthy of Blues legend Roberto Di Matteo!

2) Fran Kirby, Chelsea 3 Arsenal 1, Women's FA Cup Final, 5 May 2018

Fran Kirby has scored some wonderful goals for the Blues and this stunner in the 2018 Women's FA Cup Final at Wembley was right out of the Eden Hazard playbook. Receiving the ball on the edge of the penalty area, Chelsea's 'mini Messi' surged past a couple of Arsenal defenders before curling a lovely left-footer into the far corner.

3) Beth England, Chelsea 1 Tottenham 0, WSL, 8 September 2019

Playing in front of an excited crowd of 24,564 at Stamford Bridge, Blues striker Beth England produced a strike fit for the occasion after just four minutes, brushing past a Tottenham defender before powering a left-foot shot into the far corner from 25 yards out for what proved to be the winner. A goal to match any scored by Blues great Frank Lampard!

4) Ji So-Yun, Liverpool 0 Chelsea 4, WSL, 27 September 2015
A right-wing cross from Blues winger Gemma Davison seemed to be overhit, but silky-skilled midfielder Ji So-Yun conjured up a piece of Zola-style magic to pull the ball out of the night sky with a superb touch as it floated over her head. Spinning quickly, she then lashed a fierce shot high into the net at the near post for a wonderful individual goal.

5) Sophie Ingle, Arsenal 1 Chelsea 4, WSL, 19 January 2020
In one of the best Chelsea performances ever, the Blues were already leading 2-0 against reigning champions Arsenal when a loose ball bobbled towards defensive midfielder Sophie Ingle on the edge of the Gunners box. Showing admirable technique, the Wales captain smashed a blistering left-footer high into the far corner to notch the best goal of her career.

6) Pernille Harder, Chelsea 4 Everton 0, WSL, 8 November 2020
The Danish international showed why she is rated as one of the best players in the world with this goal, which wrapped up a convincing 4-0 win for the Blues against Everton. On the ball in midfield, Harder passed forward to Beth England and then collected her lay-off before blasting an unstoppable left-footer into the far corner from 20 yards.

7) Sam Kerr, Arsenal 1 Chelsea 4, WSL, 19 January 2020
Shortly after joining the Blues, Australia captain Sam Kerr got off the mark for her new club with a fine goal in a 4-1

demolition of London rivals Arsenal. She was indebted to Norwegian midfielder Guro Reiten, however, for a pinpoint cross from the left wing, which Kerr met with a textbook downward header into the far bottom corner.

8) Gilly Flaherty, Chelsea 2 Notts County 1, WSL, 6 September 2015

Signed from Arsenal with Katie Chapman in January 2014, centre-back Gilly Flaherty scored the best goal of her four-year stint with the Blues 18 months later, rocketing a volley high into the net after a spot of head tennis in the Notts County box.

9) Erin Cuthbert, Arsenal 1 Chelsea 2, WSL, 13 January 2019

The tireless Scottish midfielder enjoyed one of her best games for the Blues against eventual champions Arsenal in January 2019, scoring both goals in an excellent 2-1 win. Her second was a real peach, rising above two Gunners defenders to meet Hannah Blundell's right-wing cross with a Drogba-style power header.

10) Eni Aluko, Chelsea 1 Liverpool 0, WSL, 19 April 2015

The prolific Blues striker showed off her pace and finishing ability with this well-taken winner against Liverpool, racing on to a lofted pass from midfielder Laura Coombs and then calmly lobbing the ball over the Reds goalkeeper and into the empty net.

TOP 10 WORST MANAGERS

The men in the dugout who had Chelsea fans chanting en masse, 'You don't know what you're doing!'

1) Danny Blanchflower

In his playing days, Blanchflower was famously the brains behind the magnificent Tottenham Double team of 1961, but he had never managed a club before taking over a struggling Blues team in December 1979. Somewhat out of touch with the modern game, he struggled to inspire a young squad who were often bemused by his training methods which, bizarrely, included practice matches with two balls on the pitch at the same time. After winning just five of his 33 matches in charge and seeing the Blues plummet out of the top flight after their worst-ever season statistically, the Northern Irishman left the club in September 1980.

2) Andre Villas-Boas

A protégé of José Mourinho, Villas-Boas had previously worked under his fellow Portuguese at the Bridge before returning to west London in the summer of 2011 following a successful spell in charge of Porto. Relatively inexperienced, with no playing career to speak of and projecting a somewhat arrogant demeanour, he soon clashed with senior pros in the dressing room, who on one occasion questioned his tactics in front of Chelsea owner Roman Abramovich. An eyebrow-raising team selection for a vital Champions League match against Napoli put him on the brink before he was given the chop following a defeat at West Brom in March 2012, his assistant Roberto Di Matteo taking charge as caretaker.

3) David Calderhead

The Scot was poached from Lincoln City in the summer of 1907, having impressed the Chelsea board when his team knocked the Blues out of the FA Cup earlier that year. A shy man who made few public pronouncements, Calderhead was dubbed 'The Chelsea Shinx' by the media. However, his low-key style suited the times and he went on to manage the club for nearly 26 years – making him easily the Blues' longest-serving boss. Highlights, though, were few and far between: two promotions, a first FA Cup Final appearance in 1915 and a third-place finish five years later. Given the amount of money he spent in the transfer market, the star names he had at his disposal and the club's massive fanbase, these were decidedly slim pickings over such a long reign.

4) Geoff Hurst

The 1966 World Cup winner arrived at the Bridge as Danny Blanchflower's assistant in 1979 before taking over as manager, initially on a caretaker basis. His Chelsea team were unlucky not to gain promotion in 1980, and the following season were riding high in the Second Division until a disastrous run in the second half of the campaign – the Blues scoring in only three out of 22 games – led to a free-fall slide down the table. Having lost the confidence of a shell-shocked squad and with fans calling on him to go, it was no surprise when Hurst was sacked in April 1981.

5) Luiz Felipe Scolari

Manager of World Cup winners Brazil in 2002, 'Big Phil' was appointed Chelsea boss in the summer of 2009 after a stint in charge of Portugal. Although his inability to pronounce the name of the club grated with fans – 'Chel-say-ah' was the best he could manage – the early signs were initially promising. Soon, though, opposing teams realised that the Blues' attacking threat could be nullified by blocking the forward runs of their attacking full-backs and, amazingly, Scolari appeared to have no tactical 'Plan B'. Inevitably, results fell away badly and, following a dire 0-0 home draw with lowly Hull City, he was sacked in February 2009, Dutchman Guus Hiddink taking over on a caretaker basis.

6) John Hollins

An energetic and bubbly figure in Chelsea's midfield in the 1960s and 70s, John Hollins returned to the club as player-coach in 1983 and helped the Blues win promotion a year later. He was promoted to manager in 1985 but, after an excellent start, the team's form imploded and relations between the young boss and key players deteriorated. The sale of popular figures like David Speedie and Nigel Spackman went down badly with the fans, while the replacements Hollins brought in were generally of inferior quality. Finally, after a long run without a win in the 1987/88 season, he was sacked and replaced with his recently appointed assistant, Bobby Campbell.

7) Leslie Knighton

Formerly manager of Arsenal, Bournemouth and Birmingham City, Leslie Knighton took over as Chelsea boss from the long-serving David Calderhead in 1933. Despite making some excellent signings, such as Northern Ireland striker Joe Bambrick, he was unable to turn a team packed full of talented internationals into one that challenged for honours. A string of FA Cup defeats to lower-league opposition disappointed the club's vast army of fans, but the final straw came when the Blues only avoided relegation to the second tier in 1939 by a single point, leading the board to announce that he would be replaced by Billy Birrell.

8) Ron Suart

Formerly manager of Wigan, Scunthorpe and Blackpool, Ron Suart arrived at Chelsea to become assistant to Tommy Docherty in July 1967. He stayed on under Dave Sexton and then stepped up to become manager following Sexton's dismissal in October 1974. However, he could do little to prevent a demoralised team from sliding towards relegation and, with the trap door beckoning, he passed on the baton to Eddie McCreadie in April 1974 and took on an upstairs role as general manager. He later worked as chief scout before joining Wimbledon in the mid-1980s.

9) Avram Grant

A personal friend of Roman Abramovich, Avram Grant was promoted from Director of Football to manager following Jose Mourinho's shock departure in September 2007. Having previously only worked in Israel, he lacked experience in elite-level football, his deficiencies as a coach prompting some players to complain that his training methods were decades behind the times. Nonetheless, he had the good sense to change little from the successful Mourinho era and he took Chelsea to two cup finals. However, the sight of John Terry giving the on-pitch team talk before the start of extra time in the 2008 League Cup Final against Tottenham suggested that the senior players were running the show rather than the lugubrious Israeli, and it came as no shock when Grant's contract was terminated at the end of the season.

10) Ian Porterfield

Previously Bobby Campbell's assistant at the Bridge, Ian Porterfield returned to west London as Chelsea manager in the summer of 1991 after an unsuccessful spell in charge of Reading. His first season at the helm was fairly nondescript, notable mostly for a disappointing FA Cup quarter-final exit at the hands of second-tier Sunderland. The following campaign began reasonably well, but a dismal run of 13 games without a win after Christmas saw him become the first Premier League manager ever to be sacked, Blues legend David Webb filling in as caretaker boss until the end of the season.

TOP 10 SONGS WITH 'CHELSEA' IN THE TITLE

OK, none of these numbers are about the Blues as such but, on the other hand, how many non-football songs are there that even refer to Arsenal, Tottenham or West Ham?

1) 'Chelsea Dagger', The Fratellis
The Scottish band's stomper was a big hit, reaching number five in the UK charts in 2006. After the single became part of the pre-match build-up at the Bridge, the Celtic-supporting trio announced that they had all adopted Chelsea as their favourite Premier League team.

2) '(I Don't Want to Go to) Chelsea', Elvis Costello
Liverpool fan Costello had a Top 20 hit with this ska-influenced rocker, which came out in March 1978 just two months after the Blues had dumped the reigning European champions out of the FA Cup after a famous 4-2 victory at the Bridge. Might that event have inspired the song title? We'd like to think so.

3) 'Midnight in Chelsea', Jon Bon Jovi
Reaching number four in the charts in 1997, this song was Jon Bon Jovi's biggest-ever UK hit. Although the music video was filmed in the Chelsea district of New York, the lyrics are clearly about west London with references to 'a lone Sloane ranger' and 'a big red bus'.

4) 'Chelsea Morning', Joni Mitchell
Joni's shrill vocals on this folksy late-60s ballad about the quirky Manhattan neighbourhood may not be to all tastes, but this is a great song to blast out before the Blues line up for a lunchtime kick-off. Famously, the song inspired Bill and Hillary Clinton to call their only child 'Chelsea'.

5) 'Chelsea Hotel #2', Leonard Cohen
Gravel-voiced singer/songwriter Cohen wrote this song, from his 1974 album *New Skin for the Old Ceremony*, about a brief affair he had had some six years earlier with rock star Janis Joplin while both were staying in the Chelsea Hotel in New York.

6) 'Chelsea Girls', Nico

Lou Reed and Sterling Morrison of The Velvet Underground wrote this rather dirge-like song in 1967 for deep-voiced German songstress Nico, referencing the louche characters staying at New York's most bohemian hostelry, the Chelsea Hotel.

7) 'Chelsea Monday', Marillion

A song about the Blues finishing off the weekend's Premier League programme in the Monday evening slot? Er, no. It's actually a vaguely depressing album track by the Fish-fronted prog rockers about a young woman stuck in a west London bedsit who dreams of becoming an actress. Oh well, at least she's living in lively Chelsea rather than dreary Tottenham.

8) 'Chelsea Girl', Simple Minds

This track – about a girl who changes her name and turns her back on her old friends – appeared on Simple Minds' 1979 debut album *Life in a Day* but failed to chart as a single. Never mind, the Glasgow rockers were soon bashing out the hits and selling out stadiums around the world.

9) 'Third Week in the Chelsea', Jefferson Airplane

A folksy track on the 1971 album *Bark* by psychedelic rock pioneers Jefferson Airplane, the song sees the San Francisco-based band relocated to New York for a three-week stay at the Chelsea Hotel which, considering the establishment's notorious reputation, is probably about two and a half weeks longer than most sane people could stand.

10) 'Chelsea', Counting Crows

A previously unreleased track on the Californian rockers' 1998 double live album *Across a Wire*, the song is about a man coming to terms with the loss of a loved one. And that completes our Top 10 chart rundown, pop pickers!

TOP 10 PENALTIES

The most important goals in the club's history scored from precisely 12 yards:

1) Peter Sillett, Chelsea 1 Wolves 0, First Division, 9 April 1955

A superb deadball taker, right-back Peter Sillett scored a number of crucial penalties in the Blues' 1954/55 championship-winning season, but there is no doubt about the most important one. At home to title rivals Wolves on Easter Saturday, Chelsea were pushing for a winner in the final 15 minutes when Seamus O'Connell's goalbound shot was punched off the line by England captain Billy Wright. Incredibly, the referee awarded a corner before being persuaded to consult his linesman by a crowd of angry blue shirts and the howls of the home fans in the 75,000 crowd. Eventually, he pointed to the spot, Sillett stepping forward to power his drive into the bottom left-hand corner of the net to secure a vital win for the Blues. Two weeks later, the dependable Sillett was on target from the spot again as the Londoners clinched the title with a 3-0 win against Sheffield Wednesday.

2) Eden Hazard, Chelsea 1 Manchester United 0, FA Cup Final, 19 May 2018

A supremely confident player, Belgian wizard Eden Hazard had his own individual way of taking penalties, which always gave the impression that he was in control of this uniquely pressurised situation. When he was fouled by Manchester United defender Phil Jones in the 2018 FA Cup Final, it was almost a foregone conclusion that Hazard would score from the spot, and that's exactly what happened as he sent David de Gea the wrong way by slotting the ball in the opposite corner for what proved to be the only goal of the game.

185

3) Frank Lampard, Chelsea 3 Liverpool 2, Champions League semi-final second leg, 30 April 2008

Frank Lampard scored a club-record 49 penalties for Chelsea, but this was easily the most memorable, coming in extra time in the 2008 Champions League semi-final against Liverpool. Adding to the pressure as he stepped forward to take the kick, Lamps had only just returned to the team after taking compassionate leave following the death of his mother, Pat. Fans in the stadium held their breath – would the emotion of the occasion prove too much for the Chelsea vice-captain? They needn't have worried. Focusing solely on the job in hand, the Blues midfielder drilled the ball into the bottom corner before raising his arms to the sky in a clear tribute to his much-loved mum. A vital goal, yes, but also a moment that neither Frank nor the fans present will ever forget.

4) Terry Venables, Chelsea 3 Leicester City 2, League Cup Final first leg, 15 March 1965

Chelsea skipper Terry Venables took over penalty duties from Bobby Tambling in 1963 and continued in the role for the next three years before departing for Tottenham. Back in the days when the League Cup Final was played over two legs, 'Venners' notched from 12 yards past England goalkeeper Gordon Banks as the Blues beat Leicester in the first leg at the Bridge before going on to lift the trophy after a battling 0-0 draw in the return at Filbert Street.

5) Frank Leboeuf, Chelsea 1 Leicester City 0, FA Cup fifth-round replay, 26 February 1997

An unerring deadball specialist, no fewer than 15 of Frank Leboeuf's Chelsea goals came from the spot. This was the most important of the lot, controversially awarded after Blues defender Erland Johnsen charged forward in the closing minutes of an FA Cup replay against Leicester and tumbled in the box. As ever, the nonchalant French stopper calmly took his opportunity, sending Foxes goalkeeper Kasey Keller the wrong way as the ball nestled in the bottom corner.

6) John Hollins, Chelsea 3 Tottenham Hotspur 2, League Cup semi-final first leg, 22 December 1971

Midfield dynamo John Hollins enjoyed his most prolific season in 1971/72, scoring an impressive 18 goals in total, including eight from the spot. The most crucial of these came four minutes from the end of the first leg of the League Cup semi-final against Tottenham at the Bridge in 1971, when he smashed the ball down the middle past legendary Spurs goalkeeper Pat Jennings. Holly's goal proved to be the winner in the tie as the Blues drew 2-2 in the second leg at White Hart Lane to claim a famous 5-4 aggregate victory.

7) Roy Bentley, Chelsea 2 Wolves 1, First Division, 25 April 1951

The Blues pulled off one of the most incredible relegation escapes ever in 1951, winning their last four games to avoid the drop on goal average ahead of Sheffield Wednesday and Everton. One of these vital victories came at home to Wolves, despite the Black Country side taking an early lead. That advantage was quickly wiped out by skipper Roy Bentley from the spot – surely one of the most significant of the then-record 150 goals he scored for the club – before Ken Armstrong grabbed the all-important winner.

8) Michael Ballack, Chelsea 2 Manchester United 1, Premier League, 26 April 2008

Classy midfielder Michael Ballack had already scored once in this top-of-the-table clash when the Blues were awarded a late penalty for handball against Michael Carrick. With Frank Lampard absent following the death of his mother, the German placed the ball on the spot and, ignoring the delaying tactics of United goalkeeper Edwin van der Sar, blasted the ball into the corner to give Chelsea a valuable win.

9) Mark Stein, Chelsea 4 Tottenham Hotspur 3, Premier League, 27 February 1994

A thrilling London derby was tied at 3-3 when Blues midfielder Gavin Peacock was felled in the box in the last minute of normal time. Striker Mark Stein, who had already netted in the first half, stepped up to the spot at the Shed End and made no mistake, smashing a thunderous drive past Spurs goalkeeper Ian Walker for a dramatic and ecstatically received winner.

10) Jorginho, Tottenham Hotspur 0 Chelsea 1, Premier League, 4 February 2021

The Blues continued their unbeaten start under new boss Thomas Tuchel thanks to a penalty awarded for an Eric Dier foul on Timo Werner and converted by Jorginho. Eschewing his usual hop, skip and jump run-up, the Italian international simply whacked the ball into the left-hand corner of the goal past Spurs keeper Hugo Lloris to give the Blues a win their overall performance thoroughly deserved.

TOP 10 WELSH BLUES

The best Chelsea players to hail from the Valleys:

1) Mark Hughes

A bargain £1.5m recruit from Manchester United in the summer of 1995, experienced striker Mark Hughes helped transform Chelsea from frustrating underachievers to serial cup winners. Forming a terrific attacking partnership with Gianfranco Zola, Hughes starred in the Blues' FA Cup-winning run in 1997, the same year he was voted Chelsea Player of the Year. The following year, a memorable strike at the Bridge secured a famous win for the Blues against Vicenza in the European Cup Winners' Cup semi-final, before he joined Southampton that summer for £650,000. Considered to be one of Wales' greatest-ever players, Hughes played 72 times for his country and later managed the team between 1999 and 2004.

2) Eddie Niedzwiecki

Signed by Blues boss John Neal from his old club Wrexham in 1983, Eddie Niedzwiecki was an ever-present in the Londoners' Second Division title-winning campaign the following season. A commanding goalkeeper who rarely made a mistake and was capable of producing saves of the highest quality, the Welshman of Polish origin was first choice between the sticks until 1986, the year he was voted the club's Player of the Year, when a series of crippling knee injuries sadly ended his career. A great Chelsea servant, Niedzwiecki stayed at the Bridge in a coaching capacity until 2000.

3) Mickey Thomas

Signed from Stoke in January 1984 by his former Wrexham boss John Neal, shaggy-haired winger Mickey Thomas made an immediate impact at Stamford Bridge, scoring twice on his home debut against promotion rivals Sheffield Wednesday in a 3-2 victory. The Welsh international didn't experience defeat in Chelsea colours until the following season, cementing his quickly earned status as a Shed cult hero. However, his reluctance to relocate from his home in north Wales meant his stay in London was always likely to be brief and he moved on to West Brom in September 1985.

4) Joey Jones

A European Cup winner with Liverpool in 1977, Joey Jones joined Chelsea from Wrexham in October 1982. The tough-tackling left-back had a nightmare debut, being booed by the travelling Blues fans after being sent off at Carlisle. However, his unstinting commitment soon won over the supporters and he was voted Chelsea Player of the Year at the end of the campaign. The following season he helped the Blues win promotion to the top flight, his clenched-fist salute to the fans in the Shed a much-loved pre-match ritual. After losing his place to new recruit Doug Rougvie, he moved on to Huddersfield in August 1985.

5) John Phillips

Signed from Aston Villa for £25,000 in August 1970 as back-up for Peter Bonetti, 19-year-old John 'Sticks' Phillips soon proved that he was a more-than-capable understudy with some excellent displays in the Chelsea goal, notably during the Blues' march to the European Cup Winners' Cup Final. The Welshman finally replaced 'The Cat' as first-choice keeper in 1974 but a broken leg deprived him of a long run in the side and, after a spell in America with St Louis Stars, Bonetti was recalled by boss Eddie McCreadie, leaving Phillips sidelined once again. After making 149 appearances for the Blues and winning four caps for Wales, he joined Crewe on loan in 1979 before playing for Brighton, Charlton and Crystal Palace.

6) Vinnie Jones

Eyebrows were raised at Stamford Bridge when Blues boss Ian Porterfield signed Vinnie Jones from Sheffield United in August 1991. The midfield enforcer was better known for his appalling disciplinary record than his football skills, his notorious reputation as a shin-hacking hardman forged with the aptly named 'Crazy Gang' of Wimbledon in the late 1980s. However, Watford-born Jones soon won over the majority of Chelsea fans with his wince-inducing tackles and fighting spirit, and his cult status was secured when he smashed in a 25-yarder in front of the Kop to help the Blues achieve a first league win at Anfield for 57 years. Soon after the start of the 1992/93 season he returned to Wimbledon and in 1994, aged 30, he won the first of his nine caps for Wales.

7) Peter Nicholas

An experienced midfielder, Peter Nicholas added steel and grit to a just-relegated Blues team when he arrived from Aberdeen for £350,000 in August 1988. During the following season, he was outstanding as Bobby Campbell's side romped to the Second Division title but his flair-free, no-frills approach to the game failed to find favour with the Bridge crowd. After making nearly 100 appearances for the Blues and winning a then-record 73 caps for Wales, Nicholas joined Watford in 1991.

8) Danny Winter

A stylish and dependable right-back, Danny Winter first featured for the Blues towards the end of World War II as a guest player, having previously seen action at Dunkirk and El Alamein with many of his Bolton team-mates in the 53rd Field Regiment. After helping Chelsea win the Football League (South) Cup at Wembley in April 1945, the Welshman from Tonypandy made a permanent move south and went on to make over 150 appearances for the club before joining Worcester City in 1951.

9) Graham Moore

Something of a teenage prodigy at Cardiff, Graham Moore won the first of his 21 caps for Wales in 1960 aged just 19. The following year, he joined Chelsea for £35,000 but was unable to prevent Tommy Docherty's young side from dropping out of the First Division. An attacking midfielder with a goalscorer's instincts he fared better in the second tier, contributing eight goals as the Blues won promotion at the first attempt. In November 1963 he moved on to Manchester United, where he struggled with injuries, and he later played for Northampton, Charlton and Doncaster.

10) Gareth Hall

A Chelsea youth product, Gareth Hall came through the ranks to make his Blues debut as an 18-year-old in May 1987. Over the next eight years, he competed for the right-back berth with Steve Clarke, often being preferred over the Scotsman by bosses Bobby Campbell and Ian Porterfield. However, when Glenn Hoddle took over the reins in 1993 the Croydon-born Welsh international became very much second choice and it was no surprise when, after making over 170 appearances for the Blues, he joined Sunderland on loan in 1995, with the deal becoming permanent the following year.

TOP 10 AMUSING FAN CHANTS

The Chelsea choir have come up with some very witty chants over the years, including these:

1) 'Steve Gerrard, Gerrard, he slipped on his f***ing arse, he gave it to Demba Ba, Steve Gerrard, Gerrard'

When Chelsea visited Liverpool in late April 2014, Reds fans were almost frothing with excitement: a win against the Londoners would just about guarantee the Merseysiders their first league title for nearly a quarter of a century, while even a draw would leave their fate very much in their own hands. However, the pre-match script was turned upside down when

Liverpool skipper and talisman Steven Gerrard slipped inside his own half, allowing Chelsea striker Demba Ba to pounce on the loose ball and plant it in the net at the Kop end to give the Blues a first-half lead. When Willian doubled the Blues' advantage late on, the Scousers' balloon was well and truly deflated, but it was Gerrard's uncharacteristic error that came to symbolise Liverpool's ultimately fruitless title quest and the following season he was taunted with this memorable ditty by opposition fans up and down the country.

2) 'You're shish, and you know you are!'
An inventive chant, riffing on an old standard set to the tune of the Pet Shop Boys hit 'Go West', directed at the kebab-loving fans of Turkish outfit Galatasaray who visited the Bridge for a Champions League group fixture in 1999.

3) 'Normal service has resumed'
In January 2002, Tottenham crushed Chelsea 5-1 in the League Cup semi-final second leg at White Hart Lane, going through to the final 6-3 on aggregate. Incredibly, this was Spurs' first win against the Blues in any competition for 11 years, a run encompassing 26 matches (17 Chelsea wins and nine draws). The heavy defeat was hard to take for the west Londoners, but six weeks later their fans were crowing that 'normal service has resumed' as the Blues cruised to a 4-0 win at the Lane in a one-sided FA Cup quarter-final.

4) 'Feed the Scousers, let them know it's Christmas time'
A festive season favourite, set to the tune of the famous Band Aid charity single 'Feed the World', which reflects Chelsea fans' deep-seated concern and compassion for the good people of Liverpool, a city that, sadly, has suffered more than most from long-term unemployment and urban deprivation over the years.

5) 'We love the Old Bill in Seville'

In April 2007, Tottenham fans endured a miserable trip to Spain for a UEFA Cup tie against Sevilla. Not only did they see their team lose 2-1, but a section of their supporters were attacked by baton-wielding riot police midway through the first half. The Spurs fans claimed they were victims of 'police brutality' but, when the two teams met at the Bridge just two days later, their Chelsea counterparts were less than sympathetic and showed their support for the muscle-flexing Andalucian authorities with this appreciative chant. To complete a depressing week for the north Londoners, Chelsea won the match 1-0.

6) 'Live round the corner, you only live round the corner'

Set to the tune of Cuban classic 'Guantanamera', this is a jibe aimed at 'travelling' Manchester United fans at the Bridge, most of whom it is alleged live in Hammersmith, Earl's Court or Putney and have never actually been to Old Trafford. Indeed, a 2020 survey revealed that United have over two million fans in London – 50 per cent more than they can boast in their home city!

7) 'Arsene Wenger, we want you to stay!'

From the high point of winning the Premier League with his so-called 'Invincibles' in 2004, Arsene Wenger's reign at Arsenal rapidly subsided into underachievement and mediocrity. Gunners fans argued constantly among themselves during this extended period: should the professorial Frenchman remain in charge or sling his hook tout de suite? Overwhelmingly, Chelsea fans tended towards the former view and made their feelings clear when the Blues hammered the Gunners 6-0 at the Bridge in March 2014. Happily, the Arsenal board adopted the same position, and allowed Wenger to stay in situ for another four rather aimless years before finally showing him the door at the end of the 2017/18 campaign.

8) 'Have you ever seen Gerrard win the league?'

Even the most dyed-in-the-wool Chelsea fan would have to admit that Steven Gerrard was a fantastic footballer – in his way, almost as good as our very own Frank Lampard. Gerrard also enjoyed a hugely successful career with Liverpool, winning the Champions League, UEFA Cup, FA Cup and League Cup with the Reds and scoring in all four finals. However, there was one trophy he never won despite craving it more than any other – the Premier League. Chelsea fans liked to remind Gerrard of this Grand Canyon-sized gap in his CV, especially as the Blues won the league title no fewer than four times during the Liverpool icon's playing days.

9) 'One Ranieri, there's only one Ranieri'

In May 2016, Tottenham came to the Bridge still with an outside chance of pipping surprise packages Leicester City to the Premier League title. Winning 2-0 at half-time, it all looked rosy for Spurs, but a superb Chelsea fightback capped by a brilliant Eden Hazard goal saw the Blues level the score at 2-2 – a result that would confirm the Foxes as unlikely champions. As the final seconds ticked away, Blues fans sang the praises of Leicester manager Claudio Ranieri, a former occupant of the Bridge hot seat, while the Spurs supporters were left to contemplate yet another trophyless campaign.

10) 'Champions of Europe, you'll never sing that'

Chelsea's magnificent Champions League triumphs of 2012 and 2021 mean the Blues have bragging rights over the numerous English clubs who have yet to get their hands on European football's premier chunk of silverware. As Chelsea fans like to remind them, these clubs include Arsenal, Tottenham, Everton, Newcastle, Leeds and, of course, Manchester City!

TOP 10 FINALS

The matches that had Blues fans jumping for joy:

1) Bayern Munich 1 Chelsea 1 (won 4-3 on penalties), Champions League Final, 19 May 2012

Four years after enduring Champions League agony against Manchester United in Moscow, the Blues made it through to the final again. But they faced a daunting challenge in the shape of a strong Bayern Munich side on their own patch, with a weakened team missing key players like John Terry and Branislav Ivanovic through suspension. On the back foot for long periods, Chelsea fell behind seven minutes from the end when Thomas Muller headed in at the far post. Five minutes later, though, the Blues equalised, Didier Drogba powering in Juan Mata's corner with a bullet header. Early in extra time, Bayern missed a chance to regain the lead when Arjen Robben's penalty was brilliantly saved by Petr Cech. It proved to be an omen of things to come as the Blues came out on top in the penalty shoot-out that followed the 1-1 draw. Drogba calmly slotted in the winning spot kick to round off the greatest night in Chelsea's long history.

2) Manchester City 0 Chelsea 1, Champions League Final, 29 May 2021

Thanks to Covid restrictions, a crowd of just 14,000 saw the Blues lift the Champions League for a second time after a tense 1-0 win against Premier League rivals Manchester City in Porto. The key moment came shortly before half-time when Kai Havertz took Mason Mount's defence-splitting pass in his stride, rounded City goalkeeper Ederson and coolly stroked the ball into an empty net. After that, a brilliant Chelsea rearguard action restricted City to few clear-cut chances, the best falling to Riyad Mahrez in the final minute when he blazed over the bar from the edge of the box.

3) Chelsea 2 Leeds United 1, FA Cup Final replay, 29 April 1970

After a hard-fought 2-2 draw at Wembley, Chelsea and Leeds resumed hostilities at Old Trafford with both clubs aiming to win the FA Cup for the first time in their history. After falling behind to a first-half goal by Mick Jones and with goalkeeper Peter Bonetti struggling with a knock, the Blues' prospects of victory looked slim. However, Dave Sexton's side never gave up and deservedly equalised when Peter Osgood flung himself full length to head home Charlie Cooke's cross. A riveting, and at times brutal, final was settled in extra time, Blues defender David Webb nodding in at the far post after the Leeds defence failed to clear Ian Hutchinson's long throw.

4) Chelsea 2 Real Madrid 1, European Cup Winners' Cup Final replay, 21 May 1971

Two days after a 1-1 draw in the Greek port of Piraeus, Dave Sexton's Blues locked swords again with six-time European Cup winners Real Madrid. The Londoners enjoyed a magnificent first half, taking the lead with a crashing volley by defender John Dempsey and then doubling their advantage when Tommy Baldwin set up strike partner Peter Osgood to score with a low shot off the post. The Spanish giants hit back with a goal of their own from Paraguayan substitute Sebastian Fleitas 13 minutes from the end, but it wasn't enough to prevent Ron Harris from becoming the first Chelsea skipper to lift a European trophy.

5) Chelsea 2 Benfica 1, Europa League Final, 15 May 2013

A year after winning the Champions League, the Blues became the first English club to lift all three historic UEFA trophies with victory over Benfica in the Europa League Final in Amsterdam. Fernando Torres put Chelsea ahead early in the second half, scoring with aplomb after being put through by Juan Mata. However, the Portuguese outfit soon equalised with a penalty, awarded for handball against Cesar Azpilicueta. With extra time looming, the Blues gave it one more push and were rewarded with a dramatic last-gasp winner, Branislav Ivanovic outjumping the Benfica defenders to head in Mata's corner.

6) Chelsea 4 Arsenal 1, Europa League Final, 29 May 2019

Baku, the capital of Azerbaijan, was always an odd choice for the Europa League Final, but even more so after two London clubs made it through to the showpiece event. The inconvenient location meant relatively few fans travelled over from England, but the muted atmosphere certainly didn't affect the Blues, who recorded their biggest-ever victory in a major final. Playing in his last match for Chelsea before moving to Real Madrid, playmaker Eden Hazard signed off in some style, scoring twice and setting up Pedro for a goal after striker Olivier Giroud had headed the Blues in front early in the second half. All Arsenal could manage in reply was a solitary goal by Alex Iwobi on a night to forget for the Gunners – but one to remember for all Chelsea fans.

7) Chelsea 2 Middlesbrough 0, FA Cup Final, 17 May 1997

Chasing a first major trophy for 26 years, the Blues got off to the perfect start when midfielder Roberto Di Matteo carried the ball forward before unleashing a thunderous shot from 30 yards, which crashed into the net off the underside of the bar. The goal was timed at 43 seconds – at the time the fastest-ever in a Wembley cup final. With seven minutes to play, nervous Chelsea fans could finally stop biting their nails when Eddie Newton scored from close range after Gianfranco Zola's clever flicked pass. A 'Blue Day' to remember for all those present.

8) Chelsea 1 Stuttgart 0, European Cup Winners' Cup Final, 13 May 1998

A tight match in Stockholm turned Chelsea's way midway through the second half when the mercurial Gianfranco Zola entered the fray as a substitute. Less than a minute after coming on, the little Italian raced on to a Dennis Wise pass and powered a drive into the top corner for what proved to be the winning goal. 'I hit the ball perfectly and it went where I wanted it to go – it was absolutely magnificent,' beamed the Blues striker afterwards.

9) Chelsea 2 Everton 1, FA Cup Final, 30 May 2009

Returning to the new Wembley after winning the first FA Cup Final to be played there two years earlier, the Blues had a nightmare start when Everton striker Louis Saha scored after just 25 seconds. Midway through the first half, however, Didier Drogba levelled the scores, meeting Florent Malouda's left-wing cross with a powerful header into the bottom corner. The Londoners began to dominate after that, and eventually took the lead when Frank Lampard fired in left-footed from 20 yards, celebrating his strike with a jig around the corner flag. Five minutes later, a shot from Malouda appeared to cross the line after bouncing down off the crossbar, but with no goal-line technology to help them the Blues had to be satisfied with a narrow 2-1 victory.

10) Chelsea 3 Liverpool 2, League Cup Final, 27 February 2005

Three years after losing in the FA Cup Final at the Millennium Stadium, the Blues returned to Cardiff aiming to win the League Cup for the third time in their history. They got off to a terrible start, though, falling behind to John Arne Riise's first-minute volley. Chelsea had to wait until ten minutes from the end to get back into the game, Reds skipper

Steven Gerrard heading into his own net after Paulo Ferreira pumped a free kick into the box. Two quickfire goals in extra time by Didier Drogba and Mateja Kezman completed the turnaround, making Antonio Nunez's late header for the Merseysiders no more than a consolation.

TOP 10 TATTOOED BLUES

Who has the most impressive inkings among past and present Chelsea players?

1) Raul Meireles
The Portuguese midfielder is one of the most tattooed footballers in the world, up there with the likes of David Beckham and Zlatan Ibrahimovic. The ex-Blue has two full sleeves, a giant dragon on his back and two Mayan skulls on his chest. Add his trademark Mohawk haircut and you've got one extremely scary-looking dude!

2) Kenedy
The Brazilian winger is a walking Who's Who with tattoos of boxing legend Muhammad Ali, reggae star Bob Marley, rapper Tupac Shakur and screen goddess Marilyn Monroe – possibly a nod to her close friendship with his near namesake, President Kennedy?

3) Christian Pulisic
The American wideman has a full left sleeve, including the eyes of a tiger on his forearm. Play that *Rocky* theme tune!

4) Olivier Giroud
The Blues hitman has a striking Maori tattoo on his upper right arm and 'The Lord is my shepherd, I shall not want' written in Latin on his left forearm. Slightly strange, but the

Frenchman has definitely not been wanting for goals since he joined Chelsea from Arsenal.

5) Emerson
The heavily inked left-back has two full sleeves and a number of other tattoos, including the flags of both Brazil and Italy, reflecting his mixed heritage, and, rather bizarrely, PlayStation commands on his left leg.

6) Juan Sebastian Veron
Famously, the Argentinian midfielder has a tattoo of fellow countryman and iconic revolutionary Che Guevara on his right shoulder. Sadly, Veron's time at Stamford Bridge was about as successful as Che's in Bolivia, where the guerrilla commander was killed in October 1967.

7) Willy Caballero
The Blues back-up goalkeeper has a large tattoo of Mary and Jesus on his left arm, providing a small hint that he may be a devoted Christian.

8) Didier Drogba
The legendary Chelsea striker has the names of his four children inked on his lower left arm along with a rosary and the number he wore for most of his goal-filled time at the Bridge: 11.

9) Eden Hazard
When he was a youngster the Belgian sorcerer had the birth dates of his mum, dad and three brothers inked in above his left wrist – handy, no doubt, for remembering when to send birthday cards! More recently, Hazard popped into the Fulham Tattoo Centre near Stamford Bridge to have a rose and cherubs tattooed on his right arm.

10) Gonzalo Higuain

The Argentinian striker unveiled a new tattoo of the Che Guevara slogan 'Hasta la victoria siempre' ('Always until victory') the season before joining Chelsea on loan from Juventus. However, fans of rival clubs were quick to mock online, changing 'hasta' to 'pasta' while suggesting that Higuain was a tad flabby.

TOP 10 TWO-TIME BLUES

The players who loved Chelsea so much they returned to Stamford Bridge later in their careers. But who made the biggest impact second time around? And who should have heeded the old advice 'never go back'?:

1) Nemanja Matic

After making only a handful of appearances for Chelsea, 22-year-old Nemanja Matic joined Benfica in January 2011 as a bit part in the deal that brought David Luiz to the Bridge. The willowy midfielder filled out during a three-year stint in Lisbon, and when he returned to west London for £24m in January 2014 was a strong and authoritative figure in the holding role. The following season, he was named in the PFA Team of the Year as the Blues won the Premier League title and he was also an integral part of the Chelsea side that topped the table again in 2017. Surprisingly, that summer the Serbian enforcer was allowed to leave for Manchester United for £40m, teaming up again with former Blues boss Jose Mourinho.

2) David Luiz

Chelsea fans had mixed feelings when new boss Antonio Conte shelled out £34m to bring David Luiz back to the Bridge in August 2016 after two years with Paris St-Germain.

On the one hand, the Brazilian central defender had starred in the Blues' Champions League victory in 2012, even scoring with an emphatically taken penalty in the shoot-out victory against Bayern Munich; on the other hand, the frizzy-haired Luiz was notorious for his lapses in concentration that often resulted in the gifting of goals to the opposition. However, Conte's gamble paid off big time as Luiz fitted seamlessly into the Italian manager's back three, which provided the bedrock of Chelsea's 2017 Premier League success. Two years later he played his last game for the Blues, helping them to victory in the Europa League Final against Arsenal – the club he would join that summer for £8m.

3) Graeme Le Saux

In one of the worst swap deals in Chelsea's history, talented left-winger Graeme Le Saux was traded by caretaker boss David Webb for journeyman Blackburn striker Steve Livingstone in February 1993. Converted to an attacking left-back by Rovers boss Kenny Dalglish, the Jersey-born Le Saux won the Premier League with the Lancashire club in 1995 before returning to west London for £5m two years later. In his first season back at the Bridge, he helped the Blues win two trophies and he remained a first-team regular until joining Southampton in 2003 in part-exchange for Wayne Bridge.

4) Peter Bonetti

The legendary goalkeeper's Chelsea career seemed to be at an end when he was one of a number of senior players released by new manager Eddie McCreadie following the Blues' relegation in 1975. 'The Cat' played that summer in America with St Louis Stars before returning to train with Chelsea, initially on a weekly contract. Almost immediately, he was back in the first team following an injury to John Phillips and a poor run of form by his deputy, Steve Sherwood. Over the next four years, the evergreen Bonetti re-established himself as Chelsea's top keeper, helping the Blues win promotion in 1977 and taking his total appearances for the club to 729 – a tally only bettered by his team-mate Ron 'Chopper' Harris – before retiring in 1979.

5) Charlie Cooke

After starring in the glamorous Chelsea side of the late-1960s and early-1970s, skilful Scot Charlie Cooke was sold to Crystal Palace in a job lot with full-back Paddy Mulligan in the autumn of 1972. However, to the delight of Blues fans, he only stayed at Selhurst Park for 16 months before returning to the Bridge for a bargain £17,500 in January 1974. His excellent form back in blue earned him a recall to the Scotland team and although his first-team appearances became less regular as the years passed, he remained a joy to watch until leaving in 1978 to see out his career in the States.

6) Nigel Spackman

A hard-running member of Chelsea's 1983/84 promotion-winning team, midfielder Nigel Spackman returned to the Bridge in September 1992 after spells with Liverpool, QPR and Rangers. Despite suffering his share of injuries, he used his experience to good effect in the holding role over the next four seasons before moving into management with Sheffield United.

7) Didier Drogba

After spells with Shanghai Shenhua and Galatasaray, Blues legend Didier Drogba returned to the Bridge in the summer of 2014 on a one-year deal. 'He is coming with the mentality to make more history,' said Chelsea manager Jose Mourinho, and he was proved right as the veteran Ivorian striker chipped in with seven goals in all competitions to help the Blues win the League Cup and the Premier League before winding down his trophy-filled career in the MLS with Montreal Impact.

8) John Hollins

The midfield dynamo in the exciting Chelsea side of the 1960s and early-1970s, John Hollins came back to the Bridge in 1983 as player-coach after stints with QPR and Arsenal. Long since converted to a right-back, the 37-year-old Hollins played in the majority of the games as the Blues stormed to the Second Division title the following year, before taking over as manager from John Neal in 1985.

9) Allan Harris

The older brother of Chelsea legend Ron, full-back Allan Harris was a bit-part player with the Blues between 1960 and 1964 before leaving for Coventry City. He returned to the Bridge in May 1966 and the following season played in the FA Cup Final defeat to Tottenham. That, though, proved to be his last game for the club as he was sold to QPR, helping them gain promotion to the top flight for the first time in their history, in 1968. He was later assistant to Terry Venables at Barcelona.

10) Peter Osgood

'The King of Stamford Bridge' returned to Chelsea in December 1978 after a disappointing stint in America with Philadelphia Fury. The young Blues he teamed up with were struggling at the wrong end of the table and, now in the twilight of his illustrious career, Ossie was unable to prevent them sliding into the Second Division. However, strikes against Middlesbrough and Manchester City took his Chelsea goals tally to 150 before he hung up his boots the following year.

TOP 10 COMEBACKS

The matches where all seemed lost for the Blues – until they remembered the old adage 'it's never over until the final whistle'!

1) Chelsea 4 Bolton Wanderers 3, First Division, 14 October 1978

A fifth consecutive home defeat of a miserable season seemed inevitable when the Blues were three goals down against the Trotters at half-time. Finally responding to loud pleas from the terraces, Chelsea boss Ken Shellito brought on pacy winger Clive Walker midway through the second half and his direct runs soon put the Bolton defence on the back foot. On 75 minutes, Walker crossed for Tommy Langley to score, and when Kenny Swain added a second nine minutes later the Blues were back in the game. Urged on by the home crowd, Walker raced down the wing again before drilling a fierce low shot into the net with just three minutes left to play. Then, in the very last minute of a remarkable game, the 'super sub' tormented the Trotters one final time, firing in a cross that Bolton centre-back Sam Allardyce could only divert into his own net to complete one of the most amazing recoveries in Chelsea's history.

2) Chelsea 4 Liverpool 2, FA Cup fourth round, 26 January 1997

The Blues' cup dreams appeared to be over for the season when they trailed a dominant Liverpool by two goals at half-time. Throwing caution to the wind, Chelsea boss Ruud Gullit brought on striker Mark Hughes for defender Scott Minto, and the Welshman made an instant impact, scoring with a sharp shot on the turn. Just before the hour mark, Gianfranco Zola equalised with a powerful left-footer from the edge of the box, and five minutes later fellow Italian

Gianluca Vialli scored from Dan Petrescu's defence-splitting pass. A brilliant second-half performance by the Blues was capped when Vialli headed in Zola's pinpoint free kick.

3) Blackpool 3 Chelsea 4, First Division, 24 October 1970

Young goalkeeper John Phillips endured a difficult Chelsea debut, conceding three goals in the first half, but the match turned on its head when Blues boss Dave Sexton introduced Charlie Cooke for Tommy Baldwin. Three goals in ten minutes – two from winger Keith Weller and one from defender David Webb – gave the initiative to the away side and the Blues sealed an unlikely victory in the last minute when Blackpool's Dave Hatton turned the ball into his own net.

4) Portsmouth 2 Chelsea 3, League Cup third-round replay, 6 November 1990

Trailing Second Division Portsmouth by two goals with just nine minutes to play, the Blues seemed to be heading for a disappointing League Cup exit. However, David Lee restored some hope when he got on the end of Kerry Dixon's flick from a Dennis Wise corner. A Wise spot kick after Andy Townsend had been chopped down then levelled the scores before a calm finish by striker Kevin Wilson in the last minute took the Blues through to the next round to the delight of the travelling fans.

5) Chelsea 6 Newcastle United 5, First Division, 10 September 1958

Having led earlier in the match, the Blues were losing 5-3 with just ten minutes left to play and seemingly set for a first home defeat of the season. But the Geordies were a flaky side themselves, and when Chelsea inside-left Tony Nicholas smashed a shot into the top corner they became jittery. Two minutes later, Blues striker Ron Tindall took advantage of a mistake by Toon defender Bob Stokoe to make it 5-5, and then he grabbed the winner by heading in Peter Brabrook's cross at the far post.

6) West Bromwich Albion 2 Chelsea 4, First Division, 9 March 1955

Chasing a first-ever league title, the Blues desperately needed to win at a snowy Hawthorns but found themselves trailing by two goals with less than half an hour to play. However, wing-half Derek Saunders chose a good moment to score his first goal for the club and it wasn't long before the away side were in front thanks to a brace from Peter Sillett, one from the penalty spot after Albion goalkeeper James Sanders needlessly kicked Les Stubbs. Just to make the points safe, skipper Roy Bentley added another late on.

7) Southampton 2 Chelsea 3, Premier League, 14 April 2018

The relegation-threatened Saints seemed destined to collect three points when they went two goals up against Antonio Conte's Blues on the hour mark. However, sub Olivier Giroud pulled a goal back on 70 minutes with a perfectly directed near-post header and the mercurial Eden Hazard soon equalised with a well-placed shot. A sensational turnaround inside just eight minutes was completed when Giroud struck a low volley into the bottom corner.

8) Chelsea 3 Sheffield Wednesday 2, FA Cup third round, 4 January 1975

A cup shock looked to be in the offing when the Blues fell two goals behind against Second Division strugglers Sheffield Wednesday. Pushed up front, giant defender Micky Droy pulled a goal back on 74 minutes and two minutes later striker Chris Garland cracked in a shot off the bar. The winner, completing a remarkable transformation, came seven minutes from time when Droy headed in Charlie Cooke's flighted free kick.

9) Leeds United 2 Chelsea 3, Premier League, 27 August 1994

The Blues got off to a terrible start at Elland Road, conceding two goals in the first 19 minutes to a side who were champions just two years earlier. However, a Dennis Wise penalty put the visitors back in contention by half-time and they were level on the hour thanks to John Spencer, who netted from close range after Leeds goalkeeper John Lukic spilled a free kick. It was the Scottish striker, too, who grabbed the winner with a shot through the hapless Lukic's legs just two minutes from the end.

10) Charlton Athletic 2 Chelsea 3, Premier League, 17 August 2002

The Blues still looked to be on their summer holidays in this opening match of the season when they went two goals behind despite the home side having defender Paul Konchesky sent off for an elbow on new signing Enrique de Lucas. Finally, Chelsea awoke from their slumbers just before half-time, Bolo Zenden setting up Gianfranco Zola for a well-taken goal. Chelsea, though, had to wait until the 84th minute for an equaliser when sub Carlton Cole finished off a driving run with a low shot into the corner from the edge of the box. After that, there was only going to be one winner, and it was Frank Lampard who delivered the *coup de grâce* with a typical piece of opportunism following a mix-up in the Charlton defence.

TOP 10 INTERNATIONAL BOSSES

The Chelsea players who went on to manage on the highest stage of all:

1) Didier Deschamps

After a stellar playing career that included winning the World Cup with France in 1998 and the FA Cup with Chelsea two years later, Didier Deschamps started out as a manager with Monaco before later taking charge of two of his former clubs, Juventus and Marseille. In July 2012, he was named as the new manager of France, and two years later led 'Les Bleus' to the quarter-finals of the World Cup in Brazil. In 2016, his French team reached the final of the European Championships but surprisingly lost 1-0 to Portugal on home soil. Two years later he more than made up for that disappointment, guiding his country to victory at the 2018 World Cup in Russia, to become only the third man to lift the trophy as both a player and manager.

2) Terry Venables

As Chelsea skipper in the early-1960s, Terry Venables demonstrated a keen tactical intelligence that marked him out as a future manager. After cutting his teeth as boss of Crystal Palace and QPR, Venables moved into the big time with Barcelona, leading the Catalans to the league title in 1985. After a turbulent spell in charge of Tottenham, 'El Tel' succeeded Graham Taylor as England manager in 1994. Two years later his team thrilled the nation at Euro '96, memorably beating Scotland and the Netherlands in fine attacking style before agonisingly losing out to Germany in a semi-final penalty shoot-out. He then accepted a new challenge Down Under, taking Australia to the brink of qualification for the 1998 World Cup before the Socceroos were knocked out by Iran on the away goals rule.

3) Walter Winterbottom

A half-back with Manchester United before the start of World War II, Walter Winterbottom was a fairly regular guest player for Chelsea during the conflict while serving with the

RAF. After the war, he was appointed England's first national manager, in 1946. Under his leadership, England gradually modernised an outmoded tactical system and competed at four World Cups, making it through to the quarter-finals in both 1954 and 1962. Winterbottom was later director of the newly formed Sports Council and in 1978 was awarded a knighthood.

4) Steve Clarke

A stalwart defender for Chelsea for over a decade, Steve Clarke moved into coaching after hanging up his boots in 1998. Six years later, he was appointed assistant manager to new Chelsea boss Jose Mourinho, staying at the Bridge for another four years. He later managed Reading, West Brom and Kilmarnock, where he was named Scottish Manager of the Year in both 2018 and 2019. In May 2019, he was appointed Scotland manager and after some disappointing early results oversaw an upturn in the team's fortunes, culminating in a penalty shoot-out victory over Serbia that took the Scots through to the finals of Euro 2020 – the first major competition the country had qualified for in over two decades.

5) Ron Greenwood

A central defender who read the game well, Ron Greenwood collected a championship winner's medal with the Blues in 1955 despite being transferred to Fulham midway through the campaign. After managing West Ham for 13 years, he was appointed England manager in 1977, to the disappointment of the many fans who would have preferred the more outspoken Brian Clough. Nonetheless, Greenwood didn't do a bad job, guiding the Three Lions to their first finals for a decade, the European Championships in 1980, and then to within a whisker of the World Cup semi-finals two years later.

6) Glenn Hoddle

Having impressed the top bods at the FA with the attractive playing style he adopted at Chelsea in his three years as the Blues' supremo, Glenn Hoddle was lined up to succeed Terry Venables as England coach after Euro '96. His side were unlucky not to progress further than the last 16 at the World Cup finals two years later, losing out in a penalty shoot-out to Argentina after being reduced to ten men when David Beckham was sent off. However, a poor start to the Euro 2000 qualifying campaign had the media gunning for him, and when Hoddle made some ill-advised comments about disabled people in a newspaper interview he was forced to resign.

7) Tommy Docherty

Briefly a Chelsea player, Tommy Docherty managed the club between 1961 and 1967 before later taking the hot seat at Rotherham, QPR, Aston Villa and Porto. In September 1971 he became the caretaker boss of Scotland, an appointment that was made permanent two months later. The following year, Scotland shared the Home International Championship with England and then got their 1974 World Cup qualifying campaign off to a great start with two wins over Denmark. At this point, however, 'the Doc' accepted an offer to become manager of Manchester United, having won a highly creditable seven of his 12 matches in charge of his country.

8) Mark Hughes

An FA Cup winner with the Blues in 1997, Mark Hughes was still playing up front for Everton when he was appointed Wales manager two years later. Under his leadership, Wales' fortunes improved markedly and the men from the Valleys came close to qualifying for the Euro 2004 finals, losing 1-0 on aggregate to Russia in a two-legged play-off in November 2003. The following year, Hughes accepted an offer to take charge at one of his old clubs, Blackburn Rovers, and he has since managed Manchester City, Fulham, QPR, Stoke and Southampton.

9) Ken Armstrong

A key member of Chelsea's 1955 title-winning team, Ken Armstrong emigrated to New Zealand two years later and shortly afterwards became player-manager of the Kiwis' national team, adding 13 international caps to the one he had been awarded for England. In six years in charge, he guided the emerging soccer nation to 11 victories in 32 matches – a significant improvement on their previous results. In 1980 he briefly returned to international management, taking charge of the New Zealand women's team.

10) Ray Wilkins

After an illustrious playing career with Chelsea, Manchester United, AC Milan and Rangers, Ray Wilkins moved into management with QPR and Fulham. In 1998, he returned to Stamford Bridge as assistant to Blues boss Gianluca Vialli, a role he later reprised under Guus Hiddink and Carlo Ancelotti. In September 2014 Wilkins was appointed head coach of Jordan, leading the country at the 2015 Asian Cup, where they finished third in their group behind Japan and Iraq. Later that year, he came back to England to become assistant manager at Aston Villa.

TOP 10 SEASONS TO FORGET

The campaigns Blues fans wish they could erase from their personal memory banks:

1) 1978/79

A 'season from hell' saw the Blues finish bottom of the First Division after winning just five of 42 league games. Cup exits at the first time of asking to Bolton (League Cup) and Manchester United (FA Cup) added to the mood of despondency around a crumbling Stamford Bridge.

2) 1987/88
A Blues side featuring a host of internationals, including Kerry Dixon, Pat Nevin and Steve Clarke, somehow managed to get relegated from the First Division in the most horrible way possible, after losing 2-1 on aggregate to second-tier Middlesbrough in a play-off final marred by serious crowd violence.

3) 1974/75
The glory days of the early 1970s came to a shuddering halt when the Blues were demoted from the top flight after failing to win any of their final half-dozen matches. To make matters worse, Tottenham and Arsenal were in the relegation mix as well but both managed to survive by narrow margins.

4) 1982/83
A third consecutive season of dreary Second Division mediocrity was on the cards until John Neal's Blues were plunged into the mire by an awful nine-match winless run in the spring. Happily, Clive Walker came up with the winner at fellow strugglers Bolton in the penultimate match and the club was saved from a first-ever relegation to the third tier.

5) 1923/24
After a dismal campaign, the Blues rallied in the final weeks of the season, winning their last four matches. However, it was not enough to avoid relegation to the second tier on goal average. A lack of goals was the main problem, the Blues scoring just 31 in 42 league games, with top scorer Andy Wilson getting a meagre five in total.

6) 2015/16

Premier League champions a season earlier, Chelsea's campaign imploded on the opening day against Swansea when boss Jose Mourinho verbally abused club doctor Eva Carneiro for running on to the pitch to treat Eden Hazard. Shockingly bad results and player discontent led to Mourinho's departure shortly before Christmas, with Guus Hiddink arriving to reprise his caretaker role of 2009. Although the Dutchman steadied the ship, it remained a real dog's dinner of a campaign with the Blues finishing behind the likes of Southampton, West Ham and Stoke in tenth place and failing to make much headway in the cup competitions.

7) 1961/62

Somewhat predictably, the loss of goal machine Jimmy Greaves to AC Milan had a major impact on the Blues' fortunes as they were relegated to the Second Division after 25 consecutive seasons in the top flight. To be fair, strikers Bobby Tambling (20 goals) and Barry Bridges (19 goals) did their best to fill the gap left by Greavsie, but a midfield lacking firepower allied to a leaky defence (94 goals conceded) spelt doom for Tommy Docherty's young side, who finished bottom of the table.

8) 1909/10

After winning their first promotion to the top flight in 1907, the Blues dropped down to the second tier again after losing 2-1 at Tottenham on the final day of the season. If David Calderhead's men had won at White Hart Lane, they would have stayed up with Spurs heading through the trap door instead. Painful!

9) 1973/74

Following a run of four consecutive defeats in December, a training ground bust-up between Blues boss Dave Sexton and star players Peter Osgood and Alan Hudson resulted in the two Shed heroes being transfer-listed and eventually sold. Even the return of fans' favourite Charlie Cooke from Crystal Palace could not dispel the gloom around west London, the depressing mood exacerbated by delays to the construction of the new East Stand and poor results, which saw the Blues only survive the drop by a single point.

10) 1914/15

Although Chelsea enjoyed a great run in the FA Cup – reaching the final, which they lost 3-0 to Sheffield United at Old Trafford – it was a different story in the league, the Blues finishing in the bottom two with Tottenham after winning just eight of 38 games. Relegation should have been on the cards, but World War I came to the aid of the west Londoners with the suspension of the league programme for the remainder of the conflict. When the league resumed in 1919, it was decided to expand the top flight from 20 to 22 clubs and Chelsea were reinstated in the First Division. Spurs, though, were not so lucky!

TOP 10 NICKNAMES

The Chelsea players with the best alter egos:

1) Ron 'Chopper' Harris

One of the hardest players around in the often-brutal era of the 1960s and 1970s, Ron Harris' unflinching and sometimes ruthless approach to defending was perfectly summed up by his legendary moniker.

2) Peter 'The Cat' Bonetti

Coined by early team-mate Ron Tindall, 'The Cat' was a superb nickname for the Chelsea goalkeeper of the 1960s and 1970s whose sharp reflexes and incredible agility most definitely had a feline quality.

3) Eric 'The Rabbit' Parsons

No, he didn't have teeth like Bugs Bunny! A member of Chelsea's 1955 title-winning side, Eric Parsons was known as 'The Rabbit' for his speedy runs down the right wing.

4) Marcel 'The Rock' Desailly

Whether he was playing in defence or in midfield, French international Marcel Desailly was a rock-like presence in the Chelsea team between 1998 and 2004.

5) George 'Gatling Gun' Hilsdon

The first Chelsea player to score 100 goals for the club, George Hilsdon earned his nickname for his powerful quickfire shooting.

6) Tommy 'The Sponge' Baldwin

1960s team-mate John Hollins dubbed the Geordie striker 'The Sponge' after seeing him soak up a skinful of booze on a night out – but it might just as well have applied to his prodigious capacity for hard work on the pitch.

7) Michael 'The Bison' Essien

With his powerful, surging runs from deep right into the heart of opposition territory, Michael Essien couldn't have had a more appropriate nickname than 'The Bison'.

8) Ray 'Butch' Wilkins

The Blues' captain during the late-1970s earned his ironic nickname as a child for his calm, non-aggressive style of play and it stuck throughout his long and successful career.

9) Reece 'The Beast' James

Mason Mount came up with this nickname for the young defender, whose power and strength makes him odds-on to win any 50/50 challenge.

10) William 'Fatty' Foulke

In the simpler, non-PC days of the early 20th century, when Chelsea were founded, everyone agreed that calling 22-stone goalkeeper William Foulke 'Fatty' was pretty hilarious!

TOP 10 NORTH AND SOUTH AMERICAN BLUES

The Chelsea players who travelled across the pond to light up Stamford Bridge:

1) Willian

In August 2013, Chelsea just pipped Tottenham to the signing of Brazilian international Willian, who moved to the Bridge from Russian outfit Anzhi Makhachkala. The £30m fee proved to be money well spent as the tricky winger played a full role in the Blues' many successes over the next seven years. Willian was a clever player who loved to make darting runs forward and scored some sensational goals, especially from free kicks. He was also extremely hard-working and fully deserved his Chelsea Player of the Year award at the end of the dreadfully disappointing 2015/16 season, when his committed and thoroughly professional attitude was in stark contrast to that of many of his team-mates. It was a sad day for his many admirers when he reluctantly joined Arsenal in 2020 after failing to agree a new deal with the Blues.

2) David Luiz

Signed from Benfica for around £20m in January 2011, Brazilian centre-back David Luiz returned from injury to perform heroically when the Blues won the Champions League the following year. The next season, he picked up a winner's medal in the Europa League but his high-risk style of defending was not to Jose Mourinho's taste, and in June 2014 he was sold to PSG for £50m. Two years later he returned to the Bridge, his imperious performances in Antonio Conte's three-man back line proving central to the Blues' title success as well as earning him a place in the PFA Team of the Year. His last act in a blue shirt was to help Chelsea win the Europa League again in 2019 before he left for Arsenal later that summer.

3) Gus Poyet

A free transfer from Spanish side Zaragoza in the summer of 1997, Uruguayan midfielder Gus Poyet suffered a cruciate knee ligament injury in his first season at the Bridge but returned to action to help the Blues win the European Cup Winners' Cup and then scored the winning goal in the Super Cup against Real Madrid. Tall and strong in the air, he was a consistent goal threat throughout his time in west London while his exuberant personality made him a real fans' favourite until he blotted his Chelsea copybook by joining Tottenham in 2001. He later managed Brighton and Sunderland.

4) Ramires

A £20m recruit from Benfica in August 2010, Brazilian midfielder Ramires served Chelsea superbly for five years before moving on to Chinese side Jiangsu Suning, helping the Blues win a host of honours. Famed for his hard-running style, he also came up with some memorable goals, scooping the club's 'Goal of the Season' award in 2011 for an individual effort against Manchester City and again the following campaign with an audacious lob against Barcelona in the Champions League semi-final. In the same year, 2012, he also scored the opener in the FA Cup Final win against Liverpool.

5) Oscar

The Blues paid Brazilian outfit Internacional £19m to bring Oscar to the Bridge in the summer of 2012 and the nimble midfielder enjoyed a good first season in west London, scoring twice on his Champions League debut against Juventus before helping his new club win the Europa League. Undoubtedly skilful, he was perhaps a little lightweight for the Premier League and, after falling out of favour with new boss Antonio Conte, the Blues were more than happy to accept a whopping £60 million bid for his services from Chinese club Shanghai SIPG in January 2017.

6) Christian Pulisic

Touted as one of the most exciting young players in the game, USA international Christian Pulisic cost the Blues a hefty £58m when he moved to the Bridge from Borussia Dortmund in 2019. In a first season in west London disrupted by injury and the Covid-19 pandemic, the speedy wide man showed enough glimpses of his talent to suggest he could achieve great things in the future, notably when opening his Chelsea account with a brilliant hat-trick at Burnley and then scoring a wonderful individual goal against Manchester City, which helped to confirm Liverpool as 2020 Premier League champions. His second campaign was again a bit up and down, but finished on a high in Porto as the Blues won the Champions League for a second time.

7) Alex

Signed from Santos in 2004, powerful Brazilian centre-half Alex spent three years on loan at PSV Eindhoven before finally making his Chelsea debut in August 2007. Although behind John Terry and Ricardo Carvalho in the defensive pecking order, the heavily built and shaven-headed stopper never let the Blues down when called upon, and thrilled the fans with his trademark piledriver free-kicks from as far as 40 yards out. After helping Chelsea win the FA Cup in 2009 and the Double the following year, he joined PSG for £4.2m in January 2012.

8) Hernan Crespo

A prolific striker in Italian football, Hernan Crespo joined Chelsea from Inter Milan for £16.8m in August 2003. Vying for a place up front with Jimmy Floyd Hasselbaink, Eidur Gudjohnsen and Adrian Mutu, the Argentinian fell out of favour after a bright start and spent the next season on loan with AC Milan. Recalled by Jose Mourinho for the 2005/06 campaign, he chipped in with ten goals as the Blues retained the Premier League title. It wasn't, though, enough to persuade the Blues boss to keep him as Crespo was loaned out to Inter Milan, eventually joining the Italian giants on a permanent deal in 2008.

9) Thiago Silva

With the Blues defence leaking goals at an unacceptable rate, boss Frank Lampard strengthened his back line by signing centre-back Thiago Silva on a free transfer from Paris Saint-Germain in August 2020. After a shaky Premier League debut against West Brom, the veteran Brazilian international soon showed why he is rated as one of the best players in the world, his defensive prowess and leadership skills helping the Blues to keep five consecutive clean sheets. He ended his first season at the club by helping the Blues win the Champions League, although he suffered the disappointment of being subbed off injured in the final victory against Manchester City.

10) Juliano Belletti

The Blues signed Juliano Belletti in the summer of 2007, a year after he had scored the winning goal for Barcelona in the Champions League Final against Arsenal. Over the next three seasons, the Brazilian utility man became something of a cult hero at the Bridge thanks to his work rate and ability to score spectacular goals from long range, including a memorable 30-yarder against Tottenham that won the club's 'Goal of the Season' award in 2008. After close to 100 appearances for the Blues – nearly half of them as a sub – he moved on a free transfer to Brazilian outfit Fluminense in 2010.

TOP 10 SCANDALS

The times when the Blues were front-page news for all the wrong reasons:

1) Chelsea join European Super League

In April 2021, Chelsea announced the club would be joining a new midweek European Super League (ESL) along with five other leading Premier League teams and six clubs from Italy and Spain. Fans, pundits and football bodies alike condemned the scheme, which was widely seen as an attempt by the owners of Europe's richest clubs to make even more money at the expense of fans and clubs lower down the pyramid. Two days after the announcement of the breakaway league, thousands of Chelsea fans demonstrated outside Stamford Bridge before the Blues' match with Brighton, at one point blocking the entry of the team bus into the stadium. Their efforts were rewarded when news broke that, after all, Chelsea would not join the new league, and when the other five Premier League clubs also pulled out the ESL was effectively a dead duck.

2) John Terry and Wayne Bridge spat

In January 2010, a number of tabloid newspapers gleefully reported that Chelsea skipper John Terry had had a four-month affair with Vanessa Perroncel, the ex-partner of Terry's former Chelsea and England team-mate Wayne Bridge. The allegation led to England manager Fabio Capello temporarily stripping Terry of the captaincy and the following month Bridge refused to shake his old friend's hand when his club, Manchester City, visited Stamford Bridge. However, six months later both the *News of the World* and the *Mail on Sunday* apologised to Miss Perroncel, stating that the story was 'untrue in any case'.

3) John Terry racism allegation

After Chelsea lost a tempestuous London derby 1-0 to QPR in October 2011, Blues skipper John Terry was accused of racially abusing Rangers defender Anton Ferdinand at one point in the match. The following year, Terry stood trial at Westminster Magistrates' Court but was found not guilty of racist abuse after the chief magistrate accepted his defence that he had used the offending words in a sarcastic fashion. However, Terry, who had earlier been stripped of the England captaincy over the affair, was later found guilty of racial abuse at the civil standard by the Football Association and was handed a four-match ban along with a whopping £220,000 fine – a punishment that prompted him to retire from international football.

4) Historical allegations of child abuse and racial abuse

In August 2019, Chelsea issued an apology after a QC-led inquiry published evidence from numerous witnesses that former chief scout Eddie Heath, who died in 1983, had abused young boys aged between 10 and 17 in the 1970s. A separate report by the charity Barnardo's concluded that young black players at the club in the 1980s and 1990s were subjected to 'a daily tirade of racial abuse' instigated by former coach and academy director Gwyn Williams. Chelsea again apologised but four of the players announced their intention to sue the club for damages in the High Court – a case that is expected to be heard in 2022.

5) Stamford Bridge riot

After Chelsea lost the 1988 two-legged play-off final at home to Middlesbrough and were relegated to the old Second

Division, fans from the two clubs clashed on the pitch, leading to police making over 100 arrests. Prime Minister Margaret Thatcher said she was 'deeply distressed' by the violence while the FA blamed Chelsea for the trouble, fining the club £75,000 and ordering the closure of the Stamford Bridge terraces for the first six matches of the 1988/89 season.

6) Graham Rix imprisonment

In March 1999, Chelsea assistant manager Graham Rix was sentenced to 12 months' imprisonment at Knightsbridge Crown Court after pleading guilty to two counts of unlawful sex with a 15-year-old girl and indecently assaulting her. The former England international served six months in Wandsworth Prison before being released and returning to his job at Stamford Bridge.

7) Dennis Wise arrest

After celebrating a 4-0 home win against Leicester City in October 1994 at then-England manager Terry Venables' Kensington club Scribes West, Chelsea skipper Dennis Wise became embroiled in a furious row with a taxi driver. The police were called and the Blues midfielder was arrested and charged with criminal damage and assault. Initially found guilty and sentenced to three months in prison, his conviction was later overturned on appeal but Wise lost the Chelsea captaincy as a result of the incident.

8) Jody Morris and John Terry arrest

Young Chelsea first-team players John Terry and Jody Morris were involved in an incident with a bouncer at the members-only Wellington Club in Knightsbridge in January 2002 which led to them appearing at Middlesex Guildhall Crown Court seven months later. Terry was charged with a number of offences, including wounding with intent to cause grievous bodily harm, while Morris was charged with affray. The jury found the pair not guilty on all accounts but their friend Des Byrne, a Wimbledon player, was found guilty of 'possessing a bottle as an offensive weapon'.

9) Adrian Mutu sacked

After a so-so first season with the Blues, striker Adrian Mutu was hoping for a fresh start in the summer of 2004 under new Chelsea boss Jose Mourinho. However, Mourinho quickly became suspicious of the Romania captain's behaviour and, suspecting that he may be using drugs, Mutu was 'target-tested' by the club. When the result came back positive for cocaine, Mutu was banned from playing for seven months by the FA and then sacked by the Blues for 'gross misconduct'. Chelsea had acted in a similarly decisive manner when Australian goalkeeper Mark Bosnich tested positive for the same drug two years earlier, so Mutu really only had himself to blame.

10) The Blackpool incident

Title-chasing Chelsea were preparing for their final two matches of the season, in Blackpool in April 1965, when eight players, including skipper Terry Venables, George Graham and John Hollins, disobeyed boss Tommy Docherty's instruction to stay in the team hotel and instead went out drinking on the Golden Mile. The miscreants were sent back to London in disgrace, their places being taken by a group of reserve players who were summoned to make the train journey up to the North West.

TOP 10 NON-LEAGUE BLUES

These days Chelsea are about as likely to buy a player from a non-league club as Roman Abramovich is to go shopping in Poundland. However, that wasn't always the case, and in the past the Blues have picked up a fair few gems in the lower reaches of the football pyramid.

1) Vic Woodley

Signed from Spartan League outfit Windsor and Eton in 1931, Woodley fought off stiff competition from Scottish international John Jackson to become Chelsea's first-choice goalkeeper for most of the 1930s. 'Young Woodley', as he was known after a popular West End play of the period, went on to play for England, keeping goal in a then-record 19 consecutive internationals, before the start of World War II.

2) Ian Hutchinson

A fearless striker famed for his flying headers and extraordinary long throw, 'Hutch' joined the Blues from Southern League Cambridge United for £5,000 in July 1968. Within a year, he was established as the perfect strike partner for Peter Osgood, the pair scoring 53 goals between them in the 1969/70 season, which culminated in the Blues winning the FA Cup for the first time. Sadly, Hutchinson was later bedevilled by a string of serious injuries and was forced to retire at the age of 27.

3) Jack Harrow

A bargain £50 buy from Southern League Second Division club Croydon Common in March 1911, speedy full-back Jack Harrow proved to be a real bargain, becoming the first Chelsea player to make more than 300 appearances for the club and skippering the Blues in their first FA Cup Final in 1915. After serving in the Royal Flying Corps in World War I he resumed his career, playing on until the age of 37 and then joining the club's training staff.

4) George Mills

Initially signed on amateur forms from Bromley of the Athenian League, George Mills helped the Blues win promotion to the top flight in 1930, topping the club's scoring charts with 14 goals. Although he was sometimes behind superstar strikers Hughie Gallacher and Joe Bambrick in the pecking order, Mills remained a reliable goalgetter throughout the 1930s, becoming the first Chelsea player ever to score over 100 league goals.

5) Derek Saunders

Captain of the Walthamstow Avenue team that won the FA Amateur Cup in 1952, wing-half Derek Saunders moved on to Chelsea the following year. The step up from the Isthmian League to the top flight of English football didn't trouble him in the slightest, and in 1955 he was an ever-present in the Chelsea side that won the league title for the first time. He retired in 1959, having made more than 200 appearances for the club.

6) Kenny Swain

Trainee schoolteacher Kenny Swain joined the Blues from Isthmian League club Wycombe Wanderers in the summer of 1973. He made his debut the following year, and in the 1976/77 season formed a tremendous strike partnership with Steve Finnieston, as the Londoners won promotion to the top flight. A talented and versatile player, he later converted to full-back after moving to Aston Villa, with whom he won the league and European Cup in the early-1980s.

7) Micky Droy

Man-mountain Micky Droy was snapped up by Chelsea in 1970 while playing for Slough Town in the Athenian League. Famed for his towering defensive headers, which could send the ball from the Blues' penalty area to over the halfway line, he went on to make more than 300 appearances for the club and was skipper for a number of years in the early-1980s before moving on to Crystal Palace.

8) Jim Lewis

Another recruit from Walthamstow Avenue in 1952, Lewis remained an amateur, juggling his football career with a job as a Thermos flask salesman. A useful squad player, he shared left-wing duties with the young Frank Blunstone in Chelsea's 1955 title-winning side. After scoring a more-than-respectable 40 goals for the Blues in 95 games, he returned to Walthamstow in 1958.

9) John Mortimore

A steady centre-half, Mortimore signed from Isthmian League side Woking in 1956 and went on to serve the club for nearly a decade, making 279 appearances in total and featuring in the Chelsea side that won the League Cup for the first time in 1965 before winding down his career with QPR.

10) Paul Canoville

Chelsea's first-ever black player, Paul Canoville joined the Blues from Southern League South Division side Hillingdon Borough in 1981. Subjected to vile racist abuse by a section of the club's support on his debut against Crystal Palace the following year, he gradually won over the haters with some eye-catching performances on the left wing – particularly during the Blues' Second Division title-winning season in 1983/84 – before moving on to Reading in 1986.

TOP 10 CHELSEA FC WOMEN QUOTES

The Chelsea girls have plenty to say for themselves:

1) 'I was playing in an all-girls team with other Reading Academy players and there was a match against boys where they actually all laughed at

us when we turned up. We beat them 13-0; some
went home crying.'
Fran Kirby, recalling a pivotal match from her teenage years

2) 'I went through school with people thinking
negatively of me for playing football with the
boys. I wasn't scared to be different.'
Millie Bright

3) 'I was able to follow my dream. My mother was
very supportive. I was playing with boys my own
age from a young age and was much better than
them, so my mum wasn't too fussed.'
Ji So-Yun

4) 'Do you know what, I've never done a knee-
slide in my life. I think the occasion just got the
better of me and it was just unbelievable to play in
front of that crowd.'
Beth England, on her celebration after scoring against
Tottenham at Stamford Bridge in September 2019

5) 'I'm in the best job in the world.'
Chelsea Women boss Emma Hayes after being linked with
a move to League One side AFC Wimbledon

6) 'I had to put my notice in at Morrisons to play
for Chelsea.'
Erin Cuthbert

7) 'The dream would be some day to play in the
same league.'
Magda Eriksson, shortly before her girlfriend Pernille Harder
joined Chelsea from Wolfsburg

8) 'Individual awards are just confirmation of what you're doing. It's a nice feeling, but it's not like the happiness you feel when you win a championship.'
Pernille Harder, two-time winner of the UEFA Women's Player of the Year award

9) 'The reason I came to London is to become a better footballer, to not stay in my comfort zone. It's given me everything I wanted.'
Sam Kerr

10) 'I don't like attention! I hope it doesn't get like the men's game in that way, and you can't just go to Asda.'
Sophie Ingle

TOP 10 GUT-WRENCHING FINALS

The finals that left Blues fans feeling sick to the stomach:

1) Chelsea 1 Manchester United 1 (won 6-5 on penalties), Champions League Final, 21 May 2008
The Blues have won six out of seven major European finals, but this is in the one that got away. After Frank Lampard levelled Cristiano Ronaldo's opener, the match in the Luzhniki Stadium in Moscow developed into something of a stalemate, eventually going to penalties. John Terry had the chance to win it for Chelsea but slipped and sent his kick agonisingly wide. Salomon Kalou kept the Blues in the hunt but when Nicolas Anelka had his tame spot-kick saved by Edwin van der Sar, United came out on top in the first all-English Champions League Final.

2) Tottenham 2 Chelsea 1, FA Cup Final, 20 May 1967

Playing in the club's first-ever Wembley showpiece, a young Blues outfit didn't really do themselves justice in the 'Cockney Cup Final'. Bobby Tambling's late goal for Tommy Docherty's side was a mere consolation against a Spurs team that had the upper hand throughout and, rather irritatingly, featured two ex-Chelsea players in Jimmy Greaves and Terry Venables.

3) Arsenal 2 Chelsea 1, FA Cup Final, 27 May 2017

Antonio Conte's Double-chasing Blues fell behind to an early goal by Arsenal's Alexis Sanchez, which might well have been ruled out for handball had VAR been operating then. To add to Chelsea's woes, wing-back Victor Moses was stupidly sent off midway through the second half after collecting a second yellow for a dive in the Gunners' box. Diego Costa pulled the Blues level with 15 minutes to play but just three minutes later Olivier Giroud crossed for Aaron Ramsey to head home the winner.

4) Stoke City 2 Chelsea 1, League Cup Final, 4 March 1972

Dave Sexton's men warmed up for the final by recording 'Blue is the Colour' but it turned out to be red-and-white ribbons that were attached to the trophy after Stoke's veterans pulled off a shock victory. The Potters took the lead early on through Terry Conroy but Peter Osgood levelled for the Blues with a hooked shot from a prone position just before half-time. The match was settled 17 minutes from time when 35-year-old George Eastham fired the ball past Peter Bonetti from close range.

5) Arsenal 2 Chelsea 0, FA Cup Final, 4 May 2002

The omens were not good when Chelsea were allotted the south dressing room at the Millennium Stadium in Cardiff, the previous nine clubs to have used it ending up as losers. Those fears were confirmed when the Gunners took the lead in unlikely fashion on 70 minutes, midfield journeyman Ray Parlour curling a 25-yarder past Chelsea goalkeeper Carlo Cudicini. When Freddie Ljungberg fired in an almost identical goal ten minutes from the end it was all over, Arsenal claiming the first part of their third Double.

6) Tottenham 2 Chelsea 1, League Cup Final, 24 February 2008

Incredibly, Tottenham had only beaten Chelsea in two of 42 previous matches between the clubs and that run looked set to continue when Didier Drogba put the Blues ahead shortly before half-time with a well-struck free kick. However, Spurs' Bulgarian striker Dimitar Berbatov equalised from the spot midway through the second half before Jonathan Woodgate headed the winner for the north Londoners three minutes after the start of extra time.

7) Manchester United 4 Chelsea 0, FA Cup Final, 14 May 1994

Having beaten United twice earlier in the campaign, Glenn Hoddle's Blues had hopes of a famous hat-trick, and came close to opening the scoring in the first half when Gavin Peacock smashed a shot against the bar. United, though, upped the tempo after the break and took control through two Eric Cantona penalties, the second harshly awarded against Frank Sinclair. Further goals from Mark Hughes and Brian McClair completed a miserable afternoon for the Blues and confirmed United's first-ever Double.

8) Arsenal 2 Chelsea 1, FA Cup Final, 1 August 2020

The Covid-19 pandemic cast a huge shadow over the final, causing it to be played six weeks later than planned and behind closed doors. The eerie Wembley atmosphere didn't seem to affect the Blues, though, who took an early lead through Christian Pulisic. However, Arsenal hit back with a penalty by Pierre-Emerick Aubameyang on the half-hour mark, and the same player then hit the winner for the Gunners midway through the second half. Chelsea's misery was complete when midfielder Mateo Kovacic was sent off after collecting a second yellow card.

9) Corinthians 1 Chelsea 0, Club World Cup Final, 16 December 2012

After defeating Mexican side Monterrey 3-1 three days earlier, Champions League holders Chelsea made it through to the final of the Club World Cup in Yokohama, Japan. The Blues were favourites to lift the trophy but put in a rather insipid performance and went down to a 1-0 defeat against Brazilian outfit Corinthians, Peruvian striker Paolo Guerrero heading the winning goal midway through the second half.

10) Chelsea 0 Manchester City 0 (won 4-3 on penalties), League Cup Final, 24 February 2019

Two weeks after being thrashed 6-0 at the Etihad, the Blues put on a much better performance against Manchester City at Wembley and might have nicked a win in normal time. However, the match went to extra time and penalties, with misses by Jorginho and David Luiz handing City what turned out to be the first leg of an unprecedented domestic Treble.

TOP 10 PENALTY SAVES

The Chelsea goalkeepers who thwarted the opposition from the penalty spot:

1) Petr Cech, Bayern Munich 1 Chelsea 1, Champions League Final, 19 May 2012

Petr Cech made a number of vital penalty saves for the Blues – notably in the 2010 FA Cup Final against Portsmouth – but none quite as significant as this one in the 2012 Champions League Final against Bayern Munich. The Blues were drawing 1-1 shortly after the start of extra time when Didier Drogba made a clumsy challenge on Bayern's Franck Ribery, giving the ref no option but to award a penalty. Former Blues winger Arjen Robben took the kick, firing hard and low, but Cech dived to his left to stop the shot and then quickly snaffled up the ball as it rolled away from him. Later that evening, of course, the giant goalkeeper was the hero again, saving two spot kicks as the Blues won the cup on penalties.

2) Tony Godden, Manchester United 0 Chelsea 1, First Division, 28 September 1986

Chelsea were leading through a superb early goal from Kerry Dixon when Blues goalkeeper Tony Godden was penalised on the hour mark for bringing down United winger Jesper Olsen in the box. The Dane took the spot kick himself but shot too close to Godden, who saved with relative ease. Minutes later, United had another chance to equalise when they were awarded a second penalty, again for a foul on Olsen – this time by midfielder John McNaught. Once again, though, Godden foiled the Red Devils, diving to stop Gordon Strachan's fierce drive. Fully 35 years on, he remains the last Chelsea keeper to save two penalties in the same match.

3) John Jackson, West Bromwich Albion 1 Chelsea 2, First Division, 21 September 1935

Chelsea signed Scottish international John Jackson from Partick Thistle in 1933 and two years later he enjoyed his best afternoon with the Blues, saving two penalties in a 2-1 win at the Hawthorns. First, he denied Baggies inside-forward

Teddy Sandford in the tenth minute then, in the second half, Jackson preserved the Blues' narrow lead with a save from prolific West Brom striker William 'Ginger' Richardson.

4) Peter Bonetti, Chelsea 1 Everton 1, First Division, 7 September 1968

Surprisingly, Blues legend Peter Bonetti didn't have the greatest penalty-saving record, only keeping out seven of the 57 he faced in his long Chelsea career. In this match, Everton were already a goal up when they were awarded a first-half spot kick, which World Cup winner Alan Ball stepped up to take. The ginger-haired midfielder's shot appeared to be heading for the corner of the net but, diving to his left, 'The Cat' pulled off a brilliant save that helped the Blues earn a point after Peter Osgood equalised with another penalty late on.

5) Willie Foulke, Chelsea 7 Burslem Port Vale 0, Second Division, 3 March 1906

The Blues' giant goalkeeper saved an incredible ten penalties in his one season with the club in 1905/06. Two of them came in the last five minutes of this match when, with the home side cruising to a 7-0 win, Foulke blocked two Port Vale spot kicks, to the delight of the fans at Stamford Bridge. This despite the fact that the penalty rule had just been changed, so that the goalkeeper now had to stay on his line and was no longer able to 'charge' the taker.

6) Kevin Hitchcock, Chelsea 1 Everton 0, FA Cup fourth round, 26 January 1992

Leading through Clive Allen's excellent volley, the Blues looked set to be pegged back in this FA Cup fourth-round tie when Kevin Hitchcock brought down Everton winger Peter Beagrie in the box with just ten minutes to play. However, the Chelsea goalkeeper quickly turned from villain to hero when he pounced on Tony Cottee's powerfully struck drive to ensure that the Blues would feature in the fifth-round draw for the first time in a decade.

7) Dmitri Kharine, Viktoria Zizkov 0 Chelsea 0, European Cup Winners' Cup first round second leg, 28 September 1994

Back in Europe for the first time in 23 years, the Blues travelled to the Czech Republic determined to protect a two-goal lead from the first leg at Stamford Bridge. Thanks to goalkeeper Dmitri Kharine they succeeded in their mission, the Russian's impressive display including a memorable double save from Petr Vrabec's piledriver penalty kick and Karel Poborsky's follow-up effort.

8) John Phillips, Chelsea 0 QPR 0, FA Cup third round, 5 January 1974

A tense FA Cup derby between the two west London rivals appeared to be heading QPR's way when the visitors were awarded a dubious penalty. Rangers skipper Gerry Francis struck his shot well, hard and low towards the right-hand corner, but Blues keeper Phillips dived full length to make a superb save. The match finished goalless but, sadly, even the in-form Welshman couldn't prevent Rangers winning the replay at Loftus Road thanks to a single goal from star striker Stan Bowles.

9) Eddie Niedzwiecki, Fulham 0 Chelsea 1, League Cup third-round replay, 6 November 1985

The Blues were leading through a Kerry Dixon goal when a foul by midfielder Nigel Spackman gave the Cottagers a last-gasp chance to level this League Cup third-round replay. However, Chelsea goalkeeper Eddie Niedzwiecki capped a magnificent individual display by blocking Cliff Carr's penalty with his legs. 'You always have a chance from a penalty,' he reflected afterwards. 'I just tried to make myself as big as possible. Luck was with me as I dived the right way.'

10) Carlo Cudicini, Manchester United 1 Chelsea 1, Premier League, 8 May 2004

Italian goalkeeper Carlo Cudicini saved an impressive six of the 13 penalties he faced while with the Blues, on this occasion diving low to his right to turn Ruud van Nistelrooy's well-struck shot around for a corner after Robert Huth had brought down Louis Saha. The match eventually ended in a 1-1 draw, the point ensuring Chelsea's qualification for the Champions League the following season.

TOP 10 ENGLISH BLUES

The best of the Chelsea players from Merry Olde England:

1) Frank Lampard

After signing from West Ham in 2001 for £11m, Frank Lampard enjoyed a glorious career with Chelsea over the next 13 years, during which he won three Premier League titles, four FA Cups, two League Cups and skippered the Blues to triumph in both the Champions League and Europa League. By the time he moved on to New York City in 2014 the attacking midfielder had smashed the club scoring record, notching an incredible total of 211 goals, while his total of 609 Premier League appearances puts him third on the all-time list behind Gareth Barry and Ryan Giggs. In an England career lasting 15 years he played 106 times for his country, scoring an impressive 29 goals.

2) John Terry

A Chelsea youth product who made his debut in 1998, John Terry went on to become the most successful skipper in Premier League history, leading the Blues to five titles. He also won five FA Cups and three League Cups in a 19-year Bridge career and played a full part in the club's Champions League and Europa League triumphs in 2012 and 2013 respectively despite missing both finals. A fantastic all-round defender who was renowned for his reading of the game and long-range passing as well as for his trademark blocks, clearances and tackles, Terry's total of 717 games for the Blues is bettered only by Peter Bonetti (729) and Ron 'Chopper' Harris (795). First capped in 2003, he played 78 times for England but twice lost the armband for disciplinary reasons.

3) Peter Osgood

After scoring some sensational goals in his debut season, Peter Osgood was hailed as the brightest young attacking talent in the country. A broken leg, sustained in a tackle with Blackpool's Emlyn Hughes in October 1966, hampered his progress but he bounced back to star in the exciting Chelsea side that won the FA Cup for the first time in 1970 and the European Cup Winners' Cup the following year. Tall and strong, he was a genuine threat in the air while his delicate and subtle skills on the ground could help unpick the tightest of defences. The scorer of 150 goals for the Blues, Ossie was unlucky to win just four caps for England. After his death in 2006, a statue of 'The King of Stamford Bridge' was erected outside the West Stand.

4) Jimmy Greaves

After filling his boots in youth-team football, 17-year-old Jimmy Greaves carried on scoring at a phenomenal rate for the first team, banging in 22 goals in his debut season in 1957/58. Incredibly, he was only warming up, totalling 37, 30 and a club-record 43 goals in the following three campaigns before joining AC Milan in the summer of 1961. A brilliant finisher who always remained calm in front of goal and invariably shot right into the corner of the net, Greaves was first capped by England in 1959 and went on to play 57 times for his country, scoring 44 goals.

5) Ashley Cole

A long-time transfer target for the Blues, Ashley Cole eventually moved across London from Arsenal in the summer of 2006, with William Gallas travelling in the opposite direction. Already rated as one of the best defenders in the world, the pacy left-back only enhanced his reputation at the Bridge while filling his personal trophy cabinet with silverware, including a record seven FA Cup winner's medals (four gained with Chelsea) and the Champions League in 2012. A guaranteed England starter for over a decade, he won 107 caps for his country.

6) Roy Bentley

Captain and centre-forward of the Chelsea side that won the title against the odds in 1955, Roy Bentley signed for the Blues from Newcastle seven years earlier. A superb header of the ball, he could also shoot powerfully with both feet while his mobility made him an extremely difficult man to mark. Top scorer for the club in all eight of his full seasons at the Bridge, Bentley left for Fulham in 1956 after becoming the first Chelsea player to hit 150 goals in all competitions. He also played for England 12 times, scoring nine goals.

7) Kerry Dixon

The 1980s were not the greatest decade for Chelsea, but they perked up when hotshot striker Kerry Dixon signed from Reading in the summer of 1983. After contributing 28 goals to the Blues' promotion success the following season, Dixon added another 24 in the top flight in 1984/85 – sufficient to win him a share of the Golden Boot with Gary

Lineker. Called up for England duty, Dixon scored twice on his full international debut against West Germany but he was unable to replace Lineker as the Three Lions' first-choice centre-forward, winning just seven caps in total. For Chelsea, though, the goals kept flowing until he moved on to Southampton in 1992.

8) Alan Hudson

Born and brought up around the corner from Stamford Bridge, Alan Hudson burst on to the Chelsea scene as an 18-year-old in the 1969/70 season, his probing passes and powerful forward surges from deep being central to the Blues' run to the FA Cup Final. Sadly, the midfield prodigy missed the dramatic showdown with Leeds through injury, but he was back to help the Londoners win the European Cup Winners' Cup the following season. A bust-up with manager Dave Sexton led to his departure to Stoke in 1974, and it was with the Potters that he won his two England caps – a pitiful return for such a sublime talent.

9) Ray Wilkins

A Chelsea youth product, 'Butch' made his Blues debut aged 17 in October 1973 – nine months after his brother, full-back Graham, had first featured for the club. Less than two years later, the talented midfielder with an eye for a defence-splitting pass was handed the captain's armband by manager Eddie McCreadie, and in 1977 Wilkins led the team back to the top flight while also winning the second of his Chelsea Player of the Year awards. He later played for Manchester United, AC Milan and Rangers and was capped 84 times by England.

10) Dennis Wise

An FA Cup winner with unfashionable Wimbledon, Wisey was a club-record £1.5m signing when he joined the Blues from the Dons in the summer of 1990. Moved from the wing to a central midfield role by Glenn Hoddle three years later, his incisive passing and impressive work rate made him the most influential player in the Chelsea team that developed from also-rans into serial cup winners in the late 1990s. First capped in 1991, he played 21 times for England without ever being a regular starter.

TOP 10 PREMIER LEAGUE GOALS

Despite winning a number of 'Goal of the Month' awards, no Chelsea player has picked up the 'Goal of the Season' gong in the Premier League era. Incredible, really, when you consider these beauties:

1) Eidur Gudjohnsen, Chelsea 3 Leeds United 2, 28 January 2003

Jose Mourinho once described Icelandic striker Eidur Gudjohnsen as 'the White Pele' and this outrageous strike against Leeds was straight out of the great Brazilian's repertoire of outlandish skills. After a driving forward run, Frank Lampard crossed from the right into the penalty area, the ball heading towards Gudjohnsen at around chest height. Springing backwards into the air near the penalty spot, the Chelsea forward connected with a perfect overhead kick to send the ball flying into the bottom corner for a wonderful equaliser. It deservedly won 'Goal of the Month' for January 2003 and made the shortlist for ITV's 'Goal of the Season'.

2) Eden Hazard, Chelsea 3 Arsenal 1, 4 February 2017

One of the best-ever individual goals in Premier League history began when Hazard collected Diego Costa's headed pass on the halfway line. The little Belgian then headed off on a mazy dribble, easily sidestepping Laurent Koscielny before shaking off the challenge of Francis Coquelin, the Gunners' supposed midfield enforcer. Running into the penalty area, Hazard nipped past the retreating Koscielny for a second time before clipping a shot past former Blues keeper Petr Cech for a majestic solo goal that made the top six in the BBC's 'Goal of the Season' poll.

3) Michael Essien, Chelsea 1 Arsenal 1, 10 December 2006

A goal down to Arsenal with a little over five minutes to play, the Blues needed something special to preserve an unbeaten home record in the Premier League stretching back nearly three years. Midfielder Michael Essien came up with the goods, firing in a powerful curling shot with the outside of his right foot from fully 30 yards that left Gunners goalkeeper Jens Lehmann clutching thin air.

4) Jimmy Floyd Hasselbaink, Manchester United 3 Chelsea 3, 23 September 2000

In Claudio Ranieri's first match as Chelsea manager, Jimmy Floyd Hasselbaink produced a moment of pure magic to give Chelsea an early lead at Old Trafford. Graeme Le Saux's overhit cross from the left appeared to be going out of play, but Tore Andre Flo did well to loft the ball back into the middle. Standing on the edge of the box, Hasselbaink controlled the dropping ball on his chest, let it bounce once, and then smashed an unstoppable right-foot shot past a stationary Raimond van der Gouw in the United goal and into the far corner of the net.

5) Didier Drogba, Chelsea 1 Liverpool 0, 17 September 2006

Receiving a high right-wing cross on his chest 20 yards from goal, Drogba turned in a flash to send a powerful left-foot half-volley shot scorching past Liverpool goalkeeper Pepe Reina – an utterly sensational goal three minutes before half-time that proved to be the winner for Jose Mourinho's side.

6) Gus Poyet, Chelsea 4 Sunderland 0, 7 August 1999

The Blues rounded off a wonderful opening-day display against newly promoted Sunderland with a breathtaking team effort that won 'Goal of the Month' in August 1999. French midfielder Didier Deschamps began the move with a long pass to Gianfranco Zola, who cleverly evaded a couple of Sunderland defenders while waiting for support. It arrived in the form of Gus Poyet, whose forward run was spotted by Zola, the little Italian delicately scooping the ball into his path for the Uruguayan to meet on the full with a net-bursting volley.

7) Alex, Chelsea 2 Arsenal 0, 3 October 2010

It's a measure of Alex's prowess at set pieces that he took long-range free kicks ahead of the likes of Didier Drogba and Frank Lampard, quite often with spectacular results. On this occasion, the beefy Brazilian defender stepped up to smash a swerving shot over the Arsenal wall and beyond the dive of Lukasz Fabianski five minutes from time. The stunning strike wrapped up a 2-0 home win for the Blues and secured Alex the 'Goal of the Month' trophy for October 2010.

8) William Gallas, Chelsea 2 Tottenham 1, 11 March 2006

Faced with a packed Tottenham defence determined to hang on for a rare point at Stamford Bridge, Chelsea's quest for a late winner seemed likely to be denied until William Gallas received the ball on the left-hand edge of the Spurs penalty area. Cutting inside, the Frenchman unleashed a piledriver of a shot that arrowed into the far corner at the

Shed End, sparking scenes of ecstatic celebration on and off the pitch.

9) Mario Stanic, Chelsea 4 West Ham United 2, 19 August 2000

On the opening day of the season, new boy Mario Stanic produced a stunning piece of skill against West Ham, juggling the ball three times before unleashing an unstoppable volley from 25 yards that ripped into the net past Hammers keeper Shaka Hislop. The brilliant effort was later named 'Goal of the Month' for August 2000.

10) Frank Lampard, Everton 2 Chelsea 3, 17 December 2006

Frank Lampard scored an incredible 147 Premier League goals for Chelsea, but none better than this: a fierce swerving shot from just outside the penalty area that flew past Everton keeper Tim Howard and into the far corner. Super Frank's stunner levelled the scores at 2-2 and minutes later Didier Drogba won the match for the Blues with another long-distance wonder goal.

TOP 10 WORST PREMIER LEAGUE-ERA KITS

Even diehard fans thought twice before shelling out for replicas of these shockers:

1) Away, 2020/21

What on earth were Nike thinking? Blues fans around the world were shocked when the club unveiled their third-choice shirt for the 2020/21 season, a garish pink monstrosity with fading blue stripes that looked like something Gok Wan might throw on for a glitzy party. Fortunately, perhaps, lockdown restrictions during the pandemic meant we were spared the embarrassing sight of thousands of pink-clad Chelsea supporters grouped together like a troupe of shrimp behind the goal at Anfield, the Emirates and Old Trafford.

2) Away, 1994–96

The great Ruud Gullit famously signed for Chelsea in 1995 after expressing his admiration for the club's white socks, but the dreadlocked Dutchman must have been appalled by this stomach-churning Umbro creation – a 'tangerine and graphite' affair that frequently appears in lists of the worst all-time Premier League kits.

3) Home, 2019/20

The hideous graphics on an otherwise half-decent blue top were supposed to represent different aspects of Stamford Bridge in shadowy form, but instead looked as though the Nike designers had invited a classroom of hyperactive five-year-olds to scrawl all over the shirt with black marker pens. A ghastly mess that fully deserves the title of 'Chelsea's worst-ever home kit'.

4) Away, 2007/08

A perfectly decent white kit with blue trimmings was relegated to third place in the club's pecking order behind this ugly Adidas yellow number featuring some weird black boomerang-style graphics at the sides. The overall look suggested the shirt might be better suited as a goalkeeper's jersey and the passage of time has not improved its low standing among fans.

5) Home, 1997–99

The late-1990s were a great time to be a Chelsea fan as brilliant signings like Gianfranco Zola, Roberto Di Matteo and Frank Leboeuf helped fire the Blues to repeated cup successes. However, the Umbro-designed home kit of the period did not go down well with traditionalists, being too light a shade of blue and sporting unnecessary large white panels under the arms. Wisey and co. deserved much better.

6) Away, 2020/21

Not content with creating an awful third-choice pink kit, Nike also designed a pretty naff first-change strip for the Blues to wear during the 2020/21 season. Disconcertingly, the 'arctic blue' shirt splattered with dozens of little black dashes looked rather like the upper half of a toddler's romper suit – an impression only enhanced by the giant '3' sponsorship logo on the front.

7) Away, 2018/19

Nike's design for this 'teal' blue third kit supposedly featured a semi-abstract map of west London on the front of the shirt, but it just looked like a huge dirty grey splodge – much more like the grimmest zones of north London, in fact. Fans were suitably unimpressed, but happily the kit got very few outings as the Blues' much classier yellow away strip took preference on their travels domestically and in an ultimately triumphant Europa League campaign.

8) Away, 1991–93

From today's perspective, this yellow kit with an upwardly rising jagged blue line across the front looks remarkably like one of Dr Chris Whitty's troubling graphs of increasing Covid infection rates during the global pandemic. The Umbro-designed strip proved about as popular with fans as a bad dose of the virus too, and few tears were shed when it followed failed manager Ian Porterfield out of the Bridge exit at the end of the inaugural Premier League season.

9) Home, 1993–95

Red trimmings started to creep into the Chelsea home kit in the 1980s and Umbro decided to continue the trend by controversially including a red collar on this early Premier League design. For many fans it was a step too far, but the team performed reasonably well in the otherwise acceptable strip, reaching a first FA Cup Final for 24 years in 1994.

10) Away, 2006/07

With its thin grey stripes set against a pitch-black background, this Adidas away kit looked a bit like the bleak view from inside a Guantanamo Bay cell. However, if the idea was to terrify the living daylights out of the opposition with a vaguely menacing design, then it worked a treat, as Jose Mourinho's Blues only lost once wearing this unattractive kit.

TOP 10 BIZARRE MOMENTS

Chelsea have featured in numerous weird and wacky incidents over the years, including these 'Strange but Blue' moments:

1) A cup final with no fans

As well as causing death and misery around the world, the Covid-19 pandemic created chaos in the sporting world, with the 2019/20 football season brought to a shuddering halt in the spring. When matches did eventually resume in June 2020 they were played behind closed doors, with no fans allowed anywhere near the stadiums, let alone inside. The Blues, though, responded well to the new circumstances and battled past Leicester and Manchester United to reach the FA Cup Final. The row upon row of empty seats at Wembley made for a sad sight, however, and the eerie atmosphere may have contributed to a disappointing performance by Frank Lampard's men as they lost 2-1 to London rivals Arsenal.

2) Snow joke in Norway

When the Blues travelled to northern Norway for a European Cup Winners' Cup tie against Tromso in November 1997, they ran into a heavy Arctic snowstorm that would have had Father Christmas scampering back to his cosy grotto. Indeed, midway through the second half, with the markings completely obscured by thick snow, it seemed the match would have to be abandoned. Incredibly, the ref allowed play to continue, Tromso winning 3-2. Back on the Stamford Bridge grass two weeks later things were very different in the return leg, the Blues cruising to a convincing 7-1 victory.

3) Kit cock-up

In a Premier League match at Coventry in April 1997, the travelling Blues fans were stunned to see their heroes taking to the Highfield Road pitch in an extremely odd kit: red-and-black chessboard shirt with a 'Peugeot' advertising logo, blue shorts and white socks. It quickly dawned on them that Chelsea were wearing Coventry's away jerseys, but why? The explanation was simple, though unusual: the referee had decided the two teams' first-choice kits clashed and, remarkably, nobody on the Chelsea staff had thought it might be a good idea to pack the Blues' change yellow strip. In the match itself, Coventry (home) beat Coventry (away) 3-2.

4) The goal that wasn't

In a First Division match against Ipswich at the Bridge in September 1970, Blues midfielder Alan Hudson fired in a shot from 20 yards that just missed the target, striking the outside stanchion before rebounding on to the pitch. The players expected ref Roy Capey to blow for a goal kick, but instead he pointed to the centre circle in the mistaken belief that the ball had gone in the net. Ipswich boss Bobby Robson cut a furious figure afterwards and demanded that the match, which Chelsea won 2-1, should be replayed – but to no avail.

5) Kepa refuses to go

With a penalty shoot-out looming in the 2019 League Cup Final between Chelsea and Manchester City, Blues boss Maurizio Sarri decided to make a substitution, replacing goalkeeper Kepa Arrizabalaga with penalty-saving specialist Willy Caballero. However, Kepa, who had been treated for cramp a few minutes earlier, signalled that he was fine to continue and dismissively waved away his manager. A furious Sarri then stormed off down the tunnel, apparently intent on getting away from Wembley ahead of the fans, before returning to the bench while casting dark looks at his goalkeeper. When the shoot-out did eventually take place, Kepa managed to save from Leroy Sane but City still won 4-3 to take the trophy for a second year running.

6) Four Blues clock off early

A freezing cold wind and sub-zero temperatures couldn't prevent the Blues' First Division fixture at Blackpool going ahead in October 1932, but in the second half four of the visitors decided they'd had enough of the appalling conditions and dashed off to the warmth of the changing room. Showing true northern grit, the Blackpool players all stayed on the pitch and won the match 4-0. The following week, the Chelsea club programme refused to condemn the players who walked off. 'Those ready to disparage the quitters should know that in each case the player had barely enough strength left to reach the dressing room before collapsing. Common humanity suggested the game should have been abandoned.' Still, up north at least, the incident only served to enhance the Blues' reputation as 'southern softies'.

7) Suarez gets peckish!

During a match at Anfield in April 2013, Liverpool striker Luis Suarez bit Chelsea defender Branislav Ivanovic on the right arm while the pair challenged for the ball in the Blues' penalty area. The incident wasn't spotted at the time by the officials but was picked up by the TV cameras and quickly became a hot topic. Even Prime Minister David Cameron got involved, saying that Suarez 'set the most appalling example'. The FA agreed and hit the Uruguayan striker, who had previously bitten another opponent while playing for Ajax, with a ten-match ban. A lesson learned, finally? Not really. Suarez was at it again at the 2014 World Cup, sinking his gnashers into the shoulder of Italian defender Giorgio Chiellini!

8) Out go the lights

In a fourth-round FA Cup replay against Preston at Stamford Bridge in January 1969, the Blues were in a comfortable position, leading 2-0 with just 15 minutes to play. Suddenly, though, the floodlights failed, leaving ref Ken Burns no alternative but to abandon the match. The game was rescheduled for the following Monday afternoon, ensuring that it could finish in daylight. Despite the strange kick-off time, more than 36,000 fans – many, no doubt, bunking off school or work – turned up at the Bridge to see Chelsea win 2-1 with late goals from David Webb and Charlie Cooke.

9) Ballboy barminess

Trailing Swansea 2-0 on aggregate in the League Cup semi-final second leg at the Liberty Stadium in January 2013, Chelsea were running out of time to get back in the tie. When the Blues won a corner with ten minutes to play Eden Hazard rushed to get the ball, which a ballboy had dived on when it went out of play. When the kid refused to hand over the ball, Hazard attempted to kick it from under him. Bad move! The ballboy started rolling around on the ground and clutching his stomach as though he had been shot by a sniper. Predictably, the ref was duped by the little rogue's Neymar-esque amateur theatrics and sent Hazard off, the

Belgian star subsequently serving a three-match ban for 'violent conduct'.

10) A 'home' game in Seville
Due to the Covid-19 pandemic, both legs of Chelsea's Champions League quarter-final with Porto in April 2021 were played behind closed doors at the Sanchez Pizjuan Stadium in Seville. Playing 'away' in the first game, the Blues won 2-0 thanks to goals by Mason Mount and Ben Chilwell. Back in southern Spain six days later, Porto secured a 1-0 victory on Chelsea's 'home' turf but it wasn't enough to prevent the Blues going through to the semi-finals of the competition for the first time since 2014.

TOP 10 CELEBRITY FAN QUOTES

A-listers from the worlds of music, cinema and sport reveal their love for the Blues:

1) 'For me, Chelsea is life – the rest mere detail.'
Former Olympic athlete Lord (Seb) Coe, writing in *Country & Town House*, 2020

2) 'When we were in the Second Division trying to get promoted, I went on all sorts of mad journeys following Chelsea. I remember going to Bristol Rovers, when they beat us 3-0. They weren't exactly glory years.'
Actor Phil Daniels, interviewed by the official Chelsea magazine in 2006

3) 'Good luck Chelsea.'
Actor Sir Michael Caine on Twitter, before the 2020 FA Cup Final against Arsenal

4) 'I've supported Chelsea since I moved to England – and before that. My first game was in 1985. I haven't got a box; I'd much rather be down there with everybody else.'
Canadian rock star Bryan Adams, interviewed by *Classic Rock* in 2014

5) 'I know it's strange for a North London lad but I lived in Fulham for two years in 1970 and became a Chelsea fan then and have suffered the slings and arrows ever since.'
Madness singer Suggs, talking to the *Evening Standard* in 2003

6) 'When I moved back to London, in about 1989, most of my friends were Chelsea fans and I went to a game with them – my first-ever game – which made a massive impression on me.'
Blur and Gorillaz frontman Damon Albarn, interviewed by chelseafc.com in 2013

7) 'Alright, I've been outed as a Chelsea supporter (I'm a lifer). I never talk about it because of the insane aggro – in truth, I just love footy.'
Actress Minnie Driver on Twitter, 2017

8) 'I started supporting Chelsea in the late-60s. I always had to be Peter Osgood or Peter Bonetti; I fancied myself more as a striker but played more in goal.'
Former Olympic rower Sir Steve Redgrave, interviewed by chelseafc.com in 2018

9) 'Sarri needs to go, he can't make the right decisions.'
American actor Owen Wilson on Twitter, 2019

10) 'I love Chelsea this year as much as I've loved them since 1970.'
TV presenter Jeremy Clarkson on Twitter, 2019